Women,
Crime
and the

Canadian

Criminal

Justice

System

Walter S. DeKeseredy
Carleton University

anderson publishing co.
2035 Reading Road
Cincinnati, OH 45202
800-582-7295

EDITOR Ellen S. Boyne
ASSISTANT EDITOR Sharon L. Boyles
ACQUISITIONS EDITOR Michael C. Braswell

Cover digital composition and design: Tin Box Studio, Inc.
Cover photo credit: © Barnaby Hall/Photonica

Photo credits—
p. xii CP Picture Archive
p. 36 CP Picture Archive/Ray Smith
p. 64 CORBIS/Hulton-Deutsch Collection
p. 98 CP Picture Archive/Ryan Remiorz
p. 126 Simon Wood/CORBIS/Hulton-Deutsch Collection

Women, Crime and the Canadian Criminal Justice System

Copyright © 2000
     Anderson Publishing Co.
     2035 Reading Rd.
     Cincinnati, OH 45202

     Phone 800.582.7295 or 513.421.4142
     Web Site www.andersonpublishing.com

Library of Congress Cataloging-in-Publication Data

DeKeseredy, Walter S., 1959-
    Women, crime and the Canadian criminal justice system / Walter S. DeKeseredy.
       p.   cm.
    Includes bibliographical references and index.
    ISBN 0-87084-894-1 (pbk.)
    1. Female offenders--Canada. 2. Female juvenile delinquents--Canada. 3. Criminal justice,
Administration of--Canada I. Title.
    HV6046.D34.D34   1999
    364.3 ' 74 ' 0971--dc21   99-42601
                                                    CIP

Foreword

Canadians can be justly proud of their long track record of concern about women involved with the criminal justice system. The first international conference on female offenders was held in Vancouver, British Columbia, in the fall of 1979. In 1990, the Canadian Task Force on federally sentenced women was convened, and while some of its outcomes are controversial, it remains one of the few examples of a concerted national effort to seriously address the long-ignored needs of women in prison. Walter DeKeseredy's book, *Women, Crime and the Canadian Criminal Justice System* builds on this worthy tradition—bringing together what is known about girl and women offenders in Canada in an energetic, lively, and thorough volume.

Several important strengths set this book apart from other efforts in the area of women's offending. Most importantly, DeKeseredy, because of his important and groundbreaking work in area of women's victimization, can clearly see the links between the violence that girls and women experience and their subsequent "offending." DeKeseredy correctly begins the discussion of women's pathways into crime by focusing on the immense amount of victimization that women experience, and the relationship between those experiences and women's involvement in crime— particularly violent crime, but also other forms of crime (such as prostitution). As a result of this linkage, women in prison, both in Canada and the United States have astonishing histories of both sexual and physical violence. Also, unlike with male offenders, this pattern of victimization continues after they leave girlhood and characterizes their adult lives as well. This volume also highlights the important fact that, while victimization looms large in the lives of all incarcerated women in North America, such histories of victimization are particularly pronounced among women of color. Among federally sentenced women, for example, 68 percent have been the victims of physical abuse and 53 percent the victims of sexual abuse. However, the comparable figures for aboriginal women are 90 percent and 61 percent, respectively. This intersectionality between race and gender is an important aspect of women's involvement in the criminal justice system, and goes a long way toward explaining the over-incarceration of women of color in both Canada and the United States. In the Canadian situation, as DeKeseredy powerfully notes, aboriginal women, who make up only 2 percent of the general population, account for fully 18.5 percent of federally sentenced women.

While there are numerous other aspects of DeKeseredy's offering that set it apart from other efforts on the situation of the female offender, perhaps none is so important as the fact that DeKeseredy is documenting the fact that Canadian women, like their United States counterparts, are increasingly being swept up in the imprisonment "binge" that has been haunting North America for the last two decades. While the Canadian increase of 50 percent seems "small" in comparison to the United States' increase of nearly 300 percent, it should in no way be disregarded. It signals a dangerous and unnecessary mimicking of the United States' pattern of relying on incarceration to manage, but not address, intractable social problems and injustices like racism and economic inequality.

Another strength of DeKeseredy's work is his recognition of the links between girls' problems and women's crime. For this reason, the book covers girls' pathways into trouble with the law and investigates the impact of various changes within the juvenile justice system on girls' experience with the juvenile court. Here, DeKeseredy notes that Canadian courts may well be a bellwether of punitive impulses in the area of girl's delinquency. Specifically, while Canadians may have hoped that by passing the *Young Offenders Act*, girls charged with noncriminal offenses would not be incarcerated, this book corrects that impression. In fact, the situation as documented by this book could well be worse for Canadian girls than for their United States counterparts, with Canadian courts increasing the rate of incarceration of female youth at a significant—and alarming—rate; as an example, the number of girls placed in "secure custody" increased in just the space of four years (1991-1995) by an alarming 55 percent. This increase, according to the research summarized by DeKeseredy, was virtually all explained by the incarceration of girls for "administrative" offenses (such as violating the conditions of probation) and other violations of court rules rather than criminal acts.

Another strength of DeKeseredy's work is his appreciation of the role of the media in the shaping of public opinion about crime and crime policies. Since the end of the Cold War, crime coverage has emerged as the number one topic on nightly news casts across North America. Moreover, because this crime coverage has tended to feature freakish, unusual, and violent offenses, the voting public is convinced that crime is out of control at precisely the time that crime rates are dropping to the lowest levels seen in decades.

Some of the most egregious media coverage of crime has been devoted to the violence of girls and women, and Canadians have seen an excess of this sort of media with a series of high-profile murders committed by girls and women (such as the Virk case in British Columbia and the Homolka case in Ontario). DeKeseredy quickly and correctly notes that the more typical cases of women engaging in what he has called "self-help homicide" (by which battered wives and girlfriends kill abusive boyfriends and husbands to save their own lives) rarely receive such massive and intense media attention. There is a reason for this, and it is political: cases that involve bizarre violence committed by women are the stuff of which backlash is made and backlash journalists such as Patricia Pearson have managed to parlay women's crime into national prominence for themselves precisely by avoiding the realities of women's offending—choosing, instead, to sensationalize and sexualize women's violence. The demonization of women accused of crimes serves a number of powerful political interests, particularly when the argument is made that women's participation in crime, especially traditionally "male" crimes like murder, can be blamed on the women's movement.

This book is a standout in its treatment of the emerging theories of girls' and women's crime. DeKeseredy's credentials as a feminist criminologist stand him in very good stead. He understands that gender is more than a variable, and that no complete theory of crime can be generated that does not address the sex/gender system that is created by patriarchy. His extremely useful reviews of contemporary feminist theories make this book a "must read" for all those seeking to understand the situation of girls and women in the criminal justice system.

What will make for a safe society? DeKeseredy contends that a return to a concern for social and economic justice is an essential starting point. We also need to look past punitive, and masculinist methods like punishment and imprisonment to alternatives such as restorative justice. In addition to healing rather than harming the social fabric, such interventions are also far more affordable—and we can start that experiment today with the girls and women who are needlessly being incarcerated in both Canada and the United States. Work such as DeKeseredy's important new book on the actual situation of girls and women in the criminal justice system, can, in fact, lay the important groundwork for more humane ways to reduce both crime and victimization by putting justice first and hatred last.

Meda Chesney-Lind
Professor, Women's Studies, University of Hawaii at Manoa

Preface

One does not have to read this book or others like it to discover that many Canadians see their country as being riddled with predatory violent women and girls. This is largely because on any given day, newspapers and television stations typically present at least one sensational story about a terrifying, albeit statistically insignificant, crime committed by a female, such as Karla Homolka. You will also often hear some journalists, conservative politicians, and many male members of the general public contend, "But women do it too!" This assertion is used to challenge the overwhelming empirical data showing that women are the primary targets of physical abuse in intimate heterosexual relationships. Unfortunately, Canada is now experiencing a major anti-feminist backlash, one that involves painting women and girls as demons or evil to justify resistance to feminist challenges to the patriarchal status quo.

The main objective of this book is to challenge the above and other myths about female crime in Canada. Data presented in Chapters 1 and 2 show that, like their United States counterparts, Canadian women and girls are not major criminal threats to our safety. Although it may be contrary to popular belief, the vast majority of crimes in Canada are committed by males, and most female offenders are nonviolent.

Why do women and girls commit crime? Chapter 3 provides various widely read and cited answers to this question. However, some theories are better than others. From my standpoint, feminist perspectives are superior to mainstream accounts and so are policies informed by the rigorous theoretical work done by feminists such as Susan Caringella-MacDonald, Dawn Currie, Meda Chesney-Lind, Kathleen Daly, Karlene Faith, James Messerschmidt, Jody Miller, Claire Renzetti, Martin D. Schwartz, Aysan Sev'er, and Betsy Stanko. Indeed, it is time to seriously consider progressive alternatives to the correctional facilities that are addressed in Chapter 4. Some salient examples of alternative policies are discussed in Chapter 5; however, they are not likely to be welcomed by conservatives.

In his groundbreaking book *Confronting Crime: An American Challenge*, Elliott Currie (1985, p. vii) correctly points out that "Most books about social questions are, to a much greater extent than is usually recognized, the products of collective effort." So is this one. I consider myself to be very lucky and privileged to have close friends, relatives, and colleagues who gave me an incredible amount of support to muster up the emotional, physical, and intellectual energy to write about the complex issues addressed in *Women, Crime, and the Canadian Criminal Justice System.* My strongest thanks, however, go to my family, especially my partner, Pat, and my daughter, Andrea. Their love, kindness, and sense of humor helped me maintain my strength and focus, although it often drained theirs. My mother, Eva Jantz, my father, Stephen DeKeseredy, and Marie Barger, Andrea's grandmother, were always willing to help when my work schedule created child care dilemmas. They were also a major source of inspiration.

I have learned a substantial amount about the issues covered in this book from the following colleagues and friends: Shahid Alvi, Raquel Kennedy Bergen, Susan Caringella-MacDonald, Meda Chesney-Lind, Kim Cook, Shelly Crego, Dawn Currie, Colleen Dell, Desmond Ellis, Karlene Faith, Colin Goff, Judith Grant, Donna Hale, Drew Humphries, Katalin Kennedy, Mary Koss, John Lowman, Brian MacLean, Linda MacLeod, James Messerschmidt, Jody Miller, Susan Miller, Debra Pepler, Barbara Perry, Claire Renzetti, Bernard Schissell, Martin D. Schwartz, Roberta-Lynn Sinclair, Betsy Stanko, Terry Wotherspoon, and Jock Young. Since many of these people disagree with one another, I assume full responsibility for the material presented in this book. I also deeply appreciate all of the time they took away from their busy schedules to help me sharpen my sociological imagination and to comment on my work over the last 15 years.

Of course, this book would not have been possible without the patience, co-operation and editorial assistance of Anderson Publishing Co. The staff there, especially Susan Braswell, Mickey Braswell, and Ellen Boyne, went beyond the call of duty. I can't thank them enough.

Table of Contents

Women who commit violence are very often victims of violence themselves. Note the bruised eyes of Karla Homolka, who, together with her husband, sexually assaulted and murdered three women in Ontario.

Chapter 1

Crimes Committed
by Canadian Women

INTRODUCTION

Like most Canadian teenage females, Reena Virk liked to "hang out" with friends. However, similar to many other visible-minority teenagers who grow up in predominantly white, Anglo-Saxon, middle-class Canadian suburbs, Reena, the daughter of East Indian parents, was often treated like a "left-over" (Holmes & Silverman, 1992). Like Leslie Faber,[1] the mentally retarded girl who was sexually assaulted by a group of affluent white teenage boys in Glen Ridge, New Jersey, on March 1, 1989, Reena "could never expect to break through the invisible wall that separated her from the coolest kids in the school" (Lefkowitz, 1997, p. 18), despite the fact that she "was a sweet kid" (cited in Chisholm, 1997). According to Jiwani (1998, p. 2):

> Reena Virk could not "fit in" because she had nothing to fit in to. She was brown in a predominantly white society. She was supposedly overweight in a society which values slimness to the point of anorexia, and she was different in a society which values "sameness" and uniformity.

Thus, it is not surprising that she had a low self-esteem. Her domestic life did not help. She was shuttled between three foster homes and her own parents' household. Further, her father was charged with sexually abusing her and she attempted suicide (Purvis, 1997). What may be surprising, especially

> *Women's crime, like girls' crime, is deeply affected by women's place. As a result, women's contribution to serious crime, like that of girls', is minor.*
>
> (Chesney-Lind, 1997, p. 95)

1

for people unfamiliar with social scientific research on young Canadian women's lives, opinions, fears, perceptions of the world, self-esteem, and experiences, is that she would accept an invitation on the evening of November 14, 1997, from a couple of acquaintances to join a group of their female friends at a nearby waterfront park in Saanich British Columbia, one of whom slightly earlier that day stubbed out a lighted cigarette on Reena's forehead. She suspected that Reena spread rumors about her and wanted revenge (Chisholm, 1997). After reading about this incident in *MacLean's,* Canada's weekly newsmagazine, the author of this text asked, "Why would anyone want to socialize with such a cruel person?"

The answer to this question lies in research showing that many young girls, regardless of the conflicts they have with their peers, "feel the need to be able to fit in and be part of the popular crowd" (Holmes & Silverman, 1992, p. 36). Many Canadian adolescent women "are afraid of losing friends, having no friends, not having the 'right' friends, or not having enough friends" (Holmes & Silverman, 1992, p. 36). Consider what Molly Pallmann, one of Reena's friends, said about her: "She very much wanted to belong with the cool kids" (cited in Chisholm, 1997, p. 2). Unfortunately, the "cool kids" did not want her friendship, and as described in Box 1.1, they made their position clear in a terrifying and deadly manner.

Box 1.1

Fury of Her Peers
A Teenager's Brutal Assault and Drowning
Raises Questions in a Quiet Canadian Town

Early on the evening of Friday, Nov. 14, the teenager (Reena) got a call inviting her to join a group of girls at the nearby Gorge waterway, a local hangout. Agreeing to go was one of the last decisions she made. Eight days later, her body was found half submerged on the shoreline of a tidal inlet, about 200 meters from the spot where she had been beaten almost to death, it appears, by the girls whose company she craved. Police have not released details, but rumors swirled that the corpse's arms and back were broken and the face disfigured.[2] The official cause of death was drowning.

Across Canada, which prides itself on having lower crime rates and less violence than the U.S., parents and teenagers alike struggled to make sense of a particularly senseless crime. Eight local teens have been charged in the killing, their identities shielded as juveniles under the country's *Young Offenders Act.* Seven of the eight are girls; six of them have been charged with aggravated assault, and a 16-year-old boy and the remaining girl are accused of second-degree murder.

Almost as disturbing as the death was the fact that a number of onlookers apparently did nothing to stop the beating and that the suspects' peers at several neighborhood high schools did not come forward even after news of the alleged

Box 1.1, *continued*

murder spread in school hallways. "This is not just a matter of a few bad kids," said Carole James, chairwoman of the Greater Victoria School Board. "When you have a large group of children standing and watching, they are all involved."

Reena's death and the subsequent conspiracy of silence, eerily reminiscent of the movie *River's Edge*, was a brutal awakening for Victoria, a quietly picturesque city of 304,000 on Vancouver Island. The case has spurred calls in Canada's Parliament for tougher penalties under the *Young Offenders Act*, which sets a maximum of four years' imprisonment for second-degree murder, and has raised questions about mounting violence among school-age girls.

Police at first did not suspect foul play, since Reena had gone missing on several previous occasions. But the Monday after the beating, news of the incident spread in school corridors and locker rooms. By the next day, a school official had heard enough to inform police. It took three more days—until a week after the murder—for police to begin making arrests, and another day before Reena's body was spotted by a helicopter team.

No one had any explanation for the violent outburst. Some of the accused are what police call "wannabe" gang members, who pose as *Crips* and *Bloods* but who have not—in the past—anyway—organized any criminal activity. At least two of the teens were in foster homes, and several others have required counseling by social workers in the past. Police have ruled out racism as a motive, noting that some of the accused are also nonwhite. Girls interviewed last week say the incident may have been triggered by something as trivial as a stolen agenda planner or perhaps a disputed boyfriend.

Relatives and friends have tied flowers and messages to the green railing of the bridge where the teenager was last seen alive. "Growing up trying to fit in, trying to look cool with those fools," reads a hand-lettered poem. "At least you're in a better place."

Source: This box includes excerpts from an article written by Purvis (1997, pp. 1-3) for *Time*. From "Fury of her Peers: A Teenager's Brutal Assault and Drowning Raises Questions in a Quiet Canadian Town," *Time* 12/8/97. © 1997 Time Inc. Reprinted by permission.

The vicious murder described in Box 1.1 led many Canadians to conclude that Canada is now riddled with a new wave of "violent, unruly women . . . running amuck" (Faith, 1993a, pp. 65-66). Similarly, the case of Karla Homolka and the way in which it was reported by journalists led many Canadians to believe that violence among Canadian women and girls women is "sharply on the rise" (Chisholm, 1997). In the early 1990s, Homolka, and her now ex-husband Paul Bernardo, sexually assaulted and murdered three young women from southern Ontario, one of whom was her sister. Like the Reena Virk case, this case shocked and angered many Canadians and generated an unprecedented amount of media coverage (Boritch, 1997).

Are these two cases typical examples of female crime? Are Canadians experiencing an unprecedented epidemic of violent crimes committed by "unruly" or "fallen women"?[3] The main objective of this chapter is to show that the bulk of crimes committed by Canadian women, like those committed by girls (see Chapter 2), are relatively minor. Adult female offenders tend to follow their traditional roles as shoppers, consumers, and health-care providers within the family (DeKeseredy & Schwartz, 1996). As you will soon discover, very few women commit crimes like those perpetrated by Reena Virk's peers and Karla Homolka. In fact:

> Females primarily commit thefts of value under $1,000, and men dominate in offences exceeding that amount. Males steal electronic equipment, tools and other goods of significantly higher values than those taken by females. In other words, in the age of women's liberation, female offenders primarily continue to commit primarily "feminine" offences; they write bad checks and take items useful to them as homemakers and for feminine appearances. They commit fraud against the government from need and in resistance against the destitution level of welfare allotments for their children's care (Faith, 1993a, p. 65).

THE NATURE AND EXTENT OF CRIMES COMMITTED BY CANADIAN WOMEN

In Canada, the United States, and elsewhere, there is an important battle being waged over the nature of women's behavior and its role in crime (Renzetti, 1994). For example, despite ample evidence demonstrating major gender differences in the extent, contexts, meanings, and motives of female crime in the street, in the workplace, and in domestic settings, many conservative academics, politicians, and others claim that interpersonal violence is a *gender-neutral problem*. In other words, they contend "But women do it too!" Of course, *some* women do commit nonlethal or deadly violent crimes. Still, as pointed out in the next two sections of this chapter, the number who do so pales in comparison to the high rates of male violence in a broad range of social settings. It is to murders committed by Canadian women that we turn first.

Murder

Murder is the intentional killing of one person, directly or indirectly, by another (Gartner, 1995). According to the Canadian *Criminal Code*, there are four types of murder: *first-degree murder, second-degree murder, manslaughter,* and *infanticide* (see Box 1.2). Viewed by the majority of Canadians as the most serious crime, murder is a relatively rare offence for both males and females (Boritch, 1997). Further, as pointed out in Figure 1.1, homicide data collected by Canadian police departments and compiled by the Canadian Centre for Justice statistics show that, between 1961 and 1990, most murders were committed by men. Two important points should be considered when considering the data presented in Figure 1.1. First, longitudinal homicide data provide a more stable basis for drawing conclusions than those for a single year (Ellis & DeKeseredy, 1996). Second, the people included in Figure 1.1 were *suspects* at the time the data were collected. Some were found guilty and others were found guilty of less severe charges (Silverman & Kennedy, 1993).

Box 1.2

Four Types of Murder in Canada

First-degree murder occurs when:
   a) it is planned and deliberate or
   b) the victim is a person employed and acting in the course of his/her work for the preservation and maintenance of the public peace (e.g., police worker, correctional worker) or
   c) the death is caused by a person committing or attempting to commit serious offences (e.g., sexual assault, kidnapping, hijacking).

Second-degree murder is all murder that is not first-degree.

Manslaughter is generally considered to be a homicide committed in the heat of passion by sudden provocation. It also includes other culpable homicides that are not murder or homicides.

Infanticide occurs when a female causes the death of her newborn child, and her state of mind is disordered as a result of her having given birth.

Source: Adapted from Goff (1997, p. 99) and Fedorowycz (1995).

Figure 1.1 shows that over a relatively long period of time, the number of murders committed by women is much smaller than that committed by men. For example, 87 percent of the suspects were male, while 13 percent were female. Obviously, most Canadian killers are male. Further, men mainly kill other men and they are slightly more likely to kill strangers than their spouses (Ellis & DeKeseredy, 1996; Johnson, 1996). On the other hand, between 1961 and 1990, most female offenders (40%) killed their husband or common-law partner. Twenty-two percent killed one of their children (Silverman & Kennedy, 1993).

Figure 1.1
Suspect Characteristics, Murder in Canada, 1961-1990

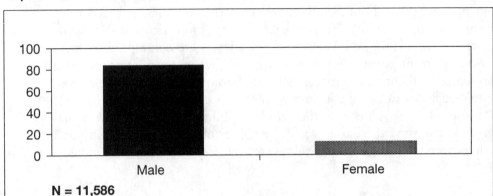

Source: Adapted from Silverman and Kennedy (1993, p. 11). From *Deadly Deeds*, 1st edition, by R.A. Silver-man and L.W. Kennedy, © 1992. Reprinted with permission of INelson Thomson Learning, a division of Thomson Learning. Fax: 800/730-2215.

After hearing about a case in which a woman killed her husband or another family member, many people immediately ask, "How could she do that?" According to Chesney-Lind (1997: 98-99) and other feminist criminologists, this is the wrong question. Rather, we should ask, "Why do so few women murder?" This is not an odd or perverse question when you consider the staggering amount of wife beating that occurs in North America. For example, Table 1.1 show that annually at least 11 percent of Canadian women in marital/cohabiting relationships are physically assaulted by their male partners.

Physical assault and other types of woman abuse (e.g., sexual assault, psychological abuse, etc.) also occur at alarming rates in Canadian dating and estranged marital/cohabiting relationships. For example, DeKeseredy and Kelly's (1993a) national representative sample survey of woman abuse in heterosexual university/college dating relationships generated the following results:

- 13.7 percent of the 1,307 men in their sample indicated that they had physically assaulted their dating partners in the year before the survey, while 22.3 percent of the 1,835 female respondents stated that they had been victimized in such a way during this same time period.

- Close to 35 percent of the women reported having been physically assaulted, and 17.8 percent of the men stated that they had been physically abusive since leaving high school.

Table 1.1
North American Wife Abuse Surveys

	Description of Surveys				Abuse Rates			
Survey	Survey Location & Date	Sample Description	Interview Mode	Measure of Abuse	Abuse Past Year (%)	Severe Abuse Past Year (%)	Abuse Ever (%)	Severe Abuse Ever (%)
Straus et al. (1981)	U.S. National 1975	2,143 married or cohabiting men and women	Face-to-face	CTS (aggregate)[1]	12.1	3.8	–	–
Schulman (1979)	Kentucky 1979	1,793 presently or formerly married and cohabiting men and women	Phone	CTS[2]	10.0	4.1	21.0	8.7
Straus & Gelles (1986)	U.S. National 1985	3,520 presently or formerly married or cohabiting men and women	Phone	CTS (aggregate)	11.3	3.0	–	–
Brinker-hoff & Lupri (1988)	Calgary 1981	526 men and women	Face-to-face and self-admin-istered question-naire	CTS (men only)[3]	24.5	10.8	–	–
Kennedy & Dutton (1989)	Alberta 1987	1,045 men and women	Face-to-face and phone	CTS (aggregate)	11.2	2.3	–	–
Lupri (1990)	Canada National 1986	1,530 married or cohabiting men and women	Face-to-face and mail question-naire	CTS (men only)	17.8	10.1	–	–
Smith (1986)	Toronto 1985	315 women aged 18-55	Phone	CTS/open questions and 1 supp-lementary question	10.8	–	18.1	7.3
Smith (1987)	Toronto 1987	604 presently or formerly married or cohabiting women	Phone	CTS & 3 supp-lementary questions	14.4[4]	5.1	36.4[5]	11.3
Statistics Canada (1993)	Canada National 1993	12,300 women 18 years of age and older	Phone	CTS[6]	3.0	–	29.0	–

[1] Men-as-aggressors and women-as-victims from different couples.
[2] Women-as-victims.
[3] Men-as-aggressors.

[4] Past year rates based on CTS alone.
[5] Abuse ever rates based on CTS (25.0, 7.8) plus supplementary questions.
[6] Includes a sexual assault item.

Source: This table is a modified version of tables constructed by Ellis and DeKeseredy (1996) and Smith (1989). Except for Brinkerhoff and Lupri's (1988) study, the surveys described in this table include separated and divorced respondents. Table 6.1 (Wife Abuse Surveys) on p. 182 of Ellis and DeKeseredy's *The Wrong Stuff: An Introduction to the Sociological Study of Deviance*, 2nd ed. Toronto: Allyn & Bacon. Reprinted with permission of Prentice Hall Canada, Inc.

- Approximately 28 percent of the female participants stated that they were sexually abused in the past year, while 11 percent of the males reported having victimized a female dating partner in this way during the same time period.

- 45.1 percent of the women stated that they had been sexually abused since leaving high school, and 19.5 percent of the men reported at least one incident of such abuse in the same time period.

In response to these and other data on male-to-female "intimate intrusions" (Stanko, 1985), many Canadians say, "Why do these women stay? I wouldn't put up with that." Well, most abused women do leave the men who victimize them (Schwartz, 1989). For many women, however, separation, divorce, or breaking up with a boyfriend does not solve the problem of abuse. As described by Sev'er (1997, pp. 579-580) in Box 1.3, some dangerous male partners keep showing up, and when they do, their visits can be deadly. For example, in 21 percent of the cases of *intimate femicide*[4] recorded in Toronto, Ontario, between 1974 and 1990, the victims were separated from either their legal or common-law male partners (Crawford & Gartner, 1992). Moreover, Canadian national homicide data analyzed by Wilson and Daly (1994) show that compared to co-residing couples, separation entails a *sixfold increase* in risk to wives.

Box 1.3

Some Canadian Examples of Woman Abuse After Termination of Intimate Relationships

Mr. Morrison was put on probation and ordered to stay away from his ex-wife for 3 years after he tried to "rape [her] on the street in front of witnesses, including children." The victim remains terrified of Morrison (*Toronto Star*, 1995a). Another man who cannot be named so as to protect the identity of his children, raped his estranged wife on the kitchen floor "and said, if she reported the incident to the police, he would kill her and their son." The next week, he again forced her to perform oral sex, all the while spreading lies that his (ex)wife was trying to "seduce" him (*Toronto Star*, 1995b).

A survivor of long-term abuse, Daisy claimed that her husband literally locked her into the apartment, without money or food. Daisy was an immigrant woman with no relatives in Canada and no understanding of the English language. Her only means of escape was a women's shelter, where she felt neither welcome (because of cultural disparities) nor safe. Her husband found the address of the shelter, physically assaulted the receptionist on duty, and dragged Daisy home. She refused to testify against him, saying time and time again that he would kill her and have her family (in her country of origin) killed if she ever left.

Box 1.3, *continued*

Ann, a 23-year-old woman I interviewed, is legally disabled as a result of repeated beatings she has suffered from her common-law partner. She said the frequency and severity of abuse increased when she wanted to return to her parents' home. One attempt to leave resulted in Ann's being taken for a ride in a remote nature conservation area under the auspices of reconciliation. She was violently raped and then asked to take off her remaining clothes and walk. She walked, totally exposed, for seven miles while he drove ahead, watching from his rearview mirror. Ann said, "it was a marshy area, the road was full of slithery things; he knew I was deadly scared of slithery things!" When Ann collapsed from heat exhaustion and fear, her still nude body was "dumped" on the front lawn of her parents' house. Although the partner was convicted of assault, he served less than a month in jail and only on weekends. He continued to make harassing calls from jail, as well.

Source: Sev'er, A. (1997). "Recent or Imminent Separation and Intimate Violence Against Women: A Conceptual Overview." *Violence Against Women*, Volume 3, pp. 579-580, copyright © 1997 by Sage Publications. Reprinted by permission of Sage Publications.

Many separated and divorced women are also victims/survivors of sublethal assaults, that is, physically and sexually violent acts that do not result in death (see Box 1.2). For example, Statistics Canada's national Violence Against Women Survey (VAWS) found that about 20 percent of the women who reported violence by a previous partner stated that the violence occurred following or during separation. In 35 percent of the cases, the violence increased in severity at the time of separation (Johnson & Sacco, 1995; Rodgers, 1994). In sum, these results as well as other post-separation woman abuse data[5] "support the widespread apprehension that wives often experience elevated risk when deserting a violent proprietary husband" (Wilson et al., 1995, pp. 340-341).

Male-to-female violence is not restricted to domestic relationships. Many women who sell sexual services are also beaten, raped, and so on by "bad dates" on the streets and in other locations. Consider the Vancouver data presented in Table 1.2. These findings are derived from Lowman and Fraser's (1995, p. 56) descriptive analysis of "Bad Trick Sheets" for the period 1985-1993. They were filled out by female sex trade workers and published by the Alliance for the Safety of Prostitutes (ASP), Prostitutes and Other Women for Equal Rights (POWER), and the Downtown Eastside Youth Activities Society (DEYAS). Box 1.4 provides one terrifying example of a "bad date" uncovered by Lowman and Fraser (1995, p. 219) in their interview with Mary, a sex trade worker in Vancouver.

The male-to-female violence data presented in this chapter and other sources (e.g., Alvi et al., 2000; DeKeseredy & MacLeod, 1997; Duffy & Momirov, 1997) show that woman abuse is endemic to Canada and that many Canadian women's lives "rest upon a continuum of unsafety" (Stanko, 1990). As stated earlier, given the alarming amount of violence

Canadian women suffer at male hands, the incredible story is that the number of female murderers is so low (Chesney-Lind, 1997). What would you do if you were in Mary's position? What would you do if your ex-partner raped you and threatened to kill you and your children? Well, chances are that you, like most female victims of serial attacks by male partners, would not resort to murder—even to save your life. Nevertheless, based on a review of the murder data presented here and elsewhere, we can safely conclude that most women who kill do so after enduring a shocking number of physical and sexual attacks by intimate partners (Browne, 1987; DeKeseredy & Schwartz, 1998; Jones, 1994; Silverman & Kennedy, 1993).

Box 1.4

A Bad Date

The date I told you about—D.P.—he picked me up on Fraser between 8th and 9th. We made a deal and I took him back to my place. He was nervous. He didn't want to be at the house. He wanted to check the house out. I was living at 14th and Fraser. I had it set up so that the front room was my work room. The back room was where people would hang out so dates wouldn't see them. On this occasion Joe, my boyfriend was there. D.P. just happened to check out that room. When he saw Joe he got really nervous and wanted to leave. He said "I can't do anything with your boyfriend here." I said, "That's not my boyfriend. It's just a friend. I guess he needed a place to stay so he came back to hang out." Anyway, I didn't want to lose the money because I was hurtin,' [Mary was using heroin at the time] so I put my shoes back on, ran down the stairs and followed him out to his car. He wanted to know where we could go. There was a club a block away and we went and parked behind it. That's where it all started. After we parked, he turned and got something from the driver's door—I thought he was reaching for his wallet. But he pulled out a pencil real quick, reached over, grabbed me and stuck the pencil in my neck. He said, "I can't afford your prices, bitch." He started struggling with me. When I grabbed the pencil, it broke into three pieces. I started to fight with him. I managed to get the door open and I was screaming for help hoping that people in the house next door would hear. The more I screamed, the more violent he got. He managed to throw me across the console.

I had six inch heels on—I kept pushing against the door keeping it open so somebody might be able to hear me. He kept trying to close the door. Then he started smacking me with his fists. By this time, he was almost right on top of me using his weight; I couldn't keep the door open any longer. We must have fought for at least ten minutes. I kept blocking his punches. On the street, you learn how to defend yourself.

Source: Lowman, J. & Fraser, L. (1995). *Violence Against Persons Who Prostitute: The Experience in British Columbia.* Ottawa: Department of Justice. Reprinted with permission.

Table 1.2
Types of Bad Dates

Experience	1985-1988		1988-1993	
	Count	Percent of Cases	Count	Percent of Cases
Physical assault	246	39.7	328	33.4
Sexual assault	176	28.4	242	24.6
Rip-off/money back	101	16.3	197	20.1
Robbed of all cash	128	20.7	151	15.4
Had or used a knife	90	14.5	133	13.6
Verbal abuse/harassment	19	3.1	96	9.8
Threatening	70	11.3	96	9.8
Confinement	83	13.4	84	8.7
Refused safe sex	37	6.0	68	6.9
Unacceptable request	18	2.9	65	6.6
Had or used a gun	47	7.6	62	6.3
Thrown from car			50	5.1
Acted weird/crazy	31	5.0	57	5.8
Drunk/stoned	32	5.3	35	3.6
Couldn't get off	31	5.0	30	3.1
Chased/followed by car			27	2.8
Pimp/possible pimp			24	2.4
Dumped			23	2.3
Had or used other weapon	31	5.0	51	5.2
Posed as cop	27	4.4	23	2.3
Given drugs/drugged			6	.6
Property damage	5	.8	4	.4
Other	7	1.1	91	9.3
Number of Offenses/Problems	1,180		1,943	
Number of cases	ASP/POWER = 619		DEYAS = 997	

Source: Lowman, J. & Fraser, L. (1995). *Violence Against Persons Who Prostitute: The Experience in British Columbia*. Ottawa: Department of Justice. Reprinted with permission.

In sum, the bulk of domestic murders committed by Canadian women are "self-help homicides" (Jones, 1994). A large number of women find themselves in physical danger and without any help from friends, family, or the police. Thus, as pointed out in Box 1.5, some abused women, like Manitoba resident Angelique Lyn Lavallee, find their best hope of protecting themselves is to commit what some legal scholars refer to as *self-help homicide* (Jones, 1994); that is, kill the men who sexually assault and beat them.

Box 1.5

A Canadian Example of Self-Help Homicide

I was scared. All I thought about was all the other times he used to beat me. I was scared. I was shaking as usual. The rest is a blank. All I remember is he gave me the gun and a shot was fired through my screen. This is all so fast. And then the guns were in another room and he loaded [a gun], the second shot, and gave it to me. And I was going to shoot myself, I was so upset. OK and then he went and I was sitting on the bed and he started going like this with his finger [Lavallee made a shaking motion with an index finger] and said something like "you're my old lady and you do as you're told" or something like that. He said "wait till everybody leaves, you'll get it then" and he said something to the effect of "either you kill me or I'll get you"—that was what it was. He kind of smiled and then he turned around. I shot him but I aimed out. I thought I aimed above him and piece of his head went that way.

Source: *R. v. Lavallee* (1990, p. 101).

The incident described in Box 1.5 occurred on August 30, 1986. Under law at that time, Lavallee (and other battered women who committed self-help homicide) could expect to be charged and convicted of murder because when she fired the gun she was not at great risk of being attacked by her partner and thus could not claim self-defense. However, at her trial, a psychiatrist testified on her behalf and stated that she was a victim of the **battered woman syndrome**. He argued that Lavallee was terrorized to the point of feeling trapped, vulnerable, worthless, and unable to escape a violent relationship.[6] He further claimed that she shot her partner because she sincerely thought that he was going to kill her that night.

The jury concurred with the psychiatrist and acquitted her. However, the Crown appealed this decision, and the verdict was subsequently overturned by the Manitoba Court of Appeal, which sent the case back for retrial. According to the appeal court, the trial judge inadequately warned the jurors of the dangers of relying on the psychiatrist's opinion, which they did not consider to be "real evidence" since the bulk of his testimony was based on his interviews with Lavallee (DeKeseredy & MacLeod, 1997).

The case was taken to the Supreme Court of Canada in 1990 (see *R. v. Lavallee, 1990*). The judges upheld the original acquittal, ruling that expert testimony on the battered woman syndrome is admissible and credible. Consider the following statement made by Madam Justice Bertha Wilson:

Expert evidence on the psychological effect of battering of wives and common-law partners must, it seems to me, be both relevant and necessary in the context of the present case. How can the mental state of the applicant be appreciated without it? The average member of the public (or of the jury) can be forgiven for asking: Why would a woman put up with this kind of treatment? Why would she continue to live with such a man? How could she love a partner who beat her to the point of requiring hospitalization? We would expect the woman to pack her bags and go. Where is her self-respect? Why does she not cut loose and make a new life for herself? Such is reaction of the average person confronted with the so-called "battered wife syndrome." We need help to understand it and help is available from trained professionals (cited in *R. v. Lavallee*, 1990, p. 112).

Assault

Assault occurs when a person uses, attempts to use, or threatens to use physical force (e.g., hitting, kicking, etc.) against another person without his or her consent. Assault may also occur without violence; however, it must include a threatening act or gesture (Goff, 1997). Some assaults are more injurious than others; thus, there are variations in the severity of the charges that can be laid. Depending on the type of violence used, an offender can be charged with (1) *assault*, (2) *aggravated assault*, or (3) *assault with weapon or causing bodily harm*. Assault, like murder, is a crime committed mainly by men. For example, in 1993, 19,446 Canadian men were charged with assault with a weapon or causing bodily harm, while only 2,827 women were charged with this offence (Silverman et al., 1996; Statistics Canada, 1995). Nevertheless, many conservative policymakers, police officers, academics, journalists, and members of the general public dismiss this fact and claim that female violence "is rocketing ever upward" (Gavigan, 1993, p. 222).

Well, things have hardly "gotten worse." In fact, they seem to have gotten better. For example, Table 1.3 describes a decrease in the national rate of adult females charged with nonsexual assault, with an increase from 1992-1994 followed by a decline to slightly less than the 1992 rate in 1996. Thus, many people "grossly exaggerate the level of violence that women commit and, in the process, reinforce myths of increasing violence by women . . ." (Faith, 1993b, p. 1987).

Table 1.3
Canadian Women Charged by the Police for Nonsexual Assaults, 1992-1996

	1992		1993		1994		1995		1996	
Offence	Number	Rate	Number	Rate	Number	Rate	Number	Rate	Number	Rate
Non-Sexual Assault	13,809	1.2	13,580	1.2	14,260	1.3	13,365	1.2	13,247	1.1

Source: This is a modified version of a table constructed by Dell and Boe (1998, p. 25).

Table 1.3 includes only incidents recorded by the police and compiled by the Canadian Centre for Justice Statistics. Police statistics do not provide accurate estimates of the extent and distribution of assault and other nonlethal crimes discussed in this chapter for reasons such as the following:[7]

- Many incidents are not reported to the police because they go unnoticed, or victims are not aware that they have been harmed by a criminal offence.

- Many victims do not want to "get involved" with the police.

- Some people do not want to report their victimization experiences because they are embarrassed and do not want friends, parents, neighbors, etc., to know what happened.

- Many people, especially female victims of sexual assault, fear that they will have to deal with insensitive law enforcement officials who will not take their suffering seriously or who will blame them for their victimization.

- Some people are not "allowed" to be crime victims. For example, some police departments stamp all reports of violent crimes against prostitutes as NHI—"No Human Involved"—and do not follow up on them.

- Police inflate crime statistics to make the crime problem look worse or to inflate arrest statistics to make themselves look like better crime fighters.

Thus, it is common for crimes such as assaults to take place but for many of these events to be missing from police statistics. This is often termed the *dark figure of crime*. Some people, then, contend that police statistics are misleading and that there are probably more assaults committed by females than meets the eye. This point is well taken and widely recognized by criminologists around the world. However, many assaults by men, including those directed at intimate female partners, are also excluded from the purview of the law. For example, despite both federal and provincial directives to police to treat male-to-female violence as seriously as other types of assault (e.g., male-to-male assaults in public settings), charges are still "far from typical" (Ellis & DeKeseredy, 1996; Kantor & Straus, 1990b). Consider the data presented in Box 1.6. The results support those who contend that it is "clear that a double standard for criminal justice processing of extra-family and intrafamily crime remains" (Kantor & Straus, 1990b, p. 486).

Box 1.6

The Inadequate Police Response to Wife Beating: Some Toronto Examples

Based on their analysis of 89 callers' responses to a survey administered in Toronto by the Assaulted Women's Helpline,[8] Farge and Rahder (1991) report the following disturbing findings:

- Of those who called the police about at least one previous assault (47 percent), 75 percent stated that their previous encounter with the police was negative, and approximately 60 percent stated that they either would not or did not call them again.

- Of the 62 percent of the women sampled who called the police about a recent incident, only 51 percent stated that their call was taken seriously, and 38 percent reported that their call was not taken seriously.

- The police laid charges in only 40 percent of the cases where they were called in.[9]

- Of those who called the police, 83 percent reported that they did not receive adequate support or protection from further abuse, while only 17 percent stated that they felt helped or protected because of police intervention.

- Of the respondents who called the police, 20 percent stated that they were assaulted again by their partner after the police left.

Source: The box includes modified sections of material published by Ellis and DeKeseredy (1996, pp. 191-192).

How can we obtain more accurate data on assaults committed by women and others that break the law? The answer to this question is to conduct representative *self-report surveys*. Simply put, self-report surveys ask people if they have committed any crimes. Unfortunately, there has never been a Canadian national representative sample survey specifically designed to elicit data on a wide variety of crimes committed by adult women. To the best of this author's knowledge, the only Canadian national self-report surveys of adult female involvement with crime have focused specifically on drugs (e.g., Health Canada, 1995) and dating violence (DeKeseredy & Kelly, 1993a; DeKeseredy & Schwartz, 1998; DeKeseredy et al., 1997). Thus, we need much more information on self-reported adult female crime.

There are, however, rich self-report survey data on female-to-male violence in Canadian university/college dating relationships. For example, DeKeseredy et al. (1997) analyzed data generated by DeKeseredy and Kelly's (1993a) national survey and found that almost one-half (46.1%) of the 1,835 female respondents reported physically assaulting their male dating partners or boyfriends since leaving high school, while 17.8 percent of the men victimized their female partners in such a way during the same time period. At first glance, these results seem to show that women are more violent than men. However, when women's motives for violence are taken into account, a dramatically different picture emerges—one that seriously challenges the increasingly common assertion that women are extremely violent, perhaps more violent than men.

DeKeseredy et al. (1997) found that only a distinct minority of women reported that they had ever initiated a physical attack since leaving high school. For example, 37 percent of the women who used "minor" forms of violence (e.g., slapping, pushing, shoving) initiated an attack at some time, and 43 percent initiated "severe" violent acts (e.g., punches) at least once. However, only 7 percent of the women who used "minor" violence always (100% of the time) attacked first, while only 10 percent of the women who reported using "severe" violence were always the ones who initiated an attack.

As pointed out in Table 1.4, a substantial amount of violence reported by women was in self-defense, but most women did not report using "minor" (60.9%) or "severe" acts (56.5%) of violence in self-defense. Table 1.4 also shows that many women were "fighting back." Many (though not most) of the women's acts are either self-defensive or "fighting back." Within each level of severity, self-defense and "fighting back"

Table 1.4
Percentage of Women Using Different Motives for Violence in Dating by Frequency of Violence

Motive	Number	0%	1%-49%	50%-99%	100%
"Minor Violence"					
Self-defense	678	62.3	20.1	10.7	6.9
Fighting back	677	53.6	23.2	16.1	7.1
Initiate attack	663	63.3	19.7	9.7	7.3
"Severe Violence"					
Self-defense	367	56.5	21.6	13.4	8.5
Fighting back	359	48.9	26.7	15.2	9.2
Initiate attack	359	56.8	20.9	12.4	9.9

Source: This is a slightly modified version of a table constructed by DeKeseredy, W. and Schwartz, M. (1998). *Woman Abuse on Campus: Results from the Canadian National Survey*, p. 77, copyright © by Sage Publications. Reprinted by permission of Sage Publications.

were positively and significantly correlated with each other. Initiating an attack, however, was very weakly and nonsignificantly correlated with either self-defense or "fighting back."

Several other results of DeKeseredy et al.'s (1997) study are also worth noting here. For example:

- The women who report higher levels of self-defensive violence also report higher levels of violence committed against them.

- Women who used self-defensive violence experienced much higher rates of sexual abuse in dating since leaving high school than other women in the survey.

- Women who report that their violence was always used in self-defense were about twice as likely to claim that they were made upset because their male dating partners tried to get them to engage in behavior they had seen in pornographic media.

- Women who experienced psychological abuse, threats, and physical abuse in combination since leaving high school were much more likely to respond with self-defensive violence (about 80%, compared with 36-42% of all other victimized women).

Studies like DeKeseredy et al.'s (1997) demonstrate the importance of moving beyond simply counting acts of violence and using reliable measures of motives. DeKeseredy et al.'s (1997) study also tells us that much of the violence by Canadian women in university/college dating relationships should not be labeled "male partner abuse." Unfortunately, these and similar findings are typically ignored or dismissed by much of the mainstream media, anti-feminist academics (e.g., Fekete, 1994), and other prominent conservatives who have not demonstrated expert knowledge of intimate violence. Consider Liberal Member of Parliament Roger Gallaway, Co-Chair of the Senate-Commons Committee on Child Custody and Access. Despite hearing a presentation by the author on DeKeseredy et al.'s (1997) data, in mid-June 1998, Gallaway stated that: "The empirical evidence that exists . . . shows that in society at large women are as equally violent as men. There have been tons of studies to confirm that" (cited in Cobb, June 15, 1998, p. A3).

Robbery

Defining *robbery* is a subject of debate. For example, some researchers view robbery as a property offence because the intent is theft. In fact, Desroches' (1995) study of 80 Canadian bank robbers shows that these "bandits" do not intend to hurt their victims and they are primarily motivated by money. On the other hand, although the Canadian *Criminal Code* defines robbery as a property offence, the National Parole Board, Statistics Canada, and many criminologists consider robbery to be a violent offence because it may cause physical harm (Desroches, 1995). In fact, the maximum sentence for robbery in Canada is life imprisonment.

Many people confuse robbery with break-and-enter offences, which are crimes that generally do not involve interpersonal violence. Robbery, however, involves face-to-face confrontations between offenders and victims; thus, there is the potential for violence to occur. Therefore, robbery is defined here as "theft with violence or theft with the threat of violence against persons" (Goff, 1997, p. 103).

[handwritten margin note: robbery is more interpersonal]

The rate for Canadian women charged with robbery is significantly lower than that for men. Still, the male-female ratio has decreased since the mid-1970s. For example, in 1974, the male-female ratio for those charged with robbery was 15.5 to one, while in 1992 it was 10.9 to one (Boritch, 1997; Hatch & Faith, 1991; Statistics Canada, 1994). However, the rate for women charged with robbery (per 10,000) decreased from 1992 to 1996 (.65 and .55, respectively) (Dell & Boe, 1998). It also should be noted that when Canadian women rob banks, they typically do so with men, rarely carry weapons, and often play a secondary role in the crime (Desroches, 1995). Similar data were obtained in the United States For example, a study found that 16 of 18 female bank robbers convicted in New York City either drove getaway cars or provided other nonlethal services (Haran & Martin, 1984).

However, research shows that all adult female robbers cannot be painted with the same brush. For example, Miller's (1998) study of street robbers from poor urban St. Louis, Missouri, neighborhoods shows that most of the women in her sample (10 out of 14) reported robbing other females. She also found that those who robbed women typically used violence, such as hitting, shoving, and kicking, and most of their robberies were committed with other women and never with men. On the other hand, one-half of the women in Miller's (1998) sample committed street robberies with male accomplices (almost always against men), and women's robberies of men almost always involved guns and no physical contact. Comparable Canadian studies of adult female street robbers have not been done; thus, it is unclear at this point whether Miller's findings are relevant to the Canadian context.

Still, women who participate in robberies with men usually play "marginal roles" because they are deemed to be lacking "particular qualities . . . regarded important for success as a criminal" (Steffensmeier & Terry, 1986, p. 307), such as physical strength and emotional stability. Thus, sexism is not restricted to legitimate work like lawyering or doctoring (two professions dominated by men).

Drugs

If there are gender differences in robbery, the same can be said about contraventions of the *Controlled Drugs and Substances Act*. For example, the 1994 Canadian Alcohol and Drug survey data presented in Table 1.5 show that twice as many men 15 years of age or older reported using one or more of five types of illicit drugs in the past year than did women (10.1% vs. 5.1%). In fact, more men than women reported using each of the drugs described in Table 1.5 (McKenzie & Single, 1997).

Table 1.5
Percentage of Respondents Using Drugs in the Past Year

Sex	Cannabis	Cocaine	LSD, Speed, Heroin	Use of Any 5 Illegal Drugs
Total 15+	7.4%	0.7%	1.1%	7.7%
Male	10%	0.8%	1.5%	10.1%
Female	4.9%	0.5%	0.7%	5.1%

Source: This is a modified version of a table constructed by McKenzie and Single (1997, p. 113).

In Canada, the male lifetime rate of using any of the illicit drugs described in Table 1.5 is also considerably higher than that of women. Consider the 1994 Canadian Alcohol and Drug Survey data presented in Table 1.6. This table shows major gender differences in cocaine use, as well as consumption of LSD, speed, or heroin. Canadian men are also much more likely to ingest cannabis in their lifetime than are women.

Table 1.6
Percentage of Respondents Using Drugs in their Lifetime

Sex	Cannabis	Cocaine	LSD, Speed, Heroin	Use of Any 5 Illegal Drugs
Total 15+	23.1%	3.8%	5.9%	23.9%
Male	27.7%	4.9%	8.1%	28.5%
Female	18.7%	2.7%	3.6%	19.4%

Source: This is a modified version of a table constructed by McKenzie and Single (1997, p. 112).

In sum, then, Canadian females are less likely than males to ingest illegal substances. However, the lower female rates described in Table 1.5, Table 1.6, and elsewhere (e.g., Boritch, 1997) are related in part to women's greater consumption of legal drugs, such as alcohol (Faith, 1993a). Further, adult men and women typically use illegal drugs for different reasons. For example, men mainly use these substances for excitement, pleasure, or because of peer pressure, while women are more likely to ingest them for "self-medication" to dull the pain of poverty, unemployment, family violence, and other symptoms of class, race, and gender inequality (Chesney-Lind, 1997; Inciardi et al., 1993; Pettiway, 1997).

Consider Stephanie, a 35-year-old homeless methamphetamine (referred to on the streets as *ice*) addict interviewed by Chesney-Lind (1997). Her alcoholic parents started beating her when she was five years old "with extension cord wires, water hoses, punches, everything" (1997, p. 131). She ran away, and after high school, got married and became pregnant. Her husband died shortly after the birth of her son and, since then, Stephanie has endured numerous hardships. Consequently, she "takes refuge in ice" and told Chesney-Lind that, "I can't get no help finding me and my boy a place. So because I'm homeless, that's why I do the drug, I get so depressed cause I don't have no roof over my head for me and my boy" (1997, p. 132).

When addicted to drugs, many women turn to prostitution (Mahan, 1996; Pollock, 1999), which often culminates in them being beaten, raped, and psychologically abused by their pimps, customers, or drug dealers (Miller & Schwartz, 1994). Further, for some drug-dependent prostitutes, the crack pipe becomes a pimp (Ratner, 1993), and they "will tolerate extreme levels of verbal and physical abuse in . . . pursuit of a vial of crack" (Bourgois & Dunlap, 1993, p. 123).[10] For example, crack often interferes with men's ability to maintain an erection or achieve orgasm (Inciardi et al., 1993). These consequences of being "too high" commonly result in male customers flying into a macho rage and blaming their sexual problems on the "crack whore's" failure to satisfy them (Maher, 1997).

Prostitutes who exchange sex for crack sometimes end up in **crack houses**. These are "organized places where cocaine smokers can find the privacy and paraphernalia to smoke and sometimes cook cocaine into crack or rocks" (Mahan, 1996, p. 8). Drugs may also be bought at crack houses, places where some women reach a level of degradation that few of us can imagine. Below, one of Mahan's (1996, p. 21) respondents describes some of her experiences in a crack house:

> No morals, no principles. . . . I let them treat me like a dog. . . . I'm on my knees in the bathroom . . . there's an unbelievable stink. The water is off, but they still use it, and there is every kind of filth. When they open the door it smells bad. It gags you. And this disgusting guy pulls out his filthy, smelly dick, and I would suck it anyway.

Such sex-for-crack exchanges may be normal in crack houses, but they are not typical on the streets. Moreover, those who exchange sex-for-crack on the street do not frequently, easily, or readily do it. Consider Candy, one of Maher's (1997, p. 143) respondents. Such "work" for her was a "necessary compromise," and she would only do it "If I was stressin' real bad and a guy tell me he's got two or three caps I might do it."

Prostitution

By now, you are aware that prostitution can be dangerous work. However, an important question has yet to be answered in this chapter: What is prostitution? According to the Canadian *Criminal Code* (see Sections 210 to 213), there are three types of prostitution-related crimes: (1) *procuring and living on the avails of prostitution*; (2) *bawdy-house offences*; and (3) *communicating in a public place for the purpose of buying or selling sexual services* (Lowman, 1995). These offences are described in Box 1.7.[11]

Box 1.7

Canadian *Criminal Code* Definitions of Prostitution-Related Offenses

KEEPING COMMON BAWDY-HOUSE—Landlord, inmate, etc.—Notice of conviction to be served on owner—Duty of landlord on notice.
210. (1)   Every one who keeps a common bawdy-house is guilty of an indictable offence and liable to imprisonment for a term not exceeding two years.
    (2)   Every one who
        (a) is an inmate of a common bawdy-house,
        (b) is found, without lawful excuse, in a common bawdy-house, or
        (c) as owner, landlord, lessor, tenant, occupier, agent or otherwise having charge or control of any place, knowingly permits the place of any part thereof to be let or used for the purposes of a common bawdy-house, is guilty of an offence punishable on summary conviction.
    (3)   Where a person is convicted of an offence under subsection (1), the court shall cause a notice of the conviction to be served on the owner, landlord or lessor of the place in respect of which the person convicted or his agent, and the notice shall contain a statement to the effect that it is being served pursuant to this section.
    (4)   Where a person on whom a notice is served under subsection (3) fails forthwith to exercise any right he may have to determine the tenancy or right of occupation of the person so convicted, and thereafter any person is convicted under subsection (1) in respect of the same premises, the person on whom the notice was served shall be deemed to have committed an offence under subsection (1) unless he proves that he has taken all reasonable steps to prevent the recurrence of the offence.

Box 1.7, *continued*

TRANSPORTING PERSON TO BAWDY-HOUSE.
211. Every one who knowingly takes, transports, directs, or offers to take, transport, or directs, or offers to take, transport, or direct any other person to a common bawdy-house is guilty of an offence punishable on summary conviction.

PROCURING—Idem—Presumptions—Offence in relation to juvenile prostitution.
212 (1)   Every one who
    (a) procures, attempts to procure or solicits a person to have illicit sexual intercourse with another person, whether in or out of Canada,
    (b) inveigles or entices a person of known immoral character to a common bawdy-house or house of assignation for the purpose of illicit sexual intercourse or prostitution,
    (c) knowingly conceals a person in a common bawdy-house or house of assignation,
    (d) procures or attempts to procure a person to become, whether in or out of Canada, a prostitute,
    (e) procures or attempts to procure a person to leave the usual place of abode of that person in Canada, if that place is not a common bawdy-house, with intent that the person may become an inmate or frequenter of a common bawdy-house, whether in or out of Canada,
    (f) on the arrival of a person in Canada, directs or causes that person to be directed or takes or causes that person to be taken, to a common bawdy-house or house of assignation,
    (g) procures a person to enter or leave Canada, for the purpose of prostitution,
    (h) for the purposes of gain, exercises control, direction or influence over the movements of a person in such a manner as to show that he is aiding, abetting or compelling that person to engage in or carry on prostitution with any person or generally,
    (i) applies or administers to a person or causes that person to take any drug, intoxicating liquor, matter or thing with intent to stupefy or overpower that person in order thereby to enable any person to have illicit intercourse with that person, or
    (j) lives wholly or in part on the avails of prostitution of another person, is guilty of an indictable offence and liable to imprisonment for a term not exceeding ten years.
    (2)   Notwithstanding paragraph (1) (j), every person who lives wholly or in part on the avails of prostitution of another person who is under the age of eighteen years is guilty of an indictable offence and liable for imprisonment for a term not exceeding fourteen years.
    (3)   Evidence that a person lives with or is habitually in the company of a prostitute or lives in a common bawdy-house or in a house of assignation is, in the absence of evidence to the contrary, proof that the person lives on the avails of prostitution, for the purposes of paragraph (1) (j) and subsection (2).

Box 1.7, *continued*

(4)   Every person who, in any place, obtains or attempts to obtain, for consideration, the sexual services of a person who is under the age of eighteen years is guilty of an indictable offence and liable to imprisonment for a term not exceeding five years.

OFFENCE IN RELATION TO PROSTITUTION—Definition of "public place."
213. (1)   Every person who in public place or in any place open to public view
        (2)   stops or attempts to stop any motor vehicle,
        (2)   impedes the free flow of pedestrian or vehicular traffic or ingress to egress from premises adjacent to that place, or
        (2)   stops or attempts to stop any person or in any manner communicates or attempts to communicate with any person for the purpose of engaging in prostitution or obtaining the sexual services of a prostitute is guilty of an offence punishable on summary conviction.
    (2)   In this section, "public place" includes any place to which the public have access as of right by invitation, express or implied, and any motor vehicle located in a public place or in any place open to public view.

Source: Canadian *Criminal Code.*

Procuring and *living on the avails* were created to deter third parties from financially profiting from the prostitution of other people. Only a few people are prosecuted each year for these offences (Lowman, 1995). According to the *Criminal Code* (see Section 197(1), a *bawdyhouse* is "a place that is (a) kept or occupied, or (b) resorted to by one or more persons for the purpose of prostitution or the practice of acts of indecency" (Watt & Fuerst, 1990, p. 281). Bawdy-house offences are prosecuted more frequently than the crimes listed above, and most *communicating* offences result from a prostitute or customer communicating with an undercover officer "for the purpose of engaging in prostitution or of obtaining the sexual services of a prostitute . . ." (Lowman, 1995; Watt & Fuerst, 1989, p. 314).

If you carefully read Box 1.7, you will see that in Canada, prostitution itself is not against the law; but the combined effect of the provisions described there "makes it virtually impossible for a prostitute to work without breaking a prostitution-related law" (Boritch, 1997, p. 97). Obviously, then, Canadians are given contradictory messages. They are told that they have the right to prostitute but they cannot legally do so. For Lowman (1992, p. 78), this is an excellent example of "legislative finesse," a problem addressed below by a Vancouver police officer (quoted in Lowman, 1989, p. 211):

> The politicians are afraid to go one way or the other—it could be political suicide. . . . We're not willing to condone prostitution even though it would be easier to do so—it comes down to being a moral question. Right now, we're left with the politi-

cians being able to satisfy both sides. You can say, "I think it should be legalized," and they can say, "Well, yes, it is legal." Somebody else can say, "I think it should not be legalized, I think it should be illegal" and they can say, "Well, yes, that's why we've got these laws to control it." Why would any politician rock the boat and take a hard and fast stand in either direction?

If the prostitution laws described in Box 1.7 are problematic, the same can be said about dominant social images of the "oldest profession." Most people and dictionaries define a prostitute as a woman who engages in sex for money in a "relatively indiscriminate way" (Boritch, 1997; Lowman, 1992, p. 50; Shaver, 1993). Some researchers contend that this image ignores the fact that other types of heterosexual relationships are characterized by "sexual liaisons . . . devoid of any emotional attachment" (Lowman, 1995, p. 335). Consider women (and some men) who marry for money and "kept women" (Salamon, 1984). The latter are those who provide sex in exchange for financial support (e.g., an apartment, car, etc.) (Boritch, 1997). What about homeless women who have sex with men in exchange for a warm meal and a temporary roof over their heads (Lowman, 1995)?

A much longer list of relationships involving sex in return for money or other material advantages could be provided here. The most important points to consider here are that prostitution can take many shapes and forms (Lowman, 1991) and that not all women who engage in sexual acts for gain are viewed as prostitutes. Thus, "prostitution" is a label or "designation" (Becker, 1973; Schur, 1984). Because sex-for-money exchanges are so widespread, the decision to criminalize or condemn some types rather than others is "largely a subjective judgement call" (Boritch, 1997, p. 92).

In Canada, adult prostitution is primarily a female occupation (Lowman, 1995), with some studies suggesting that the ratio of female to male prostitutes is three or four to one (Crook, 1984; Fraser Committee, 1985). Moreover, at first glance, it seems that women are much more likely than are men to be charged for prostitution-related offences, as described in Table 1.7. However, the data presented in this table should be read with caution because most of the statistics relate to street prostitution and exclude people involved in less visible types of prostitution (e.g., "call girls"). Less visible prostitutes are at lower risk of arrest and prosecution because they work in houses, apartments, hotels, massage parlors, strip clubs, and other "off-street" locations (Boritch, 1997, p. 94). Moreover, street prostitutes do not dominate the market (Shaver, 1993). For example, in 1983, street prostitution only made up 20 percent of all the prostitution in Toronto (Bureau of Municipal Research, 1983). In sum, the figures presented in Table 1.7 are not representative of all adult Canadian prostitutes.

Table 1.7
Canadian Men and Women Charged With Prostitution-Related Offences (1975-1991)

	Women		Men	
Year	Number	%	Number	%
1975	2,372	5.3	696	0.2
1980	960	0.2	596	0.0
1985	566	0.9	385	0.1
1986	3,863	5.9	2,939	0.9
1987	4,938	7.0	5,340	1.6
1988	5,445	7.5	5,179	1.5
1989	5,277	7.3	4,411	1.3
1990	5,523	7.2	4,944	1.4
1991	5,596	6.7	5,075	1.3

It should be noted that this table includes all prostitution-related offences described in Box 1.7, as well as transportation and communicating offences (up to and including 1985).

Source: This table includes data presented in a table constructed by Shaver (1993, p. 156) from *In Conflict with the Law: Women and the Canadian Justice System*, eds. Ellen Adelberg and Claudia Currie, Press Gang Publishers, Vancouver, Canada, 1993. Reprinted with permission.

As pointed out in Table 1.8, men also get arrested for prostitution-related offences. For example, except for 1988, more men than women were arrested for procuring between 1975 and 1991. Women, on the other hand, were much more likely than men to be arrested for bawdy-house and other prostitution-related offences, except for communicating, in 1987. There is also some evidence showing that women represent only a small number of people involved in prostitution. Consider Shaver's (1993) Montreal study, which found that, in 1991, 96 percent of those involved in communicating for the purpose of prostitution were men, and the bulk of these men (99%) were clients.

The bulk of Canadian research on prostitution has focused on street prostitutes, and thus a brief description of their social and economic backgrounds is warranted here. Although street prostitutes come from a variety of backgrounds, like their United States counterparts, most have been sexually and physically abused as children, come from broken homes, and have few economic options (Chesney-Lind, 1997; Crook, 1984; Faith, 1993a; Gemme, 1984; Lowman, 1984). They are clearly not motivated by a desire for sex; they work the streets strictly for financial gain (Lowman, 1992). Street workers do not get "easy money," but it is "fast money" (Chesney-Lind, 1997, p. 139). Street prostitution, then, is a way to make a living—a means of survival in "gender-stratified" society. More will be said in Chapter 2 about the factors that contribute to women's "qualified choice" (Faith, 1993a) to become street prostitutes.

Table 1.8
Distribution of Charges Against Canadian Women for Prostitution-Related Offences By Type of Prostitution (1975-1991)

	Bawdy House		Procuring		Other	
Year	%	Number	%	Number	%	Number
1975	62	998	35	95	87	1,975
1980	63	668	23	78	67	783
1985	66	714	22	108	53	129
1986	58	756	38	178	57	5,868
1987	52	779	33	311	48	9,188
1988	64	587	55	292	50	9,745
1989	58	600	14	159	55	8,929
1990	65	482	29	177	53	9,808
1991	62	550	27	216	52	9,905

The category "other" includes data on soliciting and transporting up to and including 1985, and transportation and communicating after 1985.

Source: This is a slightly modified version of a table constructed by Shaver (1993, p. 156) from *In Conflict with the Law: Women and the Canadian Justice System*, eds. Ellen Adelberg and Claudia Currie, Press Gang Publishers, Vancouver, Canada, 1993. Reprinted with permission.

Property Crimes

Under the heading of property crimes fall: *fraud, theft, breaking and entering*, and *possession of stolen goods*. As described in Table 1.9, between 1992 and 1996, Canadian women were much more likely to be charged by the police for these offences than for others discussed in this chapter. Table 1.9 also shows that there was a major decrease in the number of women charged with property offences from 1992 to 1994, followed by a gradual decrease to 1996. Further, Table 1.10 shows that, between 1993 and 1997, women were less likely to be charged than were men for committing property offences.

Data described in Table 1.11 show that as was the case in 1992,[12] in both 1996 and 1997, most women charged with property crime were arrested for the least serious offences, such as theft under $5,000. The second highest number of arrests in both years was for fraud (e.g., writing bad checks and credit card fraud). Table 1.11 also tells us that while the rate of arrests for all female property offences increased from 1996 to 1997, the number of women charged for each of these crimes pales in comparison to that of men during this time period.

Table 1.9
Canadian Women Charged by Police*

Offence	1992		1993		1994		1995		1996	
	Number	Rate per** 10,000	Number	Rate per 10,000	Number	Rate per 10,000	Number	Rate per 10,000	Number	Rate per 10,000
Crimes of violence	14,287	13.1	14,706	13.2	15,284	13.5	14,325	12.5	14,258	12.3
Property Crimes	47,118	43.2	44,235	39.7	37,490	33.2	36,110	31.6	36,005	31.0
Drugs***	5,860	5.4	5,631	5.1	5,442	4.8	5,143	4.5	5,213	4.5
Other****	25,997	23.8	24,957	22.4	21,982	19.5	22,476	19.6	21,097	18.2
TOTAL	93,242	85.5	89,529	80.4	80,198	71.0	78,054	68.2	76,573	66.0

*Source: Uniform Crime Reports
**Rate per 10,000 total adult female (aged 18+ years) population
***Drugs = Narcotics Control Act & Food and Drugs Act
****Other = Federal Statutes and Other Crime
*****Traffic offences (Criminal Code and Impaired Driving) are excluded

Source: This is a slightly modified version of a table crafted by Dell and Boe (1998, p. 3).

Table 1.10
Men and Women Charged by the Police for Property Crimes

	1993	1994	1995	1996	1997
Adults Charged	181,220	161,748	159,128	162,946	146,910
Men	136,982	124,273	122,940	125,861	113,280
Women	44,238	37,475	36,188	37,085	33,630

Source: This is a modified version of a table constructed by Statistics Canada (1998).

Men and women commit property crimes for different reasons. Men steal as a means of "doing masculinity" (Messerschmidt, 1993) and tend to steal goods like stereos and tools, items that are not necessary for their survival (Chesney-Lind, 1987). On the other hand, women steal items that are lower in value but are useful to them as mothers, homemakers, or for feminine appearances, such as clothing, groceries, and makeup. They also write bad checks mainly to get these items. Moreover, women who defraud the government do so because they and their children cannot afford to live on minimal welfare payments or wages accumulated from "pink ghetto" work (e.g., working as a store clerk) (Faith, 1993a).

The increase in number of Canadian women charged for property crimes in 1997 is in large part due to the fact that societal reactions to their behaviors have become more punitive (DeKeseredy & Schwartz, 1996; Faith, 1993a; Messerschmidt, 1986). This is what Chesney-Lind (1997, p.

152) refers to as "equality with a vengeance"—the dark side of the equity or parity model of justice that emphasizes the need to treat women offenders as though they were "equal" to male offenders." Still, economic factors, such as poverty, also play a key role. So does family disruption, a problem that is significantly related to women's financial difficulties.

Table 1.11
Men and Women Charged For Various Types of Property Offences

Offence	1996		1997	
	Number of Men	Number of Women	Number of Men	Number of Women
Break & Entering	26, 595	1,678	24, 181	1,542
Theft over $5,00	2,102	527	1,723	457
Theft under $5,000	53,612	23,690	48,411	21,068
Possession of Stolen Goods	14,406	2,178	12,408	1,777
Fraud (credit card and writing bad checks)	20,477	8,485	18,429	8,202

Source: The data described in this table are derived from the Uniform Crime Reporting System and were given to the author by Shelly Crego, an Information Officer at the Canadian Centre for Justice Statistics.

For many Canadian women, these problems are getting worse (Alvi et al., 2000), and the linkage between family problems, economic factors, and women's increasing involvement in property crime is perhaps best explained below by Steffensmeier (1993, p. 17):

> Rising rates of divorce, illegitimacy, and female-headed households, coupled with continued segregation of women in low-paying occupations, have aggravated the economic pressures on women and have left them more responsible for child care than they were two or three decades ago. Growing economic adversity increases the pressure to commit consumer-base crimes, such as shop-lifting, check fraud, theft of services, and welfare fraud.

Given Canadian women's high levels of unemployment and poverty,[13] it is surprising that more women are not being arrested for property offences (Messerschmidt, 1986). A growing number of Canadian women are living in a "cold new world" (Finnegan, 1998). This world is characterized by the following major economic changes: globalization, the rise of the "contingent" work force, the North American Free Trade Agreement, transnational corporations moving to Third World countries to use cheap labor, the implementation of high technology in workplaces, and the shift from a manufacturing economy to a service-based economy (Alvi & DeKeseredy, 1997; W. Wilson, 1996). Thus, it is likely that we will see even more women committing, and being arrested for, property offences. An increase in the number of men charged for these crimes is also likely because many men are also faced with the problem of trying to make a living in a "harder country" (Finnegan, 1998).

White-Collar, Corporate, and Organized Crime

So far, this chapter has focused on interpersonal crimes committed mainly by socially and economically disenfranchised men and women. Of course, many such offences cause Canadians a great deal of pain and suffering. Still, the social, economic, psychological, environmental, and physical costs of these crimes are much smaller than the costs of those committed in "suites" (e.g., corporate boardrooms) by corporate executives and other white-collar workers. Consider *corporate violence*, a problem defined by DeKeseredy and Hinch (1991, p. 100) as:

> any behavior undertaken in the name of the corporation by decision makers, or other persons in authority within the corporation that endangers the health and safety of employees or other persons who are affected by that behavior. Even acts of omission in which decision makers, etc., refuse to take action to reduce or eliminate known health and safety risks, must be considered corporate violence. It is the impact the action has the victim, not the intent of the act, which determines whether or not it is violence.

In Canada, exposure to toxic elements due to hazardous working conditions and similar circumstances is at least 30 times greater than the rate of interpersonal violence (Ellis & DeKeseredy, 1996). Further, it is estimated that a Canadian dies in the workplace every six hours as a result of corporate violence. This type of crime causes more deaths in a month than do all of the mass murders in a decade (Snider, 1993). What role do women play in corporate and white-collar crime? Women are underrepresented relative to men in "crimes of the powerful" (Pearce, 1976). For example, although, government statistics reported in this chapter and elsewhere show increases in charges laid against women for fraud, most of these crimes are actually instances of welfare fraud and not really white-collar crime (Daly, 1989; Freidrichs, 1996).

According to Sutherland (1949, p. 9), *white-collar crime* is an offence "committed by a person of respectability and high status in the course of his occupation." A major reason why there is so little female white-collar crime is that Canadian women are significantly underrepresented in high-status jobs (Alvi et al., 2000; Forcese, 1997). In fact, most women have traditional "pink ghetto" jobs (e.g., nursing, sales, teaching etc.). Statistics Canada (1996) data presented in Table 1.12 show that women are "more proletarianized" than men (Carroll, 1987). This is also why so few women commit *corporate crimes*, offences defined here as those "committed by corporate officials for their corporation and the

Table 1.12
Canadian Women Employed by Occupational Group, 1982 and 1989

Occupational Group	% of Employed Women		Women as % of Sector of Employment	
	1982	1989	1982	1989
Clerical	33.9	30.5	79.0	80.4
Service	18.3	17.0	54.5	56.7
Sales	10.1	9.9	39.8	46.4
Nursing/Health	8.9	8.6	85.1	85.4
Teaching	5.7	5.6	64.3	66.1
Managerial/admin	6.0	10.7	29.2	38.1
Professional social science	1.9	2.3	47.5	57.1
Professional natural science/engineering/ mathematics	1.3	1.6	14.7	19.2
Diagnostic/ treat-ment health professionals	0.3	0.5	18.3	33.3
Other Professionals	2.0	2.5	34.5	41.0
Processing/machining	1.9	1.8	14.1	15.9
Product fabricating/ assembling/repairing	4.4	4.2	21.2	22.0
Construction	0.2	0.3	1.4	2.2
Transportation	0.5	0.7	6.0	8.6
Material handling/ Crafts	1.8	1.8	19.5	22.2
TOTAL	100.0	100.0	41.3	44.1

Source: This is a modified version of tables constructed by Forcese (1997, p. 93) and Statistics Canada (1996, p. 23). Adapted from "Canadian Social Trends," Catalogue No. 11-008, Autumn 1990, p. 23.

offences of the corporation itself" (Clinard & Quinney, 1973, p. 188). As in the United States, Canadian women, then, have relatively few chances to commit white-collar or corporate offences (Messerschmidt, 1993). A more in-depth account of why men have a "virtual monopoly" on crime "in the suites" is offered in Chapter 3 (Messerschmidt, 1993).

What about *organized crime* (e.g., money laundering, loan sharking, pornography, etc.), a term that is not found in the Canadian *Criminal Code* (Beare, 1996)?[14] For the purpose of this chapter, organized crime "is a process—an activity possessing certain attributes and characteristics" (Lupsha, 1986, p. 33). Very little is known about the extent of Canadian and American women's involvement in this process (Pollock, 1999). Further, to the best of the author's knowledge, not one systematic study on the extent, nature, and distribution of organized crimes committed by women has been done in Canada. Still, because United States research shows that organized crime groups are dominated by "old-boy" networks and women are either excluded or underrepresented in criminal syndicates (Beirne & Messerschmidt, 1995; Steffensmeier, 1983), it is fair to assume that a similar situation exists in Canada. Obviously, much more research on this topic is needed.

SUMMARY

Who commits the vast majority of crime in Canada? As elsewhere, men do. Crime is clearly a gendered social problem, and gender is consistently the strongest predictor of criminal involvement (Messerschmidt, 1993). What else can we conclude from the data described in this chapter? First, contrary to popular belief, in Canada, there has not been a dramatic increase in violent crimes committed by women. On the contrary, police data show a slight trend decrease overall (Dell & Boe, 1998). Further, in intimate relationships, such as dating, much of female violence is in self-defense or fighting back (DeKeseredy et al., 1997).

We can also conclude that most adult female offenders, like their American counterparts, mainly commit property offences. Within this category, they commit the least serious types of offences, such as theft under $5,000, and they do so out of economic necessity, most notably in order to meet their family responsibilities (Daly, 1989; Zietz, 1981). Of course, many men suffer from poverty as well, but not to the same extent as women. Unemployed women get lower unemployment benefits because of lower wages, and tend to be jobless longer than men. Further, single women and those heading single-parent families are usually coping with wages well below the poverty line, while single working men get about 33 percent more total income than unattached females (Forcese,

1997). Again, it is surprising that the rates of adult female property crime reported here are not higher than they are. The same can be said about adult female violence, given that an alarming number of Canadian women are beaten, raped, and brutally victimized in a variety of ways by male intimates.

In sum, as pointed out in numerous studies of and books on women in conflict with the law (e.g., Adelberg & Currie, 1993; Boritch, 1997; Faith, 1993a), Canadian women do not constitute a major threat to our safety. Nevertheless, much of the data reported in this chapter are derived from problematic official data that fail to tell us about crimes that do not come to the attention of police and other agents of social control. Moreover, we know very little about women's involvement in white-collar and corporate crime, and even less about their role in organized or enterprise crime. Thus, more and better studies are necessary, such as those that use self-report survey techniques and ethnographic methods (e.g., participant observation).

NOTES

[1] This is a pseudonym Lefkowitz (1997) used to protect the identity and maintain the privacy of this rape survivor and her family.

[2] Reena did, in fact, suffer multiple fractures, including fractured arms, a broken neck, and a broken back (Chisholm, 1997).

[3] *Fallen Women* is the title of Boritch's (1997) book on female crime and criminal justice in Canada.

[4] Following the lead of Ellis and DeKeseredy (1997), intimate femicide refers here to the killing of females by male partners with whom they have, have had, or want to have, a sexual and/or emotional relationship.

[5] See DeKeseredy and MacLeod (1997), Ellis and DeKeseredy (1996), and a special issue of *Violence Against Women: An International Journal* (Vol. 3, No. 6, 1997) for in-depth reviews of research on post-separation woman abuse.

[6] See Walker (1979) for more information on this concept.

[7] These criticisms are derived from the writings of DeKeseredy and MacLean (1991), DeKeseredy and Schwartz (1996), Fairstein (1993), Karmen (1990), Miller and Schwartz (1994), and the Solicitor General of Canada (1986).

[8] Eighty-one percent of these calls were from Metropolitan Toronto, and 11 percent were from the Peel region. The rest of the calls came from surrounding regions, such as York and Durham.

[9] National Canadian data also show that charges are not usually laid. For example, female respondents to the Violence Against Women Survey stated that while the police responded to 84 percent of the abusive incidents reported to them, charges were laid in only 28 percent of the cases (Rodgers, 1994).

[10] For more in-depth information on sex-for-crack exchanges, see Bourgois & Dunlap (1993), Feldman et al. (1993), Inciardi et al. (1993); Mahan (1996), Maher (1997), Ouellet et al. (1993), and Ratner (1993).

[11] See Watt and Fuerst (1989, pp. 307-315) and Lowman (1995, pp. 335-342) for more information on these *Criminal Code* provisions

[12] See Bortich (1997) and Statistics Canada (1994) for more in-depth information on the 1992 data on females charged for property offences.

[13] See Alvi et al. (2000) and Forcese (1997) for comprehensive overviews of the empirical literature on female poverty in Canada.

[14] However, the *Proceeds of Crime* legislation refers to the term *enterprise crime*, which includes 24 offences considered as enterprise/organized crimes and certain drug offences that are enforced under the Proceeds of Crime legislation (Beare, 1996).

DISCUSSION QUESTIONS

1. What role do the mass media play in leading Canadians to believe that female violent crime is increasing?

2. What are the key factors that contribute to property crimes committed by women?

3. How can we obtain more accurate estimates of female crime?

4. Men and women use drugs for different reasons. Explain.

5. What role do women play in robbery?

6. Should prostitution be considered "victimless" or harmless work?

PROBLEM-SOLVING SCENARIOS

1. Get together with a few people and discuss ways in which researchers can influence the media to provide more accurate accounts of the extent and nature of female violence.

2. Clip five articles on the extent of crimes committed by Canadian women from newspapers and articles. Identify whether these articles are consistent with the data presented in this chapter.

3. In a group, try to develop a theory that explains why more men than women commit crime.

4. In a group, identify the ways in which you, your friends, or your classmates have been directly or indirectly affected by women's involvement in crime.

5. In a group, discuss the strengths and limitations of police statistics, as well as means of overcoming their shortcomings.

6. Generate a group discussion on the possible reasons why women's involvement in organized crime has not been give much scientific attention.

SUGGESTED READINGS

Adelberg, E., & Currie, C. (eds.). (1993). *In Conflict with the Law: Women and the Canadian Justice System*. Vancouver: Press Gang.

> This book includes a collection of important essays on various issues surrounding women's involvement in crime and the Canadian criminal justice system's response, all of which are written from a feminist perspective. Some of the topics covered are prostitution, imprisonment, and aboriginal women and crime. Like the other books recommended here, this one has an outstanding bibliography.

Boritch, H. (1997). *Fallen Women: Female Crime and Criminal Justice in Canada*. Scarborough, ON: Nelson.

> Written by one of Canada's leading experts on female crime, this is an excellent resource for students and researchers alike who are looking for a comprehensive book on key empirical, conceptual, theoretical, and political issues surrounding female crime in Canada.

Chesney-Lind, M. (1997). *The Female Offender: Girls, Women, and Crime*. Thousand Oaks, CA: Sage.

> Chesney-Lind provides a comprehensive, intelligible overview of female offenders (both adults and juveniles) in the United States and the criminal justice system's response to their offences. Written from a decidedly feminist standpoint, her path-breaking book also provides progressive and effective alternatives to hard, "law and order" methods of social control.

DeKeseredy, W.S., & MacLeod, L. (1997). *Woman Abuse: A Sociological Story*. Toronto: Harcourt Brace.

> This textbook is designed to give students an in-depth overview of sociological perspectives on psychological, sexual, and physical variants of woman abuse in intimate, heterosexual relationships. The voices of

women who have been victimized are also included throughout this text, and the authors devote a substantial amount of attention to describing the strengths and limitations of various policies aimed at curbing woman abuse.

Faith, K. (1993). *Unruly Women: The Politics of Confinement and Resistance*. Vancouver: Press Gang.

This widely read and cited book offers an excellent overview of women's involvement in crime, the ways in which women are oppressed by social control practices, and the techniques these people use to resist various modes of sexist oppression.

Suman Virk, mother of murder victim
Reena Virk, talks to media representatives
outside court. The extensive media
coverage of the brutal crime has
contributed to public misperceptions
regarding the extent of crime by
Canadian women and girls.

Chapter 2

Crimes Committed by Canadian Girls

INTRODUCTION

Like many conservative United States politicians, academics, journalists, and members of the general public, a growing number of Canadians are accessing "one of the oldest traditions within criminology—sensationalizing women's violent crimes" (Chesney-Lind, 1999, p. 1). Canadian girls' violent crimes are also sensationalized. The Reena Virk case discussed in Chapter 1 is an outstanding example of a statistically insignificant incident used by conservatives to help them justify a "war" on young female offenders. Consider what Schissel (1997a) refers to as the "condemnatory images" of teenage girls described in Box 2.1 by Canadian journalist Patricia Chisholm (1997, p. 7).

> [P]ublic images of typical delinquents are primarily about males. When female youth are targeted, the depictions are couched in "paradox talk": it is so unusual for girls to act aggressively or antisocially that bad genes must be at work. The "sugar and spice" understanding of femaleness is often the standard upon which young female offenders are judged, and in effect, the images of "bad girls" are presented as biological anomalies and/or sinister products of a feminist movement. A general woman-hatred appears to underlie the "sugar and spice" conception of femaleness in articles that discuss the wild, passionate and out-of-character woman who has to be constrained or held back, revealing a dual stereotype of women in Western society—nice but emotional and unpredictable.
>
> (Schissel, 1997a, p. 107)

Box 2.1

Condemnatory Media Images of Teenage Girls

Whatever the reasons, some teenage girls clearly are experiencing acute—at times uncontainable—levels of anger and are showing far more willingness to strike out. Researchers and clinicians are also discovering a chilling lack of empathy among young girls—a quality that, until recently, appeared to be more common among adolescent boys. Miriam Kaufman, a Toronto pediatrician and author of *Mothering Teens: Understanding the Adolescent Years*, says many girls she counsels seem devoid of even a basic moral sense. "It's as if right and wrong are not even part of their experience and vocabulary," she says. Such detachment appears to have been very much present among some of those charged in Virk's death: according to the mother of one of the accused, her daughter is a habitual troublemaker utterly lacking in remorse. "If you don't like the person, beat them up. Whatever you want you can have," she says, describing her daughter's mentality.

Source: Chisolm, P. (1997). "Bad Girls: A Brutal B.C. Murder Sounds an Alarm About Teenage Violence." Maclean's (December 8). Reprinted with permission.

The information presented in Boxes 2.1 and 2.2 has fueled a *moral panic* about girls in conflict with the law. The concept of the moral panic was developed by Stanley Cohen (1980) to describe a situation in which a condition, episode, person, or a group of persons come to be defined as a threat to society. The objects of moral panics are usually people. The media, together with some sociologists, lawyers, psychologists, and other "experts," have quickly jumped on the bandwagon to help transform Canadian girls into *folk devils*. A folk devil is "a socially constructed, stereotypical carrier of significant social harm" (Ellis, 1987, p. 199). Now, instead of being viewed as vulnerable and socially and economically marginalized, many Canadian girls are seen as made up of "sugar and spice and everything evil" (Schissel, 1997a, p. 51).

Box 2.2

Killer Girls

Girls, it used to be said, were made of sugar and spice. Not anymore. The latest crop of teenage girls can be as violent, malicious and downright evil as the boys. In fact, they're leading the explosion in youth crime. It's an unexpected byproduct of the feminist push for equality.

Source: This box appeared in the *Alberta Report* (July 31, 1995a, p. 1). See Schissel (1997a) for more condemnatory media accounts of Canadian girls in conflict with the law.

Boxes 2.1 and 2.2 include "stereotypical presentations," that lack journalistic and scientific integrity (Schissel, 1997a, p. 71). Like girls in the United States, except with regard to prostitution and shoplifting, Canadian girls are much less involved in crime than are boys (Boritch, 1997).[1] Further, the gender gap in official crime rates has not significantly decreased since the implementation of the *Young Offenders Act* (see Box 2.3) (Schissel, 1997a). The purpose of this chapter, then, is to present more accurate information on the extent and nature of female youth crime than stories told by ***criminal mythmakers*** (Kappeler et al., 1996). These are journalists who use ***techniques of myth characterization*** outlined by Kappeler et al. (1996, pp. 25-26), which are summarized in Box 2.4,[2] to shape the presentation of crimes committed by girls, to create images for uncritical audiences, and to promote a punitive societal reaction.

Box 2.3

A Brief Description of the *Young Offenders Act* (YOA)

The *Young Offenders Act* (YOA) has been in force in Canada since 1984. It prescribes how the police, courts and correctional system handle young people who come into contact with the justice system. This law applies equally across Canada to all youths aged 12 to 17 (up to the eighteenth birthday) at the time the criminal offence is committed. It does not apply to children under 12 years old.

The YOA has been developed around a set of guiding principles that balance the rights and responsibilities of youths and society. These principles, which guide the interpretation of the YOA, can be summarized as follows:

- Society has both the right to be protected from youth crime, as well as the responsibility to take reasonable steps to prevent it. Multidisciplinary approaches to crime prevention that identify and respond to children and youths at risk are essential to reduce and prevent crime.

- Young people who commit crimes are responsible for their actions and should be held accountable in a way that is suitable given their age and level of maturity.

- Youths who commit crimes require supervision and discipline but, because they have special needs, they also require assistance. Programs that focus on rehabilitation are the best way to protect society and address the needs of young offenders.

- Alternatives to judicial proceedings should be considered for young offenders. In many cases, this means that youths who commit less serious, nonviolent crimes can make amends to victims by apologizing, agreeing to mediation, or doing volunteer work in the community.

Box 2.3, *continued*

- Young people accused of committing crimes have the same rights as accused adults, as set out in the *Canadian Charter of Rights and Freedoms* and the *Canadian Bill of Rights*. This guarantee of rights means that youths have: the right to be consulted on decisions that affect them, the right to the least possible interference with their freedom (when compatible with the protection of society), and the right to be informed of their rights and freedoms. Previously, the youth system (*Juvenile Delinquents Act*) was very different from the adult system.

- Parents are responsible for the care and supervision of their children. Young persons should be separated from their families only when the parents have failed to provide adequate supervision.

A Brief Note About Children Under 12

Children under 12 are not covered by the *YOA*, but are governed by child welfare and mental health legislation. Agencies that administer these laws are specific to each province and territory but generally intervene when children become involved in serious delinquent activities and/or when parents are not able to deal with them. These agencies also become involved in cases of abuse, neglect or parental death. They have access to a wider range of services than the formal criminal justice system and can address the needs of the family and community when dealing with the children's problems.

Source: Stevenson et al. (1998). "A Profile of Youth Justice in Canada," Catalogue No. 85-544, pp. 9-10. Reprinted with permission. See Alvi (2000) for more information on the *Young Offenders Act* (*YOA*), how it has changed over time, and the law governing Canadian young offenders prior to the *YOA*.

Box 2.4

Techniques of Crime Characterization

- *Creating criminal stereotypes.* This involves using phrases such as "bad girls," which characterize girl offenders as "sinister products of the feminist movement" or as "biological anomolies" (Schissel, 1997a, p. 107).

- *Presentation of opinion as fact.* This practice involves injecting personal opinion into media presentations without factual basis. An example of a phrase that presents an opinion as fact is the following part of a headline that appeared in the July 31 issue of the *Alberta Report* (1995b, p. 24): "Prodded by feminism, today's teenaged girls embrace antisocial male behavior."

- *Masking opinions through sources.* This involves collecting opinions of others that closely match the journalist's view on a given issue. Recall in Box 2.1, journalist Patricia Chisholm did not present the opinions of some of Canada's leading experts on young offenders (e.g., University of Saskatchewan sociologist Bernard Schissel) who did not find evidence of young girls "showing far more willingness to strike out."

Box 2.4, *continued*

- *Value-loaded terminology.* Biased language is used to characterize and label girls' crimes or criminals. Some examples of such language are: "malicious," "evil," "ruthless monsters," and "feminist cults of androgyny" (*Alberta Report*, July 31, 1995b).

- *Selective presentation of fact.* Presenting certain facts to the exclusion of others strengthens biased arguments about female youth crime. Consider magazine and newspaper articles that ignore data described in this chapter.

- *Information management.* The editorial process by which a particular news story is shaped and selected for presentation to the exclusion of other stories is one way to manage information. Presenting stories about sensational crimes like the murder of Reena Virk (see Chapter 1) to the exclusion of stories on the alarming rates of male-to-female violence in intimate relationships is an example of such management.

- *Undocumented sources of authority.* Vague references, including statements like "many people feel" or "many people are saying" without specific reference to who is saying what and what constitutes "many," is a misleading reference to authority.

- *Stripping fact from its context.* Also referred to by Schissel (1997a) as the "decontextualization of crime," this practice involves using facts or statements of authorities appropriate in one context and transferring them to another to support a particular position or injecting facts that are unrelated to the issue. A media presentation on three Calgary girls who stabbed a Calgary man that focuses on recording artist Courtney Love and her band *Hole* without addressing whether there is an empirical link between the two is stripping fact from its original context (see *Alberta Report*, July 31, 1995b).

- *Selective interviewing.* Another method of portraying a position as more solid than the facts indicate is interviewing one or two authorities on girls' crimes and presenting their remarks as the generalized expert opinion on a given topic. For example, interviewing one or two researchers or clinicians and giving the audience the impression that those views are reflective of the research or clinical community. Chisholm (1997) (see Box 2.1) used this method to give the impression that violent crimes committed by Canadian girls are on the rise.

THE NATURE AND EXTENT OF CRIMES COMMITTED BY CANADIAN GIRLS

The types of crimes discussed in Chapter 1, except for white-collar, corporate, and organized crime, are also examined here, as well as girls' involvement in street youth gangs. We turn to murder first.

Murder

Juvenile homicide constitutes only about 7 percent of all murders in North America, and in both Canada and the United States, most youths under the age of 18 who kill people are male. Of all the "Canadian kids who killed" between 1961 and 1983, 89 percent were male and 11 percent were female (Meloff & Silverman, 1992). Major gender differences are also evident in the number of youths charged for committing various types of "deadly deeds" in 1993 (Silverman & Kennedy, 1993), as pointed out in Table 2.1. Refer to Box 1.2 for legal definitions of these offences.

Table 2.1
Canadian Girls and Boys Charged for Homicide, 1993

Offence	Number of Boys Charged	Number of Girls Charged
Homicide		
First-degree murder	12	0
Second-degree murder	17	3
Manslaughter	4	0
Infanticide	0	0
TOTAL	33	3

Source: This table is adapted from Silverman et al. (1996, p. 295) and Statistics Canada (1995).

Attempted murder is also primarily an offence perpetrated by young males, with 61 boys and nine girls charged in 1993 (Silverman et al., 1996). So much for the notion that "killer girls" are "leading the explosion in youth crime" (*Alberta Report*, July 31, 1995a, p. 1). Still, the data and statistics on attempted murder that are presented in Table 2.1 do not speak to the question of whether the rates of homicide and attempted murder have dramatically increased in the last several years. Contrary to popular belief, they have not. Table 2.2 shows that from 1992 to 1994, the rate of girls charged for homicide has remained constant. There was a small increase in 1995, followed by a decrease in 1996. Further, the data on attempted murder described in Table 2.2 show that girls are not more likely to commit this crime today than they were in 1992.

Table 2.2
Girls Charged by Police for Homicide and Attempted Murder, 1992-1996

	1992		1993		1994		1995		1996	
Offense	Actual Number	Rate per 10,000	Actual Number	Rate per 10,000	Actual Number	Rate per 10,000	Actual Number	Rate per 10,000	Actual Number	Rate per 10,000
Homicide	4	.04	3	.03	4	.03	12	.10	3	.03
Attempted Murder	12	.11	9	.08	9	.08	4	.03	6	.05

Source: This is a modified version of a table constructed by Dell and Boe (1997, p. 24).

A comparison of Table 2.2 with Table 2.3 shows that many more boys than girls were charged with homicide and attempted murder from 1992 to 1996. Still, the male youth homicide rate decreased significantly from 1992 to 1993, and it remained stable in subsequent years. The male youth attempted murder rate was at the highest point in 1994 and dropped considerably in 1995. Thus, boys and girls alike are not becoming more deadly threats to Canadian society.

Table 2.3
Boys Charged by Police for Homicide and Attempted Murder, 1992-1996

	1992		1993		1994		1995		1996	
Offense	Actual Number	Rate per 10,000	Actual Number	Rate per 10,000	Actual Number	Rate per 10,000	Actual Number	Rate per 10,000	Actual Number	Rate per 10,000
Homicide	49	0.41	33	0.27	48	0.40	49	0.40	47	0.38
Attempted Murder	66	0.56	61	0.51	103	0.85	81	0.66	81	0.65

Source: This is a modified version of a table constructed by Sinclair and Boe (1998, p. 27).

Who are the victims of murders committed by Canadian girls? Data provided by Meloff and Silverman (1992, p. 27) in Table 2.4 answer this question. These researchers found that girls rarely commit homicide in the process of committing another crime, such as robbery. For example, from 1961 to 1983, 25 percent of the juvenile male homicides were "crime-related," compared to only 3 percent of the girl killings. On the other hand, as in the United States, the percentage of family members killed by girls is significantly higher than that for boys. Still, boys murder their parents slightly more often than do girls. Further, proportionately, girls kill strangers more than males do. However, Meloff and Silverman (1992) contend that this finding is likely an artifact of the low number of girls who commit homicide.

Table 2.4
Social Relationship by Offender Sex—Offenders Under 18, Canada, 1961-83

Sex of Offender				
	Male		Female	
Relationship	Number	%	Number	%
Parent	78	14	8	12
Sibling	49	9	9	14
Other family	46	8	15	23
Other relation	192	35	23	35
Stranger	44	8	8	12
Crime-related	138	25	2	3
TOTAL	547	100	65	100

Source: Meloff, W. & Silverman, R.A. (1992). "Canadian Kids Who Kill." *Canadian Journal of Criminology* (January): 15-34, Table 8. Reprinted with permission of the Canadian Criminal Justice Association.

Why do girls kill? It is beyond the scope of this chapter to provide in-depth answers to this question; however some brief explanations are warranted here. Table 2.4 challenges the stereotype of them being "gun-toting robbers" (Loper & Cornell, 1996). Further, while their offences may appear "psychotic," most offenders are not. Moreover, the majority are not "intellectually dull" or mentally retarded (Ewing, 1990). Rather, most come from abusive or neglectful families, and many have alcoholic or mentally ill parents. In fact, girls who kill their parents (or, in other words, commit *parricide*[4]) typically do so for revenge against, or escape from, an abusive parent. Some girls kill their fathers or stepfathers during or after incidents in which these men physically or sexually assaulted their mothers (Ewing, 1990). Consider the case of Mary Bailey, described by Ewing (1990, p. 21) in Box 2.5.

Box 2.5

An Example of Parricide

In February 1987, eleven-year-old Mary Bailey shot and killed her stepfather. Mary and her mother, Priscilla Wyers, were both charged in the killing. Testifying at her mother's trial, Mary told the jury that her stepfather physically abused her mother. Mary testified further that her mother asked her to kill her stepfather and "I told her yes. I told her right off the bat." On the morning of the killing, Mary's mother woke her up and directed her to the living room, where she found her stepfather asleep with a loaded rifle sitting nearby. Mary picked up the rifle and after three tries—succeeded in killing her stepfather. Mary was placed in a state foster home; her mother was convicted of first-degree murder.

Even where there is no conspiracy, explicit or implicit, between parent and child, the killing of one parent to protect the other parent is not an uncommon scenario in juvenile parricide.

Source: Ewing, C.P. (1990). *Kids Who Kill.* Lexington, MA: Lexington Books.

Girls who kill outside the family, such as those who murder peers and strangers, do so mainly because of an interpersonal conflict, and girls are more likely than boys to kill nonrelatives alone (Chesney-Lind, 1997; Ewing, 1990; Loper & Cornell, 1996). What about girls who kill siblings, aunts, and uncles? According to Ewing (1990), the motives for these killings are unclear; however, some of these murders seem to be related to psychopathology.

Assault

Table 2.5 shows a small, steady increase in the number of girls charged for nonsexual assault from 1992 to 1996. However, as pointed out in Chapter 1, many incidents are not reported to the police for a variety of reasons (e.g., embarrassment; incidents go unnoticed, etc.). Thus, the figures reported in Table 2.5 should be read with caution. Further, the increase in charges laid from 1994 to 1996 are likely the result of police officers, teachers, and the general public taking a more punitive approach to incidents that were previously dealt with informally, such as schoolyard fights and bullying[5] (Bala, 1997; Carrington, 1995; Gartner & Doob, 1994; Schissel, 1997a; Stevenson et al., 1998). Some other behaviors that would have likely been viewed as "incorrigibility" by parents, police, and other adult authority figures are now being labeled "assault." For example, there is evidence that police officers are now encouraging parents to block doorways when their children threaten or attempt to run away from home, and then charging these girls and boys with "assault" when they shove their parents out of the way (Chesney-Lind, 1997).

Table 2.5
Girls Charged by Police for Nonsexual Assault, 1992-1996

	1992		1993		1994		1995		1996	
Offence	Number	Rate Per 10,000	Number	Rate Per 10,000	Number	Rate Per 10,000	Number	Rate Per 10,000	Number	Rate Per 10,000
Assault	3,818	33.9	4,550	39.9	4,389	38.2	4,521	38.9	4,541	38.5

Source: This is a modified version of a table constructed by Dell and Boe (1997, p. 24).

A comparison of Table 2.5 with Table 2.6 reveals significant differences in the rate of boys and girls charged for nonsexual assault from 1992 to 1996. Obviously, a much lower number of girls are charged for this offence. Further, Table 2.6 shows a steady increase in charges laid against boys from 1992 to 1995, followed by a considerable decrease in 1996 to a little more than the 1992 rate.

Table 2.6
Boys Charged by Police for Nonsexual Assault, 1992-1996

	1992		1993		1994		1995		1996	
Offence	Number	Rate Per 10,000	Number	Rate Per 10,000	Number	Rate Per 10,000	Number	Rate Per 10,000	Number	Rate Per 10,000
Assault	10,807	91.19	11,458	95.48	11,958	98.87	12,400	101.39	11,827	95.57

Source: This is a modified version of a table constructed by Sinclair and Boe (1998, p. 27).

Self-report survey data also show that boys outnumber girls in committing physical assault (Gomme et al., 1984, Tanner, 1996), especially in heterosexual dating relationships (DeKeseredy & Schwartz, 1998). Further, research strongly suggests that when Canadian girls hit their boyfriends, they mainly do so in self-defense, while many boys hit girls as a result of a desire to dominate or control them (Gagné & Lavoie, 1993). This is also common in Canadian university/college dating relationships. Recall that, in Chapter 1, data were presented showing that much of the female violence directed against boyfriends and dates is either self-defense of fighting back (DeKeseredy et al., 1997). On the other hand, one of the strongest determinants of male-to-female violence is men's adherence to the *ideology of familial patriarchy*. This is a discourse that supports the abuse of women who violate the ideals of male power and control over women in intimate relationships (DeKeseredy & Schwartz, 1988). Relevant themes of this ideology are an insistence on women's obedience, respect, loyalty, dependency, sexual access, and sexual fidelity (Barrett & McIntosh, 1982; Dobash & Dobash, 1979; Pateman, 1988).

Like college and university men, boys are heavily influenced by the ideology of familial patriarchy (DeKeseredy & Schwartz, 1994). According to Mercer (1988, p. 16):

> Adolescence is clearly not a period when young people reject the traditional gender roles for which they have been groomed. It is characteristically a time when they act them out—sometimes to their worst extremes. The alarming revelations about this process testify to the grave personal implications that male power has for females long before they become adults.

Consider the case described in Box 2.6 by Vicki Crompton (1991, pp. 23-25). Her 15-year-old daughter Jenny was the homicide victim of an estranged boyfriend, who acted out some of the above patriarchal themes to "their worst extremes." On September 26, 1986, he stabbed Jenny more than 60 times with a butcher knife. Moreover, he repeatedly slapped her during the last few months of her life.

Box 2.6, *continued*

An Example of Patriarchal Violence in Teenage Dating

Mark ignored Jenny's attempts to break up. He still shared the locker, still walked her to class, still called. When she insisted that he stop, that she wanted to break up, he became more insistent, more possessive. The phone calls increased, the unannounced visits to the house more frequent. He would not move out of her locker. Because he made it so difficult, Jenny simply gave up and agreed to go back. When I questioned her, she said that she cared for him and wasn't sure she wanted to end it. This on-again, off-again routine continued for the next several months, into the summer, until Jenny made the final break.

As Jenny increased her attempts to pull away, Mark intensified his actions to keep her locked in. He seemed to always know her plans. At first she would unwittingly tell him where she was going. Then, as she attempted to keep this information from him, he would turn to her girlfriends and find out about her activities from them. He was so skillful that, on one occasion, he showed up at a family reunion on her dad's side of the family, having been invited by Jenny's cousin with whom he had struck up a friendship. Her trips to the mall were marred by Mark's sudden appearance. Her weekly dance lessons were punctuated by his arrival, cunningly timed just a few minutes before I arrived to pick her up. The boys who expressed interest in her were quickly squelched by a visit from Mark, who curtly told them, "She's my girl; leave her alone."

As Jenny grew more distant, he became more desperate. I realize now that he must have sat in the dark and watched our house at night. One night we decided on the spur of the moment to walk up the block for an ice cream cone. Outside our door, I noticed movement behind parked cars. Greg (Vicki's husband) investigated and discovered Mark and his friend crouching behind the cars, watching our house. Another night, at midnight, I heard noises at Jenny's second-floor window. She and I looked out to see Mark standing below, throwing rocks at her window, yelling "Jenny, Jenny."

By August 1986, Jenny had enough. Triumphantly, she called me at work one day and announced that she "had done it, really broken it off with Mark." She sounded happy, excited, relieved to be free. School would be starting in a few weeks, and Mark would not be there (he had graduated in the previous spring). I never saw Mark Smith again. I thought he had gone away. The phone calls stopped. There were no more visits.

From Jenny's perspective, however, he never did go away. He just became more deceitful. She discovered that he was entering the school grounds and breaking into her locker, the same locker they had shared the year before. He would go through her things and read the notes her friends had written. She began to suspect that he was entering our home when we were gone; she told her friends that things in her room were often not as she had left them. Mark's picture, which she had put away in a drawer, kept reappearing on top of her TV. He left her threatening notes that hinted she "would not make it to homecoming" and desperate lines that said, "I wish you would die." She told her friends about these things and even laughed the day of the homecoming parade, saying, "Well, I'm still in one piece." She never told me.

Box 2.6, *continued*

Friday, September 26, 1986, I woke Jenny to get her into the shower before I left for work. I hugged her and kissed her before leaving, as I always did. That morning I said, "I love you Jen," something I didn't always do. And she replied, "I love you too, Mom." We spoke briefly about the homecoming game that evening, and she asked if I could drive her to the dance or if she should ride with her friends. Then I rushed out the door. My day was uneventful. I was bored and had many things to do at home. I thought about asking my boss if I could leave work early, but I resisted the urge. I left work at my usual time and drove home thinking about the busy night ahead.

When I drove onto my street, the first thing I saw were groups of neighbors standing in their yards, looking toward my house. Then I saw the ambulance, the police cars, the fire truck. I saw police officers running out of my house. I started shaking so violently that I could barely park my car. I ran out, shouting, "What's happening here?" I was stopped from entering my home and told that my daughter had been stabbed, but that "the paramedics are working on her." I watched as they carried her out on a stretcher and took her away in an ambulance. I hung onto a white and shaken Greg as he described walking into the house and finding Jenny "lying in a pool of blood." I sat in the hospital emergency room and heard them tell me that my daughter was deceased. Dead? Not Jenny. I just talked to her this morning. She is only fifteen. How can she be dead?

Source: Copyright 1991 by Vicki Crompton from *Dating Violence: Young Women in Danger,* edited by Barrie Levy. Reprinted by permission of Seal Press.

Self-report survey data also show that girls are more likely to be victims of schoolyard or playground *bullying* than are boys. Further, they are less likely than boys to be perpetrators of this behavior. For example, Statistics Canada's National Longitudinal Survey of Children and Youth found that 14 percent of boys between the ages of four and 11 reported regular bullying, compared to 9 percent of the girls sampled in this age group. Girls (7%) are also slightly more likely to be victimized then are boys (5%) (Craig et al., 1998).

Bullying is not a violation of the Canadian *Criminal Code*; still, it is a problem for many children, one that often involves uttering threats and various types of physical violence. Nevertheless, girls are less likely to physically bully other children than are boys. When girls bully, they typically do so by gossiping (Craig & Pepler, 1997). It should also be noted that male bullies are typically physically stronger than are their victims (Olweus, 1987), while female bullies are usually weaker than other children their age (Roland, 1989).

Robbery

As described in Table 2.7, the rate of girls charged for robbery increased considerably between 1992 and 1996. Further, between 1987 and 1997, the female rate increased 417 percent (five per 10,000 in 1997). The male youth rate also increased considerably (166%) during this time period (25 per 10,000 in 1997), albeit to a much lesser degree (Stevenson et al., 1998). So, although the rate of girls charged for robbery has risen, many more boys commit robbery—and the gender gap in arrest rates is still very large. Also, keep in mind that when reading Table 2.7 and other data on women's and girls' arrest rates, when arrest rates are low to begin with, small changes in the rate can translate into major changes in terms of percentages (Stevenson et al., 1998).

Table 2.7
Girls Charged by Police for Robbery, 1992-1996

	1992		1993		1994		1995		1996	
Offence	Number	Rate Per 10,000	Number	Rate Per 10,000	Number	Rate Per 10,000	Number	Rate Per 10,000	Number	Rate Per 10,000
Robbery	380	3.4	418	3.7	406	3.5	517	4.4	574	4.9

Source: This is a slightly modified version of a table constructed by Dell and Boe (1997, p. 24).

Drugs

Since 1987, the number of Canadian boys and girls charged for drug offences has increased considerably. In 1997, the male rate was 35 per 10,000, while the female rate was six per 10,000. We have witnessed a 42 percent increase for boys and a 50 percent increase for girls in a 10-year period (Stevenson et al., 1998). Still, as is the case with robbery, there is a major gender gap in the rate of youths charged for drug offences. Of course, police data are not accurate indicators of drug use. Again, more accurate findings are derived from self-report surveys, such as MacLean's (1994) study of high school students in a small Canadian prairie town. His statistical analyses show that boys were more likely to use more kinds of illicit substances (e.g., cocaine, opiates, etc.) than were girls.

Other Canadian surveys generated similar results, such as the 1995 Ontario Student Drug Survey conducted by the Addiction Research Foundation of Canada (1995). For example, 3 percent of the male high school students in the sample reported using cocaine, compared to 1.6 of the females. Also, 3 percent of the males stated that they ingested heroin, while only 1 percent of the females reported using this drug.

There are several factors associated with girls' drug use, and one of the most powerful determinants is having been physically and sexually assaulted by parents (Brook & Brook, 1996; Russell, 1986). For the victims of such abuse, drugs are used to control or dull the pain of their victimization. Although drug use can be dangerous, for some survivors of incest, beatings, and other types of abuse bestowed upon them by their parents, drugs are the most effective recourse that they can find (Sleeth & Barnsley, 1989).

Prostitution is another major factor associated with some girls' drug use. For example, drug use can make "working the streets" psychologically easier, and it is often faster and more financially rewarding for some girls to finance their drug use through prostitution than through legitimate or other illegitimate means (Incidardi et al., 1993).

Drugs can also be a means of coping with poverty, a social problem that devastates many Canadian children and adolescents. In 1996, more than one in five children lived in a low-income family (Stevenson et al., 1998), and poor youths report higher levels of mental health stress and lower levels of academic achievement than their more affluent counterparts (Schissel, 1997b).[6] Thus, it is not surprising that some poor female youths use drugs to cope with the day-to-day struggle of being at the bottom of the socioeconomic ladder (Currie, 1993). Further, many poor Canadian children are raised in impoverished, transient inner-city neighborhoods (Alvi et al., 2000; Hatfield, 1997; Stevenson et al., 1998), places where many adults use drugs and legitimate means of recreation and employment are scarce, if available at all.

Such environments, as one of William Julius Wilson's (1996, p. 56-57) respondents points out, also influence poor children, males and females alike, to ingest illicit substances:

> They're in an environment where if you don't get high you're square. You know what I'm saying? If you don't get high some kind of way or another . . . and then, you know, kids are gonna emulate what they come up under. . . . I've watched a couple of generations—I've been here since '61. I've watched kids, I saw their fathers ruined, and I seen 'em grow up and do the same thing. . . . The children, they don't have any means of recreation whatsoever out here, other than their backyards, the streets, nothing. . . . The only way it can be intervened if the child has something outside the house to go to, because it is— just go by the environment of the house, he's determined to be an alcoholic or drug addict.

Prostitution

According to the law and the general public's perception, adolescent prostitutes differ greatly from prostitutes who are 18 and older (Van Brunschot, 1995). However, there is really not much difference between adult women and girls who prostitute when one considers that most adult prostitutes started their involvement in prostitution as teenagers (Lowman, 1986). For example, Lowman (1992) found that 67 percent of the female prostitutes he interviewed in Vancouver in 1984 started their careers before the age of 18. Further, Canadian research reviewed by Van Brunschot (1995) shows that adolescent and adult female prostitutes do not differ much in terms of their individual backgrounds and risk factors. Still, adolescents have fewer job opportunities than adults do,[7] and younger prostitutes are in higher demand than their older counterparts (Lowman, 1992). Thus, an adolescent's "attractiveness to customers willing to buy her services makes prostitution appear most viable to the young person with very little work experience who faces the alternative of working for minimum wage at McDonalds" (Van Brunschot, 1995, p. 303).

How many Canadian female adolescents are prostitutes? This is a difficult, if not impossible, question to answer. Prostitutes' customers (or "johns," as they are known on the street) are not likely to report their encounters with prostitutes to the police, researchers, or others because of embarrassment, fear of reprisal, and other factors. In fact, most johns are deeply concerned about keeping their sexual relations with prostitutes secret (Boritch, 1997). After all, the consequences of being caught by the police or someone telling their friends, neighbors, intimate partners, or others about their involvement with one or more prostitutes are significant. For example, in 1993, Calgary judge Sharon Vanderveen ordered a man to tell his wife about his conviction in order to deter others from buying sex on the street (Boritch, 1997; Tanner, 1993). How would you feel if your intimate partner found out that you bought sex on the street, and how would he or she react? For obvious reasons, adolescent prostitutes are also eager to keep their work hidden.

Although we may never know the true extent of female prostitution, we do know that the number of female adolescent prostitutes is much lower than the number of adult prostitutes. For example, of the 720 female prostitutes charged in Vancouver in 1986 and 1987, 13.5 percent were youths (Lowman, 1995). Since 1986, the rate of adolescents charged with prostitution-related crimes has never been greater than 12 percent of the total number of charges, and in 1991, it dropped to 4.5 percent of the total charges (Van Brunschot, 1995). Table 2.8 also shows that, except for bawdy-house offences, girls are more likely than are boys to be charged for prostitution-related offences.

Table 2.8
Canadian Boys and Girls Charged for Prostitution-Related Offences, 1993

Youths Charged		
Offense	Boys	Girls
Bawdy House	2	1
Procuring	15	19
Other Prostitution	36	230
Total	53	250

Source: This is a modified version of a table constructed by Silverman et al. (1996, pp. 298-299).

Like adult female prostitutes (see Chapter 1), adolescent females do not get involved in street prostitution because they desire sex. Rather, prostitution is a means of financial survival. Further, the key risk factors related to involvement in the sex trade are: family violence, unemployment, running away from a conflict-ridden home or having been thrown out of the home, and experiences of intrafamilial sexual abuse (Badgley, 1984; Bracey, 1979; Lowman, 1987; Van Brunschot, 1995). In Box 2.7, John Lowman (1995, p. 347), one of Canada's leading experts on prostitution, provides a perspective on becoming a street prostitute, one that addresses the contribution of most of the risk factors described here.

Box 2.7

Becoming a Street Prostitute

Generally, the weight of evidence suggests that the "typical" street prostitute enters the trade somewhere between the ages of thirteen and nineteen, and usually after running away from either a state home (group homes, foster homes, etc.) or the home of one or both natural parents. These teenagers run away because they find home life intolerable. None of these factors alone, however, explains why they turn to prostitution. This "choice"—and most of they prostitutes interviewed insist they made a choice—must be contextualized. Most prostitutes have little education and, by virtue of belonging to the age group with the highest unemployment rate, are only marginally employable. They are not eligible for welfare assistance until the age of nineteen, and they have not usually been trained in the skill of independent business. What is attractive about the street culture is that it allows the runaway or disaffiliated youth a sense of belonging, a feeling of autonomy, and a means of financial independence. Most important, street prostitution provides a means of subsistence. As the fast and substantial money that it does bring to a core group of prostitutes symbolizes much that is cherished in mainstream materialist Western culture.

Source: From John Lowman, "Prostitution in Canada" in Margaret A. Jackson and Curt T. Griffiths (eds.), *Canadian Criminology: Perspectives on Crime and Criminality*, p. 347. Copyright © 1995 by Harcourt Brace & Company Canada, Ltd. All rights reserved. Reprinted by permission of Harcourt Canada, Limited.

Street Youth Gangs

No chapter on young offenders, regardless of whether the focus is on boys or girls, is complete without addressing *street youth gangs*. However, before examining Canadian girls' involvement in these subcultures, it is first necessary to define the term *gang*. Many North Americans loosely use this term to refer to groups of youths who "hang around" street corners, malls, or other public places, and who belong to either the same class or ethnic group (Schissel, 1997a). What's wrong with this picture? Don't adults congregate in public places too? Why aren't those who do also defined as street gang members?

Just because youth with similar backgrounds hang out together does not mean that they are gang members or that they will get in trouble with the law. It is normal and healthy for youth to want to spend time with their friends, and adolescents who do not often have psychological problems (Huff, 1993). Most serious youth crime (e.g., violence) is committed in groups (Bursik & Grasmick, 1995; Currie, 1985), but the vast majority of Canadian youth who "flock together" do not belong to street youth gangs, do not engage in serious criminal behaviour, and do not see themselves as part of a gang. Thus, many popular perceptions of street gangs are distorted (Decker & Kempf-Leonard, 1995; Horowitz, 1990). These perceptions are hardly trivial because they are currently contributing to a moral panic about "kids out of control," and they target and scapegoat members of visible minorities (Schissel, 1997a).

How often do you hear or read in the newspaper statements such as, "Asian gang members responsible for violent attack?" Schissel's (1997a) research on youth crime and moral panics shows that such racial references are common in Canadian newspapers. It is likely, though, that you would be hard-pressed to read one headline referring to "white youth offenders" or "European Canadian gangs" (Schissel, 1997a). Racism is part and parcel of much of the popular discourse on youth street gangs, and the average (white) citizen responds differently to three or four youths of color "hanging out" than they do to groups of white youths doing so (Shelden et al., 1997). Keep in mind, however, that a study of gang members imprisoned in Vancouver found that 68 percent of them were born in Canada (Gordon, 1993). There are also distorted perceptions of girls' involvement in gangs and gang-related crime, an issue to be addressed further on in this section.

Not surprisingly, many social scientists disagree with popular perceptions of youth gangs. As you might expect, they do not view all groups of unsupervised youths milling around on the streets as gangs (Short, 1997). Still, there is much disagreement among sociologists and criminologists about what constitutes a street gang.[8] For example, James Short (1990, 1997), one of the leading United States experts on street youth gangs, refuses to equate street gangs with crime. He defines gangs as:

groups, whose members meet together with some regularity, over time, on the basis of group-defined criteria of membership and group-defined organizational characteristics; that is, gangs are non-adult-supervised, self-determining groups that demonstrate continuity over time (1997, p. 81).

Others, like Toronto-based community psychologist Fred Mathews (1993), contend that what distinguishes youth groups from gangs is that the latter are typically engaged in criminal activities. Klein (1995) provides a definition similar to Short's (1997), but includes "commitment to a criminal orientation." Who is right and who is wrong? Well, street youth gangs are not "purely criminal organizations" (Shelden et al., 1997). Most gang members, like others who commit crimes, spend most of their time engaging in conformist activities, like having coffee with their friends. Further, they spend a great deal of time "waiting for something to happen" (Jackson, 1989).

Further, not all crimes committed by gang members are *gang-related*. Consider a gang member who kills his estranged girlfriend because she had sexual relations with another boy who is not part of any gang. Another example would be a gang member who commits robbery on his or her own for his or her own financial gain. Such crimes are not gang-related, while the killing of a rival gang member because he or she killed a fellow gang member is gang-related (Shelden et al., 1997). For the purpose of this chapter, gang-related crimes committed by girls will be examined, although very briefly, for reasons described below.

In the United States, a disproportionately high number of street youth gang members are male (Carrigan, 1998; Ellis & DeKeseredy, 1996). For example, Esbensen and Winfree (1998) conducted a multisite survey of 5,935 eighth-grade students in 42 schools located in 11 United States cities and found that only 38 percent of the gang members in their sample are females. Unfortunately, we know very little about the extent of Canadian girls' involvement in street youth gangs. To the best of my knowledge, there are no Canadian studies comparable to Esbensen and Winfree's (1998) study, the Denver Youth Survey (Huizinga, 1997), and other widely read and cited United States surveys.[9]

Also conspicuously absent are Canadian *ethnographies* of female street youth gangs. Ethnographic research involves studying a smaller number of people in great depth, through a variety of techniques, such as *participant observation*. In the traditional sense, this type of research involves joining a group, such as a street youth gang, to experience the world as its members do, or at least as closely as possible. Thus, in Canada, "It is time for a conscientious inclusion of females in the study of gangs—not only for academic reasons, but also for identifying and designing gang prevention programs that include girls in the target population" (Esbensen & Winfree, 1998, p. 521).

Just because there is a dearth of rich Canadian social scientific research on female youth gangs and the crimes they commit does not mean that the general public and the media dismiss these issues. Frequently, the media report stories about girl gangs, which include "unsubstantiated but condemnatory statements about gang behavior" (Schissel, 1997a, p. 60). Some academics are also guilty of this. Consider history professor David Carrigan (1998), author of *Juvenile Delinquency in Canada: A History*. In his book, he devotes slightly more than one page to girl gangs and uncritically presents unsubstantiated statements made by members of the Metropolitan Toronto Police force to newspaper reporters.

Below is an excerpt from Carrigan's (1998, pp. 196-197) analysis of girl gangs:

> Although the majority of youth gangs are made up of males, young females are also a part of the contemporary scene. Some mix with males; others belong to girl gangs. In an earlier day female gangs were rare, even in big cities, but such is no longer the case. By 1989 they were numerous enough in Toronto to be targeted by the police and, by the early 1990s, they were being described as a "big problem." Some police maintain that they are as capable of violence as boys and that they show no remorse for attacking people. Membership in girl gangs is described as being more fluid than male gangs, with participants coming and going at short intervals. One Toronto detective observed that "a girl gang changes membership nightly, depending on the social setting. And because the motive is excitement, thrills and kicks, we have bored wealthy girls involved. It's not just street kids." The crimes the females engage in are usually robbery, theft of clothing and jewellery, and assault. In some cases, they extort money in schools for allowing other students to use the washroom, or in return for a guarantee of safety while walking through the halls. The girls frequently turn to beating up others, and many carry knives or weapons.

Carrigan's account is similar to those provided by many United States journalists. Quotes from "experts," who are often "people without data" (Schwartz & DeKeseredy, 1994), are generally used to support the journalist's notion that female gang activity is a major problem in the United States. For many feminist criminologists, the pattern of citing police officers and other "leading experts in the field" who have never conducted a survey or participant observation study, or who have never demonstrated any sophisticated knowledge of the field, is "more than a little familiar" (Chesney-Lind, 1997, p. 36).

Because accounts of girl gangs, such as Carrigan's, are common does not mean that they are accurate. Moreover, they contribute to a moral panic. It is time for journalists, academics, criminal justice officials, and others to either read or do "responsible work on girls in gangs" (Chesney-Lind, 1997, p. 57). Responsible research shows that North American girl gangs are not new and that girls have been in gangs for decades. Such research is also sensitive to the broader social, cultural, and economic forces that contribute to girl's involvement in gangs.

Why do girls join gangs? The shortage of Canadian social scientific quantitative and qualitative research on girls in gangs has led to a conspicuous absence of Canadian attempts to answer this question. Connell (1987) refers to the empirical and theoretical "selective inattention" (Dexter, 1958) given to girl gang members in Canada and elsewhere as the "cognitive purification of social cleavages" (quoted in Joe & Chesney-Lind, 1993, p. 3). Again, when girl gang members are discussed in Canada, it is generally through derogatory media stereotypes of "bad," "evil," or masculine female adolescents (Shelden et al., 1997). This is not to say that this problem does not exist elsewhere, such as in the United States. Several United States scholars have devoted substantial attention to examining girl gangs. Their analyses warrant attention here.[10]

In the United States, as you might expect, most girl gang members are socially and economically disadvantaged (Shelden et al., 1997). For them, the gang is seen as a collective solution to the following problems that await them (Campbell, 1990, pp. 172-173):

- A future of meaningless domestic labor with little possibility of educational or occupational escape;
- Subordination to the man in the house;
- Responsibility for children;
- The social isolation of the housewife; and
- The powerlessness of underclass membership.

Many Canadian girls currently face the same problems, especially a meaningless educational and occupational future. Unfortunately, for reasons described in Box 2.8, it does not look like things are going to get better (Cherney, 1999, p. A6). Thus, the "attraction of the gang is no mystery in the context of the isolation and poverty that is awaiting" many girls in Canada and in the United States (Campbell, 1990, p. 182).

As stated previously, many Canadian youths live in impoverished communities. So do many adolescents in the United States. Such areas are characterized by several other risk factors associated with joining a girl gang, such as boredom, lack of resources, and high visibility of crime (Joe & Chesney-Lind, 1995; Wilson, 1996). In addition to buffering girls' from the day-to-day stress associated with these problems, the gang functions as a "surrogate family" (Chesney-Lind, 1997), one that protects them from neighborhood and parental violence. For example, one of Joe and Chesney-Lind's (1995) respondents was frequently beaten by her father until she joined a gang, which taught her means of defending herself. She told Joe and Chesney-Lind (1995, p. 425), "He used to beat me up, but now I hit back and he doesn't beat me much now." It should be noted in passing that 62 percent of the girl gang members in Hawaii interviewed by Joe and Chesney-Lind had been either physically or sexually abused.

Box 2.8

Fewer than Half of Canada's Teens Find Part-Time Work

Canada's shrinking labour market for part-time, teenaged workers risks turning out a generation of inexperienced employees who falter when they finally hit the workplace in their 20s, according to the author of a new study on 15- to 19-year olds.

Dr. Jean Kunz, a sociologist with the Canadian Council on Social Development, found that in 1997, the most recent year for which figures are available, only 47% of teenagers held part-time jobs, compared with the 57% who held jobs in 1988, before the last recession.

By 1996, 16% of 19-year-olds had never held a job, compared with only 6% in 1989—and teens from low-income and immigrant families were the least likely to find jobs, according to the Youth at Work in Canada study by Dr. Kunz and Dr. Grant Schellenberg.

For me this is an alarming fact," said Dr. Kunz. "I'm worried about the future of our workplace. You need experience to get a job. It's a transition from youth to adulthood."

Youthful experience scooping ice cream, painting houses, or babysitting, is often considered a plus by employers when they evaluate young job candidates fresh out of school, said Dr. Kunz.

"A job gives you responsibility, a taste of what it's like in the workplace, and interpersonal skills."

Dr. Kunz attributes the teen joblessness to a bottleneck effect of overqualified university students and graduates holding jobs traditionally available to younger, part-time workers.

Among teenagers with family incomes of less than $20,000, less than half held jobs. Immigrant teenagers were twice as likely as Canadian-born teenagers to reach 19 without holding a job.

Dr. Kunz attributes the immigrant and low-income disadvantage to a lack of family connections and community networks which help Canadian-born, middle-income teens land their first jobs.

But while a part-time job is valuable experience, teens who worked more than 15 to 20 hours weekly lost ground at school, and were more likely to get in trouble with the police. More than 10 hours weekly cut into sleeping hours, exercise time, and breakfast.

Source: Cherney, E. (1999). "Fewer than Half of Canada's Teens Find Part-time Work." *National Post*, January 19, A6.

What can we conclude from the research on girl gangs briefly summarized here? Chesney-Lind (1997, p. 176) provides one of the best answers to this question. Based on her own research and in-depth review of other studies, she contends that girls' pathways into gangs in particular as well as crime in general are:

> affected by the gendered nature of their environments and particularly their experiences as marginalized girls in communities racked by poverty. The recent increase in girls' participation in gangs has, as we have seen, roots in the violence in the girls in these communities suffer. Sadly, though, the gang that promised safety and a sense of belonging often becomes a new site for girls' exploitation while facilitating their further involvement in violence and crime.

Property Crimes

If girls' involvement in gangs is strongly related to their marginalized position in society, the same can be said about their property offences. Consider homeless street youths. They spend a great deal of time looking for money, clothes, and places to sleep. For many of them, theft—especially stealing food—is a key source of survival (Hagan & McCarthy, 1997). Being hungry leads to property crime (Tanner, 1996). So does the pain and suffering caused by lacking proper clothing for surviving in bad weather. For example, Lisa, one of Hagan and McCarthy's (1997, p. 87) homeless respondents, described how she stole sheets and blankets so that she and her peers could get some protection from the cold:

> I went to the hospital once, because I was really, really sick, and I stole a bunch of hospital blankets, so we had sheets and blankets. [In the day, I stored them] in a locker . . . the lock was broken, so you could stick the key in whenever you want, and you didn't have to put money in.

The number of Canadian girls charged with property crimes is significantly lower than that of boys. For example, in 1997:

- The male theft rate was 155 per 10,000, while the female rate was 77 per 10,000.

- The male break-and-enter rate was 123 per 10,000, while the female rate was 14 per 10,000.

- The male motor vehicle theft rate was 45 per 10,000, while the female rate was 7 per 10,000 (Stevenson et al., 1998, p. 29).

The number of girls charged for each of the above offences has not changed much between 1987 and 1997. For example, the rate of girls charged with theft in 1997 was just 5 percent lower than the 1987 rate. Further, the female break-and-enter rate increased by only 1 percent, and the motor vehicle theft rate increased by only 3 percent. Moreover, when you combine all three offences into one category—property offences—the rate of girls charged in 1997 is the same as in 1987 (Stevenson et al., 1998).

Canadian self-report surveys of youth crime are rare (Gomme, 1993). Nevertheless, the handful that have been conducted so far show that the male-female ratio of property offences is smaller than that found in police data. For example, Gomme's (1982) analysis of 1977 survey data gleaned in Kingston, Ontario (1982) reveals smaller gender differences in minor theft (1.30:1), medium theft (2.26:1), car theft (3.08:1), and break-and-entry (2.59:1). Similarly, MacLean's (1994) delinquency survey of students in a small Saskatchewan prairie town did not uncover gender differences in theft and break-and-entry that are comparable to those in official statistics.

Of all the property offences committed by girls, shoplifting is by far the most common. Many more girls than boys are charged for this offence. Of course, for homeless youths, shoplifting is generally a means of survival. For other girls, though, consumer culture plays a major role (Chesney-Lind & Shelden, 1992). For example, both adult and adolescent women are targets of major advertising campaigns that are purposely designed to make them feel inadequate unless they have certain types of cosmetics and clothes. Unfortunately, in a capitalist patriarchal country such as Canada, a girl's status and popularity is heavily based on her physical appearance. Consequently, if she can not afford to buy something that is supposed to make her attractive, she might steal it (Campbell, 1981; Chesney-Lind & Shelden, 1992). Consider the following comment made by one Chesney-Lind and Shelden's (1992, pp. 43-44) respondents:

> I took everything. I mean from pins to makeup, and fingernail polish and fake fingernails. Even toothbrushes [laughs]. We went over there to go shopping, but I told them, "Nah, I shop for you guys," and what I went away with . . . was almost $300. I had two packages full.

SUMMARY

The research reviewed in this chapter yields several conclusions. The first one is that the Canadian media frequently present condemnatory images of girls (Schissel, 1997a). Second, the messages sent out by "criminal mythmakers" (Kappeler et al., 1996) do not coincide with the data described in this chapter. Canadian girls are not as (and certainly not more) violent than boys; moreover, the contexts, meanings, and motives of their violent crimes and other offences differ from those of boys. Further, like most Canadian women who break the law (see Chapter 1), most Canadian girl offenders commit property crimes, especially shoplifting.

Another point that stands out in this chapter is that there are strong similarities between adolescent and adult prostitutes when you consider that most members of both groups got involved in prostitution as adolescents (Lowman, 1986). Girls, though, are at greater risk of becoming prostitutes because they have fewer job opportunities and because younger prostitutes are in higher demand than older ones.

We can also conclude that there is a dearth of Canadian research on girl gangs and gang-related crimes committed by girls. It is time to do what Chesney-Lind (1997) refers to as "responsible work" on these issues. Research from the United States, however, shows that girl gangs and their members do not threaten society to the extent described by many news broadcasters, such as the one who made the following statement on NBC news:

> Gone are the days when girls were strictly sidekicks for male gang members, around merely to provide sex and money and run guns and drugs. Now girls also do the shooting . . . the new members, often as young as twelve, are the most violent. . . . Ironic as it is, just as women are becoming more powerful in business and government, the same thing is happening in gangs (cited in Chesney-Lind, 1997, p. 36).

As several studies point out, this is *not* happening in the United States, and there is good reason to believe that such is also the case in Canada (Alvi, 2000). Clearly, until more rigorous Canadian research on girl gangs is done, condemnatory statements made by journalists and academics like Carrigan (1998) need to be read with caution, at the very least.

Last, but certainly not least, this chapter also shows that although the sources of girls' involvement in crime are complex, three major risk factors stand out from the rest. These are poverty, unemployment, and family violence. As described in Chapter 5, policymakers need to address these determinants effectively in order to prevent female crime as well as crime in general.

NOTES

[1] See Chesney-Lind (1997) and Chesney-Lind and Sheldon (1992, 1998) for in-depth overviews of the empirical literature on United States girls' involvement in crime.

[2] Some of these techniques are also discussed by Schissel (1997a).

[3] See Chesney-Lind (1997) for United States data on girls who kill family members.

[4] See Heide (1992) for an in-depth analysis of parricide in the United States.

[5] See Atlas and Pepler (1997), Craig and Pepler (1997), and Craig et al. (1998) for recent Canadian data on bullying.

[6] For more in-depth national data on Canadian child poverty, see Statistics Canada's (1997) *National Longitudinal Survey of Children and Youth*.

[7] The 1997 female youth unemployment rate was 20.7 percent, compared to an overall rate of less than 10 percent (Bowlby et al., 1997; Stevenson et al., 1998).

[8] See Shelden et al. (1997) for an in-depth overview of conflicting social scientific definitions of gangs.

[9] See Esbensen and Winfree (1998) for a review of United States surveys that address the prevalence of girls in gangs.

[10] See Chesney-Lind (1997) and Shelden et al. (1997) for in-depth overviews of United States empirical and theoretical work on girls in gangs.

DISCUSSION QUESTIONS

1. Why is Canada currently experiencing what Schissel (1997a, p. 10) refers to as a "war on young offenders"?

2. How do poverty, unemployment, and family violence contribute to girls' involvement in crime?

3. How does the consumer culture influence girls to shoplift?

4. Should sex trade workers' clients or "johns" who are convicted for prostitution-related offenses be made to tell their friends, family members, or employers about their offences? What are the strengths and limitations of this punishment?

5. Why are self-report surveys of young offenders rare in Canada?

6. Who are the main victims of homicides committed by Canadian girls?

PROBLEM-SOLVING SCENARIOS

1. In a group, develop a study of girl gangs, and discuss the strengths and limitations of your research techniques.

2. Get together with a few classmates and construct a self-report survey of adolescent crime.

3. In a group, discuss the strengths and limitations of teachers, police officers, and other persons in authority taking a more punitive approach to schoolyard violence. Are there other strategies that might be more effective?

4. In a group, discuss the ways in which the ideology of familial patriarchy has directly or indirectly affected you and other members of the discussion group.

5. In a group, discuss reasons for the higher demand for young prostitutes.

6. Get together with a few people and discuss your direct and indirect experiences with crimes committed by girls.

SUGGESTED READINGS

Alvi, S. (2000). *Youth and the Canadian Criminal Justice System*. Cincinnati: Anderson.

> This book takes a sociological perspective on the causes and consequences of youth crime in Canada. Key debates and controversies are linked to their socioeconomic, cultural, and political contexts, and special attention is given to the role of the media in shaping public perceptions of the crime problem.

Chesney-Lind, M., & Shelden, R.G. (1998). *Girls: Delinquency and Juvenile Justice*, 2nd ed. Belmont, CA: West/Wadsworth.

> This widely cited book provides an in-depth overview of research on and theories of female juveniles in the United States. Major policy issues are also addressed, and the interviews with 10 girls are essential reading for students interested in learning how to do qualitative research on girls in conflict with the law.

Dell, C.A., & Boe, R. (1997). *Female Young Offenders in Canada: Recent Trends*. Ottawa: Research Branch, Correctional Service of Canada.

> This federal government report presents recent official data on Canadian female young offenders.

Schissel, B. (1997). *Blaming Children: Youth Crime, Moral Panics and the Politics of Hate*. Halifax: Fernwood.

> Written by one of Canada's leading experts on juvenile justice, this book offers a powerful scholarly account of what the author refers to as "Canada's war on youth."

Shelden, R.G., Tracy, S.K., & Brown, W.B. (1997). *Youth Gangs in American Society*. Belmont, CA: Wadsworth.

> This book is an excellent analysis of American research on gangs. Theoretical and policy issues are also examined, and Chapter 6 is an outstanding resource for those seeking an overview of the United States literature on girls' involvement in gangs.

Tanner, J. (1996). *Teenage Troubles: Youth and Deviance in Canada*. Toronto: Nelson.

> This book includes a comprehensive overview of Canadian empirical and theoretical work on delinquency and youth deviance. One chapter is devoted to female delinquency and reactions to it.

The skull of Charlotte Corday, murderer
of French revolutionary Jean-Paul Marat.
One early explanation of criminality was
Lombroso's suggestion that criminality
was related to atavistic characteristics
evident in the shape of the skull. Female
offenders showed fewer atavistic
characteristics than males.

Chapter 3

Theories of Female Crime

INTRODUCTION

Most of the empirical work (e.g., survey research, participant observation studies, etc.) discussed in criminology lectures, seminars, and textbooks is "gender-blind" (Gelsthorpe & Morris, 1988). In other words, women, girls, and their crime experiences are ignored or trivialized. When these issues are examined, they are usually "marginalized in special courses, as special topics, or in separate "token" chapters, rather than being integrated fully into the criminology/criminal justice curriculum" (Renzetti, 1993, p. 226). Most criminological theories are also "alarmingly gender-blind" (Messerschmidt, 1993). For example, the bulk of them are designed to explain why some men and boys, but not women and girls, commit crimes (Belknap, 1996). This is not surprising because criminology has been a "white man's discipline" (Schwartz, 1991), one that was "built by men and for men" (McCormack, 1987). Still, some criminologists attempt to explain crimes committed by girls and women and the societal reactions to their offences. The main objective of this chapter is to describe and evaluate these scholars' contributions. It is first necessary, however, to define the term *theory*.

> *Criminology has long suffered from what Jessie Bernard has called the 'stag effect' (Bernard, 1964, cited in Chunn and Menzies, 1996). It has attracted male scholars who wanted to study and understand outlaw men, hoping perhaps some of the romance and fascination of this role will rub off. As a result, what came to be known as the field of criminology was actually the study of male crime and victimization.*
>
> (Chesney-Lind & Bloom, 1997, p. 45)

WHAT IS A THEORY?

Many people view social scientific theories as academic products of "impractical mental gymnastics" or "fanciful ideas that have little to do with what truly motivates people" (Akers, 1997, p. 1). Like one of the detectives in the once famous fictional television show *Dragnet*,[1] they want "just the facts." Well, "facts" or data do not speak for themselves; they must be interpreted (Curran & Renzetti, 1994). Theories help us achieve this goal. Theories are, then, "things we think with" (Smith, 1996). They are conceptual tools that help us make sense of data and assist us in our attempts to understand the ways in which the social world functions (MacLean & Milovanovic, 1997a).

Theories can also be practical. For example, if you want solutions to problems, such as those examined in this text, you must first identify their causes. In fact, almost every policy or strategy developed to control and prevent crime is derived from some theory or theories (Akers, 1997). Let us consider incarceration, a crime control technique informed by theories of *neoclassical criminology*. James Q. Wilson (1985) is an example of a neoclassical criminological theorist, one who views crime as a function of "inadequate control." Wilson asserts that punishment should be used to deter crime and that punishment should be proportional to the severity of the crime committed. He also asserts that swift and certain penalties are more effective than severe punishments.

Ernest van den Haag is another neoclassical theorist. He contends that crime is like "any other exchange in the marketplace" (Currie, 1985, p. 26). For van den Haag, people commit crime because it does not cost them much. Thus, to reduce the rates of female crime discussed in this text and other types of crime, he maintains that:

> our only hope . . . lies in decreasing the expected net advantage of committing crimes (compared to lawful activities) by increasing the cost through increasing the expected severity of punishments and the probability of suffering them (van den Haag, 1982, p. 1035).

How would neoclassical theorists explain rising crime rates? They would probably agree with the following *Wall Street Journal* editorial:

> The sharp increase of crime in many states has undoubtedly resulted from the absence of punishment. . . . As the certainty of punishment rises, prison populations will rise. But so will the cost of crime. If states stay on their present course, it is reasonable to expect that the present surge in prison populations will cease. There will be less crime and fewer people going to jail. If so, it will be worth the cost of correcting those years of neglect (cited in Currie, 1985, p. 28).

For the past 15 years, the United States has gone on an "imprison-ment binge," with a 235 percent increase in the prison population between 1980 and 1995 (Irwin & Austin, 1997). Canada has also seen a major increase in the prison population during the same time period. For example, the average daily number of inmates in federal and provin-cial/territorial correctional facilities increased by 50 percent since 1980-81 (Goff, 1999). What is more alarming is that if Canada's inmate pop-ulation continues to grow at this same pace, the total number of federal and provincial/territorial inmates will increase to 45,000 by the year 2004 (Foran, 1996; Goff, 1999).

Obviously, North American politicians and criminal justice officials are putting neoclassical theory into practice. But how is prison supposed to increase the costs of crime? According to neoclassical theorists, incar-ceration acts as deterrent. **Deterrence** is "the inhibition of criminal activ-ity by state-imposed penalties . . . it is based on the idea that punish-ment should be used to prevent crime (Conklin, 1998, p. 475). There are two major types of deterrence: specific and general. **Specific deterrence** refers to the effects of imprisonment on people who are incarcerated. For example, for a woman who spends five years in prison for robbing a video store, the assumption is that the "pains of imprisonment" (John-son & Toch, 1982) will make her stop committing crimes to avoid ever returning to prison. Key examples of the pains of imprisonment are deprivation of liberty, deprivation of goods and services, deprivation of heterosexual relationships, and the deprivation of autonomy (Sykes, 1958). In Box 3.1, two of Toch's (1992, pp. 183-184) incarcerated respondents describe the stress associated from one of these pains—the deprivation of liberty.

What would you do if you had experiences similar to Toch's (1992) respondents? Keep in mind, too, that physical and sexual violence also occur in prison. This may seem like a stupid question. Why would any-one want to risk going back to prison or jail? Despite the violent and depressing nature of prison, a high number of people are willing to take this risk. Believe it or not, incarceration as a specific deterrent is highly problematic for reasons described in the next chapter.

General deterrence refers to the effects of the punishment of specif-ic individuals on the general population. If people hear about you going to prison or being executed for committing a violent crime, particularly if combined with stories similar to the one told in Box 3.2 by Sister Helen Prejean (1993, pp. 93-94), general deterrence predicts that they are not likely to commit crimes for fear of ending up like you. Sister Pre-jean's story is also told in the Hollywood movie *Dead Man Walking*, starring Sean Penn and Susan Sarandon. Her book focuses on the exe-cution of Patrick Sonnier in April, 1984 at Louisiana's Angola State Prison.

Box 3.1

The Pains of Loss of Freedom

Respondent number 1

It does hurt, being in a cell and just looking outside and seeing things. I can see the Empire State Building. Just look outside and see the Empire State Building. That puts my mind around. The pressure gets too great, just by looking at the Empire State Building. You think them people out there are allowed to walk around as free as much as possible. And you can't get out there to make love to somebody, have your wife, have your children. You can't do this. There's too much pressure on the mind.

Respondent number 2

You're in the cell most of the day. You're locked in. And you have nothing to do but think. You get tired of playing cards. That's all they got here is cards. You get tired of that after a while. You get sick of that. And you got to think. And what do you think about? You think about home, girlfriends, things that you'd be doing, like if it was Friday night or Thursday night, what you'd be doing. And, like, when I lay down, I think of things like that. I try not to, but I can't help it. And I see things that I would be doing. I know what I'd be doing, and I can see this. . . . I just couldn't take it.

Source: Toch, H. (1992). *Mosaic of Despair: Human Breakdowns in Prison.* Hyattsville, MD: American Psychological Association. Copyright © 1992 by the American Psychological Association. Reprinted with permission.

Box 3.2

The Execution of Patrick Sonnier

Pat is in the chair now and guards are moving quickly, removing the leg irons and handcuffs and replacing them with the leather straps. One guard has removed his left shoe. They are strapping his trunk, his legs, his arms. He finds my face. He says, "I love you." I stretch my hand toward him. "I love you, too."

He attempts a smile (he told me he would try to smile) but manages only to twitch.

A metal cap is placed on his head and an electrode is screwed in at the top and connected to a wire that comes from a box behind the chair. An electrode is fastened to his leg. A strap placed around his chin holds his head tightly against the back of the chair. He grimaces. He cannot speak anymore. A grayish green cloth is placed over his face.

Only the warden remains in the room now, only the warden and the man strapped into the chair. The red telephone is silent. I close my eyes and do not see as the warden nods his head, the signal to the executioner to do his work.

I hear three clanks as the switch is pulled with pauses in between. Nineteen hundred volts, then let the body cool, then five hundred volts, pause again, then nineteen hundred volts. "Christ, be with him, have mercy on him," I pray silently.

I look up. His left hand has gripped the arm of the chair evenly but the fingers of his right hand are curled upward.

Box 3.2, *continued*

The warden says over the microphone that we will wait a few minutes for the doctor to make the "final check." Then the prison doctor, who has been siting with the witnesses, goes to the body in the chair and lifts the mask and raises the eyelids and shines the light of a small flashlight into the eyes and raises up the clean white shirt and puts his stethoscope against the heart and listens and then says to the warden that, yes, this man is dead. Warden Maggio looks up at the clock and announces the time of death: 12:15 a.m. His eyes happen to look into mine. He lowers his eyes.

Source: Prejean, H. (1993). *Dead Man Walking*. New York: Vintage.

In the United States, the death penalty does little, if anything, to deter people from committing lethal and nonlethal violent crimes (DeKeseredy & Schwartz, 1996). This lethal punishment has several other major problems, such as those described in Box 3.3 (Johnson, 1998, p. A15). Canada does not execute convicted murderers,[2] although many Canadians strongly support this type of punishment (Silverman & Kennedy, 1993). A growing number of Canadian offenders are being incarcerated, though, and yet their pains of imprisonment do not act as a major general deterrent. This is because most offenders, male and female alike, rarely evaluate the negative consequences of their actions (Goff, 1999; Shover, 1996; Tunnell 1992). For example, according to a property offender interviewed by Tunnell (1992, p. 88), "I never really thought about getting caught until, pow, you're in jail, you're in juvenile or something. That's when you think about it."

Box 3.3

Seven Flaws of Capital Punishment

In early February 1998, Karla Faye Tucker was the first woman executed in Texas since Chipita Rodriguez was hanged in 1863. Donna F. Johnson was deeply disturbed by this event and expresses her opinion in the following commentary published in *The Ottawa Citizen*.

The frenzied, circus-like atmosphere that surrounded the Huntsville, Texas, prison where Karla Faye Tucker was executed last week was disgraceful and frightening. People wielding signs saying, "Forget injection, use a pick-axe." People chanting, "No mercy, no mercy," sending out for pizza from cell phones. We are all dehumanized by the atrocity of state-sanctioned killing and the side-shows that result.

Aside from the fact that it is barbaric and uncivilized, I oppose the death penalty on seven counts.

Box 3.3, *continued*

One if murder, the unlawful killing of another human being with malice aforethought, is wrong, then it should be wrong for the state as well as its citizens. It could be argued that it is in fact more morally reprehensible for the state, as capital punishment is carried out in a rational state of mind by its privileged and educated agents.

Two, it has been amply documented that a disproportionate number of poor, nonwhite and generally disenfranchised people end up on death row, and that very often these people have not had recourse to adequate legal representation.

Three, statistics show that *capital punishment is not a deterrent to murder* (emphasis mine).

Four, people do terrible things for a variety of reasons. But people can also accept responsibility, grow and change. The death penalty eliminates all possibility for the positive reconstruction of a life.

Five, the death penalty inflicts acute suffering on family members and loved ones who are innocent of any crime.

Six, because capital punishment is motivated by hatred and revenge, it can only breed further bitterness and hatred in the hearts of those who seek it. Violence begets violence.

Seven, capital punishment allows human beings, in our radical subjectivity, and with all our limitations, bias and self-interest, to be the final arbiters of life.

An Amnesty International representative said that U.S. policy on capital punishment is more likely that of Iran than Canada. A woman keeping vigil outside the Huntsville prison was quoted as saying, "I am embarrassed to be a Texan today." I think it must be noted with concern that many Canadians cheered on the execution of Karla Faye Tucker as well.

Source: This box includes excerpts from an article by Donna F. Johnson for *The Ottawa Citizen* (1998, p. A15). Reprinted with permission of the author.

Criminal justice policies are informed by theory, but it is important to note that some theories are better than others. From the standpoint of many criminologists, neoclassical theory is flawed, and so are the policies informed by it. Further, every theory described in this chapter and in other criminology and criminal justice texts has limitations. There is no "pat explanation" of female crime and delinquency, as is the case with male crime and delinquency. What we have, then, are "bad, good, and better theories of crime" (Curran & Renzetti, 1994, p. 5). It is to what many criminologists consider to be two outstanding examples of bad theories of female crime that we turn to first. These widely read and cited perspectives are generally referred to as early theories of female crime (Chesney-Lind and Shelden, 1998).

EARLY THEORIES

Lombroso and the Born Criminal

Cesare Lombroso (1835-1909) was a *positivist criminologist*. He and William Ferrero (1895) published one of the first attempts to explain female crime; it was titled *The Female Offender*. Their book is still very influential today. For example, it heavily informs Canadian journalist Patricia Pearson's (1997) controversial analysis of violent women (Chesney-Lind, 1999). Positivists such as Lombroso, were (and in many ways still are) concerned with drawing our attention to the characteristics of criminals rather than their behaviors.

Regarded as the "father of positivist criminology," Lombroso was heavily influenced by Charles Darwin's evolutionary studies. Like Darwin, Lombroso believed that the best way to study a scientific issue was to develop a research hypothesis and then go directly to relevant subjects and take measurements or engage in observation. Lombroso was an Italian physician who specialized in psychiatry. One day, while performing an autopsy on a violent criminal, he decided that the person's skull was more suited to an animal than a human. He then began to develop a perspective that criminals were "biological throwbacks" or *atavistic*. In other words, they were not as far along the evolutionary ladder as normal human beings. For Lombroso, atavistic people share a number of characteristics, such as chimpanzee-like ears, bumps on their heads, large jaws, and so on.

Lombroso and Ferrero argued that female offenders showed fewer atavistic characteristics than male criminals did because many of them were very young. According to these theorists (1895, p. 97):

> Very often, too, in women, the [degenerate] type is disguised by youth with its absence of wrinkles and the plumpness which conceals the size of the jaw and cheek-bones, thus softening the masculine and savage features. Then when the hair is black and plentiful . . . and the eyes are bright, a not unpleasing appearance is presented. In short, let a female delinquent be young and we can overlook her degenerate type, and even regard her as beautiful; the sexual instinct misleading us here as it does in making us attribute to women more of the sensitiveness and passion than they really possess. And in the same way, when she is being tried on a criminal charge, we are inclined to excuse, as noble impulses of passion, an act which arises from the most cynical calculations.

Lombroso and Ferrero maintained that women were much less likely to commit crimes than men because of their special biological traits, such as their "piety, maternity, want of passion, sexual coldness, weakness and an undeveloped intelligence" (1895, p. 151). When a woman did commit a crime, however, she was seen to be "a monster" (1895, p. 152), one whose "wickedness must have been enormous before it could triumph over so many obstacles" (1895, p. 152).

Many social scientists, especially feminists, agree with Gavigan's (1983, p. 77) assertion that it "seems almost beyond absurd" that Lombroso's theory "should have ever been given credence." However, he was a "man of his times," and his perspective is a reflection of "malestream[3] resistances to the suffragist movement and 19th century feminism" (Faith, 1993a, p. 44). In addition to being denounced for propounding misogynistic views, Lombroso and Ferrero's work is attacked on methodological grounds. They make extravagant claims without providing strong empirical support (Boritch, 1997). Their analysis also dismisses the influence of broader social, political, economic, and cultural determinants of crime (Smart, 1976). Despite these flaws, as Chesney-Lind and Shelden (1992, p. 56) point out, Lombroso's work "actually set the tone for much of the later work on female delinquency and crime," including that done in Canada. Consider the excerpt of Chesney-Lind's (1999, p. 2) critique of Pearson's (1997) *When She Was Bad: Violent Women and the Myth of Female Innocence* described in Box 3.4.

Box 3.4

Lombroso's Influence Today

Much of what Pearson's work serves up . . . is old hat. Consider that Lombroso spent a good part of his book, *The Female Offender*, combing through the sensationalistic crimes of violent women. Lombroso, though, spared no thought for the equity approach to violence; instead, he felt that "the female criminal is doubly exceptional, as a woman and as a criminal." Normal women, he argued, are kept on the path of virtue by "maternity, piety, weakness," which means that the "wickedness" of the female offender "must be enormous before it could triumph over so many obstacles" (Lombroso, 1958, p. 151-152). Lombroso then presents a series of historic and contemporary vignettes of violent women engaged in chilling and brutal crimes. His examples include mothers who killed their children, women who killed spouses and lovers, women who kill their rivals, women who killed other family members, women who instigate and entice others to kill, and women who killed for material gain.

Now consider Pearson's chapters which include discussions of women who abuse and kill children, women who assault their spouses and lovers, and women who kill with others and women who kill alone (including women serial killers). Pretty similar terrain, in my estimation. Also similar is the reliance on details (usually gruesome) of specific women's crimes.

Source: Chesney-Lind, M. (1999). Review of Patricia Pearson's *When She Was Bad: Violent Women and the Myth of Innocence*. Reprinted with permission from the Haworth Press Inc.

Contemporary academics and journalists such as Pearson (1997) are not the only ones who are influenced by Lombroso and Ferrero's (1895) perspective on female offenders. For example, if your knowledge of female crime is based only on watching U.S. movies, you would probably conclude that women in conflict with the law are masculinized monsters, lesbian villains, incarcerated teenage predators, or pathological killer beauties (DeKeseredy & Schwartz, 1996; Faith, 1993a; Holmlund, 1994). Consider movies like *Single White Female*, *Basic Instinct*, and *The Hand That Rocks the Cradle*. Another example is *Fatal Attraction*. In this film, actress Glenn Close:

> takes the lead as the prototype of the postmodern failed-woman. Close's character is a woman whose rage at "not having it all" takes nasty turns against a family that seems idyllically happy (except for the husband's secret adultery). She is the image of the beautiful, solitary, ominous, male-identified, childless, pathologically obsessive woman, "liberated" in anti-feminist terms, who would take what she wants at any cost. In the end, she pays with her life at the hand of the injured wife (Faith, 1993a, p. 265).

Pollack and the Masked Nature of Female Crime

Otto Pollack's *Criminality of Women* (1950) and his co-edited collection of readings *Family Dynamics and Female Sexual Delinquency* (Pollack & Friedman, 1969), although published more than 50 years after Lombroso and Ferrero's (1895) contribution, are heavily influenced by their positivistic approach. Pollack (1950) developed what Ellis and DeKeseredy (1996) refer to as a *dual-focus theory* of female crime, in which he focuses on both the biological causes of female crime and causes of the reactions to female offences.

Pollack (1950) asserts that biological factors cause females to commit crimes as frequently as males; however, female crimes are more likely to involve sex, or cunning and deceit, or both. At the same time, official crime statistics show that much female crime is "masked" by the greater leniency with which female criminals are treated by chivalrous criminal justice personnel, such as police officers, judges, and prosecutors. Their chivalry is rooted in the social construction of women as passive, dependent, and requiring the protection of men. Still, Pollack's key point is that women are better than men at hiding their offences (Belknap, 1996), which is why much of their crime never attracted the attention of agents of social control. He associated women's ability to deceive criminal justice officials with the passive role they traditionally play during sexual intercourse. Pollack argued that women could hide sexual arousal or pretend to have orgasms, while men could not do so because an erection is required to perform sexually.

According to Pollack (1950, p. 10), "It cannot be denied that this basic physiological difference may well have a great influence on the degree of confidence which the two sexes have in the possible conceal-ment and thus on their character pattern in this respect." Concealment and deceit are learned during childhood, a time when "natural aggres-sions are inhibited and forced into concealed channels" (1950, p. 11).

Like Lombroso and Ferrero's (1895) perspective, Pollack's theory lacks empirical support (Ellis & DeKeseredy, 1996; Smart, 1976). Fur-ther, his account does not recognize that women's passive role during sexual relations may be culturally rather than biologically determined. Another point to consider is that rather than hiding orgasms, women may not be experiencing them (Belknap, 1996). Pollack's work is also criticized for ignoring the structural (e.g., gender hierarchy) sources of male/female differences in crime and its regulation. This theory assumes that the inferior status of women in society is biologically determined, and it ignores the "dark side" of chivalry; that is, women are often treat-ed more harshly by the police (Ellis & DeKeseredy, 1996; Smart, 1976).

UNDERSTANDING FEMALE CRIME: THE CONTRIBUTION OF SOCIOLOGICAL THOUGHT

Biological factors cause *some* men and women to commit *some* crimes. In fact, research consistently shows that two of the most signifi-cant correlates of crime are "biological" factors: age and sex (Braith-waite, 1989; Currie, 1985; Wilson & Herrnstein, 1985). For example, young (age) men (sex) commit a disproportionate amount of crime in North America today. However, theories emphasizing only biological or psychological factors cannot account for most of the data described in the first two chapters of this book. Recall from reading these chapters that the key risk factors associated with the bulk of crimes committed by girls and women are family violence, poverty, and unemployment. Thus, broader social psychological and social forces are the major determi-nants of crimes committed by most North American girls and women.

There are many other problems with biological and other individu-alistic (e.g., psychological) theories of female crime; however, they will not be repeated here.[4] Rather, following other sociologists who study crime and social control, this author contends that to make better sense of the data described throughout this book, one needs to develop what C. Wright Mills (1959) refers to as the *sociological imagination*.

The Sociological Imagination

The sociological imagination calls for an understanding of the ways in which *personal troubles* are related to *public issues*. Personal troubles are just what you might think. If you are a girl who ran away from home because you were physically, psychologically, or sexually abused by your father, you have a problem and you will have to deal with it. You may need food, housing, comfort from friends, or other types of social support. Many people, however, such as a sizeable portion of adolescent prostitutes (see Chapter 2), are suffering individually from the same type of personal problem at the same time. If 100 girls have similar experiences in one year in the same city or town, each one of them has a personal problem (or personal troubles). At the same time, however, Mills would argue that something about the broader structural or cultural forces, such as patriarchal domination and control in the family, allows for so many girls who have experienced child abuse to be suffering on the streets. To be able to look beyond the personal troubles of one or two girls who have been assaulted by their fathers and see the broader problem of father-to-daughter violence and its causes is to possess the sociological imagination.

Applied to the study of crime committed by both females and males, the sociological imagination shows that North American society is structured to promote criminal activity. An excellent example of how the sociological imagination can be applied to the study of female crime in the United States is provided by Chesney-Lind (1997, p. 180), who states that:

> We must understand how gender and race shape and eliminate choices for girls, how they injure (intentionally or not), and how they ultimately create very different futures for youths who are born female in a country that promises equality yet all too frequently falls short of that dream. We must also confront the fact that the United States has the highest rates of child poverty in the industrialized world (Donziger, 1996, p. 215), and we must understand the ways in which this economic marginalization has directly affected girls and their mothers. Only with these understandings finally in mind can we imagine real solutions to the terrible problems of violence and crime in women's lives.

Just because a theorist has the sociological imagination does not mean that he or she takes female crime seriously. In fact, most sociological theories of crime developed so far were designed to explain the criminal or deviant behavior of boys or men. Consider Cohen's (1955) theory of delinquent boys. This theory is still widely read and cited today, albeit subject to much criticism by feminist scholars.

Cohen's Theory of Delinquent Boys

Cohen's *strain-subcultural theory* of delinquency is a variation of Merton's (1938) *anomie theory*. Merton argues that there is a disjunction between culturally defined *goals* of society and the acceptable or legitimate *institutionalized means* of achieving these goals. He refers to goals as financial success and the accompanying status. However, not everyone has the legitimate means of achieving these goals, such as having a high paying job, university education, and so on. Those who lack these means experience a *structurally induced strain*, which causes them to adapt in one of five ways," four of which Merton views as deviant types. For example, they might react through *innovation*, which means that they accept the culturally defined goals but reject or cannot obtain the legitimate means of achieving them. Innovators steal, sell drugs, or commit other types of crime to get money, nice clothes, and other material status symbols.

Sociologists familiar with Merton's anomie theory would probably consider one of William Julius Wilson's (1996, p. 58) respondents to be an innovator. This 35-year-old inner-city Chicago resident justified his drug dealing activities by stating:

> And what am I doing now? I'm a cocaine dealer—'cause I can't
> get a decent-ass job. So, what other choices do I have? I have
> to feed my family . . . do I work? I work. See, don't . . . bring
> me that bullshit. I been working since I was fifteen years old.

For people like this man, who are unable to work in the formal economy because of factory closures, layoffs, and so on, "how can the 'honest job' of dishwashing compete with the easy money obtained through dishonest behavior (Pfohl, 1994, p. 264)?

Cohen argues that Merton's theory best explains both instrumental (e.g., for financial gain) adult "professional crime and the "property" delinquency crimes of some older and semiprofessional juvenile thieves. But, he deemed it incapable of explaining "the distinctive content of the delinquent subculture" (1955, p. 36).

From Merton's standpoint, adult "innovators" deal with the goal of financial success by committing crimes, such as theft, that are specifically aimed at achieving this goal. So, adult crimes are viewed as financial and purposeful. When looking at young offenders, Cohen found them very different. Although they suffer from strain, their goal is to achieve respect and status, primarily from their peers. The delinquent acts of juveniles who do not get this respect are hedonistic, nonutilitarian, malicious, and negativistic. The acts are *hedonistic* in that they are aimed at having fun, with no concern about long-term rewards or costs. They are *nonutilitarian* in that there is no particular "use" to what they are doing. For example, they steal because they feel like it, not because they see any value in what they steal. The delinquent acts are *negativistic* in that they create a set of values that are, from a middle-class perspective, negative.

Cohen further argues that juveniles' destructive behavior is committed mainly by gangs made up of lower-class, male, urban youths. Delinquency, then, is an expressive group activity. But what accounts for the emergence of lower-class, urban delinquent subcultures?

Although he is heavily influenced by Merton's perspective, Cohen does not see how failure to achieve financial goals affects these male youths. Rather, he sees the problem as an inability to achieve status. For young men, the school is the main granter of status. Nevertheless, lower-class men find that any possible status from this institution is out of their reach.

According to Cohen, the school systems of the United States mainly employs middle-class teachers who use "middle-class measuring rods" to evaluate students. Teachers measure students according to the following middle-class standards (1955, pp. 88-91):

- ambition;
- individual responsibility;
- academic or athletic achievement;
- the ability to defer immediate gratification;
- rationality;
- manners, courtesy, and personability;
- aggressive behavior;
- "wholesome" or constructive leisure; and
- respect for property.

Cohen asserts that it is:

> characteristic of American culture generally—an aspect of its "democratic" ethos—that young people of different origins and backgrounds tend to be judged by the same standards so that young people of different social class, race, and ethnicity find themselves competing with one another for status and approval under the same set of rules (1955, p. 65).

Middle-class boys do well in school because their parents prepare them to meet these standards successfully. Working-class boys, on the other hand, come from families where resources such as computers, dictionaries, books, and a quiet, private place to study are likely to be in short supply. Further, low-income parents who have a relatively large number of children need and depend on the income that working children can provide. Staying in school and doing well there so that they can go to university or college tend to be viewed as options the family cannot support. Thus, working-class boys are often tossed into a highly competitive setting in which they cannot achieve status from their middle-class peers and teachers.

Consequently, these boys experience *status frustration*, which generates "guilt, self-recrimination, anxiety, and self-hatred" (Cohen, 1955, p. 126). Some boys react to this problem by working hard to meet the middle-class standards, while others withdraw from the middle class and interact with other lower-class boys. Some frustrated youths, however, withdraw from the school environment, come into contact with other working-class boys with similar status problems, and form a delinquent subculture or gang as a way of dealing with their problems of adjustment. According to Cohen (1955, p. 121), "The delinquent subculture deals with these problems by providing a criteria of status which these children *can* meet."

To achieve status in the gang, boys resort to *reaction formation*, a psychological process in which middle-class values and standards are turned upside down. So, if teachers and other authority figures value punctuality, respect for property, and nonviolent means of resolving conflict, gang members will be late for class, engage in vandalism, and commit violent acts.

In sum, for Cohen, subcultural delinquency is a collective, nonutilitarian solution to the problem of status frustration among lower-class boys. What about girls? Cohen had little to say about girl delinquents because he assumed a "natural" sex difference between men and women accounted for women's lack of involvement in crime (Messerschmidt, 1993). Consider the following statement made by Cohen in his book *Delinquent Boys* (1955, pp. 137-138):

> My skin has nothing of the quality of down or silk, there is nothing limpid or flute-like about my voice, I am a total loss with needle and thread, my posture and carriage are wholly lacking in grace. These imperfections cause me no distress—if anything, they are gratifying—because I conceive myself to be a man and want people to recognize me as a full-fledged, unequivocal representative of my sex. My wife, on the other hand, is not greatly embarrassed by her inability to tinker with or talk about the internal organs of a car, by her modest attainments in arithmetic or by her inability to lift heavy objects. Indeed, I am reliably informed that many women—I do not suggest that my wife is among them—often affect ignorance, frailty and emotional instability because to do otherwise would be out of keeping with a reputation for indubitable femininity. In short, people do not simply want to excel they want to excel as a man or as a woman.

It should also be noted that Merton had nothing to say about women or girls in conflict of the law. In fact, "A long-standing deficiency of most strain theories is their neglect of the gender issue" (Hackler, 1994, p. 187). In Box 3.5, DeKeseredy and Schwartz (1996, p. 216) provide a more detailed critique of the gender-blind nature of Merton's theory.

Box 3.5

Merton's Anomie Theory and Gender

In the United States, women's aspirations appear to be the same as men's (A. Morris, 1987). Men and women are socialized to desire things such as nice clothes, a suburban home, luxurious vacations, and perhaps an expensive car. Nevertheless, many women are excluded from the paid work force, and those who do find jobs are "concentrated overwhelmingly at the lower levels of the occupational hierarchy in terms of wages and salary, status, and authority" (Messerschmidt, 1993, p. 125). Furthermore, although there is a growing number of female executives, managers, and administrators, further examination shows that they tend to hold low-status positions (for example, personnel, research, affirmative action) within these occupations (Blau & Winkler, 1989).

Because of gender discrimination, a large number of women do not have the same legitimate opportunities as men to achieve their material goals. According to Merton's theory, these women should experience more strain than men and therefore commit more crime than men. A large body of mainstream and feminist research reveals that this is not the case. Women are clearly not more criminal than men, a fact that seriously challenges anomie theory (Chesney-Lind & Shelden, 1992). Anomie theory still may be of some value here, however. Although economic marginalization has not made women more criminal than men, it very well may explain the kind of crimes that women *do* commit (emphasis in original). The bulk of women's crimes tend to be petty property offenses such as shoplifting, passing bad checks, fraud, and whatever else people who cannot earn enough money to make ends meet might be tempted to try in order to pick up a few extra dollars (Naffine, 1987).

Source: Dekeseredy, W.S., & Schwartz, M.D. (1996). *Contemporary Criminology*. Belmont, CA: Wadsworth, p. 216.

Merton and Cohen are not the only prominent sociological criminologists who ignore girls or women. Some *control theorists* do the same, such as Travis Hirschi (1969). He argues that "delinquent acts result when an individual's bond to society is weak or broken" (1969, p. 16). His *social bond theory* is described and evaluated in the next section.

Hirschi's Social Bond Theory

Hirschi contends that the social bond has four elements: attachment, commitment, involvement, and belief. The first element, *attachment*, refers to the degree to which people have close emotional ties to conventional others, such as parents, teachers, and friends.

Commitment refers to acquiring things (e.g., reputations, family, jobs, houses, church and club memberships) that constitute "investments" in society. These investments constitute a "stake in conformity" (Toby, 1957), and the greater one's stake in conformity, the greater the likelihood of conforming behavior.

Involvement refers to the amount of time one spends doing conventional or legitimate activities, such as studying, working, or volunteering. An individual who is lonely because she or he spends all her time working at a legitimate job is thus doubly controlled. Being successful, she or he has acquired a great stake in conformity. Being so busy, he or she does not have the time to enjoy riding a motorcycle, let alone join Hell's Angels.

The fourth element of the social bond, *belief*, refers to an acceptance of conventional norms and values. Because they believe that obeying the law is the proper or right thing to do, many people do not break the law. However, those whose beliefs are less strongly held feel less obliged to conform with societal rules and/or laws. According to Hirschi, "The less a person believes he should obey the rules, the more likely he is to violate them" (1969, p. 26).

Hirschi tested his theory by analyzing self-report survey data from approximately 4,000 high school boys. Self-report survey data were also gleaned from high school girls, but he excluded their responses from his statistical analyses. In his book *Causes of Delinquency*, Hirschi states in a footnote that "in the analysis that follows the 'non-negro' becomes 'white,' and the girls disappear" (1969, pp. 35-36). This is just as true of those who followed in Hirschi's footsteps; virtually all tests of his theory have used all-male samples (Curran & Renzetti, 1994).

Many other gender-blind sociological theories of crime (e.g., Marxist, ecological, symbolic interactionist, etc.) have been reviewed elsewhere (e.g., Belknap, 1996; Chesney-Lind, 1997; Chesney-Lind & Shelden, 1992). Rather than reproduce this information here, it is more appropriate to focus on sociological theories specifically designed to explain female crime and societal reactions to this problem. These perspectives fall under three categories: (1) women's liberation/emancipation theories, (2) power-control theory, and (3) feminist theories.

Women's Liberation/Emancipation Theories

Unlike Cohen (1955) and others who argued that women are "naturally" inhibited from committing crime, in 1975, Freda Adler and Rita Simon published books challenging this popular notion. For these two theorists, female "nature" does not inhibit crime. Rather, women have lacked opportunities to break the law, and if given such opportunities, they would act just like men. Adler (1975) and Simon (1975) were among the "first wave of women" of their generation to do criminological research and to help legitimate serious research on female crime and punishment (Faith, 1993a).

Adler (1975, p. 16) analyzed FBI arrest statistics and found that between 1960 and 1972:

- the number of women arrested for robbery increased by 277 percent, while the male rate rose 169 percent;

- the female embezzlement arrest rate increased 280 percent compared with a 50 percent increase for men;

- the female larceny arrest rate rose by 303 percent compared to an 82 percent increase for men; and

- the number of women arrested for burglary increased by 168 percent, while the male rate rose by 63 percent.

What accounted for the above major increase in female crime rates? Adler argued that while the women's liberation movement opened up new roles for women in the military, education, business, and politics, it was also opening up new roles for women in crime, which was historically dominated by men. According to Adler (1975, p. 13):

> But women, like men, do not live by bread alone. Almost every other aspect of their life has been similarly altered. The changing status of women as it affects family, marriage, employment, and social position has been well documented by all types of sociologists. But there is a curious hiatus: the movement for full equity has a darker side which has been slighted even by the scientific community. . . .
>
> In the same way that women are demanding equal opportunity in fields of legitimate endeavor, a similar number of determined women are forcing their way into the world of major crimes.

Girls are not exempt from Adler's liberation/emancipation thesis. She argues that the women's movement seems to be "having a twofold influence on juvenile crimes" (1975, p. 95). She asserted that:

> Girls are involved in more drinking, stealing, gang activity, and fighting—behavior in keeping with their adoption of male roles. We also find increases in the total number of female deviancies. The departure from the safety of traditional female roles and the testing of uncertain alternative roles coincide with the turmoil of adolescence creating criminogenic risk factors, which are bound to create this increase. These considerations help explain the fact that between 1960 and 1972 nation-

al arrests for major crimes show a jump for boys of 82 percent—for girls, 306 percent (1975, p. 95).

What Adler (1975, p. 13) refers to as the "shady aspect of liberation" is also a major part of Simon's (1975) theory. However, Simon
departs from Adler by arguing that the increase in female crime is limited mainly to property offences and that violent female crime has
decreased. Further, Simon attributes the decrease in female violence to
feminism, which makes women "feel more liberated physically, emo-
tionally, and legally" and decreases their frustration and anger. Consequently, their desire to kill male objects of their anger or frustration on
whom they are dependent (e.g., lovers, husbands, and cohabiting partners) declines (1975, p. 40). Simon also predicts that female emancipation will contribute to an increase in female white-collar crime for the
following reasons:

> As women become more liberated from hearth and home and
> become involved in full-time jobs, they are more likely to
> engage in the types of crime for which their occupations pro-
> vide them with the greatest opportunities. Furthermore . . . as
> a function both of expanded consciousness, as well as occupa-
> tional opportunities, women's participation role and involve-
> ment in crime are expected to *change* and *increase* (1975, p. 1).

As Curran and Renzetti (1994, p. 166) point out, the liberation/
emancipation theories described here should be commended for forcing
"a contemporary reassessment of the relationship between sex and participation in criminal activity." Still, these perspectives have major problems. First, they are based on police statistics, which are not accurate
indicators of the extent of crimes committed by both men and women.
Second, the number of females arrested in Adler's (1975) sample were so
low to begin with that a small rise translated into major changes in percentage terms (Chesney-Lind & Shelden, 1992). For whatever reason, in
comparing male and female arrest rates, Adler (1975) did not control for
the major difference in the absolute base numbers from which the rates
of increase were calculated. Thus, the rate changes she reports in her
book *Sisters in Crime* are exaggerated (Curran & Renzetti, 1994).

Perhaps another example is warranted here. If, hypothetically, the
absolute base number of Canadian women who committed homicide
was two in 1998 and rose to four in 1999, one could claim that the
female homicide rate increased by an alarming 100 percent. On the other
hand, if the absolute number of males who committed homicide in 1998
were 750 and rose to 1,000 in 1999, the male rate change would appear
to be considerably lower than the female rate change. "Clearly, if we
look only at percent changes without taking into account these major

absolute base differences, we end up with a very distorted picture of men's and women's involvement in crime" (Curran & Renzetti, 1994, p. 166). Keep in mind, too, that most of the absolute base numbers for Canadian females that were presented in Chapters 1 and 2 are significantly lower than the figures for males.

Another major problem with liberation/emancipation theories is that several studies did not find a strong positive relationship between the women's movement and female crime. For example, feminism had only a minor direct effect on the status offences committed by the 287 young women in James and Thornton's (1980) sample. Further, the influence on their property crimes and aggressive delinquent acts was negative. Similarly, when Cernkovich and Giordano (1979, p. 479) examined the attitudes of girls in three high schools and two state institutions, they found that "the more delinquent girls were actually less liberated."

Last, but certainly not least, as pointed out in Table 1.12 (see Chapter 1), most Canadian women are segregated into "pink ghetto" jobs, such as nursing, sales, teaching, and so on. This accounts for why so few women commit white-collar and corporate crimes. Further, most of the crimes committed by women are not related to improved labor market opportunities (Curran & Renzetti, 1994). As noted in Chapters 1 and 2, women and girls primarily commit petty property offenses, such as shoplifting, which are offenses caused by an increasing "feminization of poverty" (Gimenez, 1990).

In sum, empirical attempts to locate the "shady" or "dark side" of women's liberation/emancipation have failed (Chesney-Lind & Shelden, 1992). If, as Belknap (1996) states in her critique of theories developed by Adler (1975) and Simon (1975), feminism has had any negative influence on female crime, it is that the public is more likely to report female offenders to the police, the police are more likely to arrest them, prosecutors are more likely to prosecute them, and judges and juries are more likely to convict them (Curran, 1984; Faith, 1993a; Messerschmidt, 1986). "Social changes in the 1960s led not to changes in criminality among women but to changes *in perceptions* of women and criminality among women" (emphasis in original) (Morris, 1987, p. 69).

Are the debates surrounding the liberation/emancipation theories reviewed here "intellectual dead ends" (Miller, 1983, p. 59)? One could say, "If there's no evidence supporting these perspectives, why discuss them?" As you can see from reading Chapter 2, especially the Boxes 2.1 and 2.2 (see Chapter 2), their popularity, at least in the minds of the general public, conservative politicians, and many journalists, is undiminished (Chesney-Lind, 1997). Thus, a critical response to these accounts is warranted. Moreover, some sociologists have recently developed what Chesney-Lind (1989, p. 20) refers to as "essentially a not-too-subtle variation of the . . . 'liberation' hypothesis." It is to this perspective that we turn next.

Power-Control Theory

Labeled by some criminologists as a feminist theory (e.g., Akers, 1997; Curran & Renzetti, 1994) and by others as a social control account (e.g., DeKeseredy & Schwartz, 1996; Ellis & DeKeseredy, 1996), the *power-control theory* developed by Hagan et al. (1989) and Hagan (1989) attempts to answer the question, "What differences do the relative class positions of husbands *and* wives in the workplace make for gender variations in parental control and in delinquent behavior of adolescents" (1987, p. 789)?

Delinquency is, according to Hagan, a type of risk-taking behavior. It is fun, liberating, and gives youths the "chance to pursue publicly some of the pleasures that are symbolic of adult male status outside the family (1989, pp. 152-153). However, boys are more willing to take such risks than are girls because they are supervised less closely and punished less severely by their parents. Thus, the "taste for such risk-taking is channeled along sexually stratified lines" (Hagan, 1989, p. 154). We need to examine the relationship between the family and workplace to understand this problem.

Hagan et al. (1987) contend that parents' positions of power in the workplace are reproduced at home and affect the probability of their children committing delinquent acts. These theorists identify two general types of family structure based on parents' power in the workplace. The first type is *patriarchal*. It consists of a husband who works outside the home in a position of authority and a wife who does not work outside the home and who is delegated responsibility for socializing and controlling the children. Such families are typically working-class and "socially reproduce daughters who focus their futures around domestic labor and consumption as contrasted with sons who are prepared for participation in direct production" (1987, p. 791). In these families, male children are encouraged to take risks because this prepares them for participation in the labor force, while females are closely supervised and are expected to grow up and be like their mothers and to avoid risk-taking behavior.

The second type of family structure identified by Hagan et al. (1987) is *egalitarian*. In egalitarian families, husbands and wives work outside the home in positions of authority. An egalitarian family "socially reproduces daughters who are prepared along with sons to join the production sphere" (1987, p. 792). Further, both sons and daughters are inclined to engage in risk-taking activities, such as delinquency.

So far, the only empirical support for power-control theory comes from self-report survey data gathered from 436 teenagers enrolled in Toronto-area high schools. Not one United States study supports this perspective (Hill & Atkinson, 1988; Jensen & Thompson, 1990;

Morash & Chesney-Lind, 1991). The lack of empirical support from the United States might be due to the fact that Canada is more racially homogenous than the United States. Heterogeneity makes analyses more difficult (Shoham & Hoffman, 1991).

There are several other problems with power-control theory. For example, having a job does not necessarily mean that a woman has equal power at home. While a growing number of men "help" around the house, most married working women have to do all of the cooking, cleaning, and child care, and most of them lack equal decision-making power (Armstrong & Armstrong, 1994). Moreover, many middle- and upper-class women are beaten, psychologically abused, and sexually assaulted by their husbands or cohabiting partners (Beirne & Messerschmidt, 1995; DeKeseredy & MacLeod, 1997; Finkelhor & Yllö, 1985).

In addition to neglecting the fact that a place in the paid marketplace does not automatically translate into power at home, Hagan and his colleagues ignore the influence of the following important variables: social class, negative parental sanctions, victimization, peer group influence, and the role of the school (Chesney-Lind & Shelden, 1998). However, from a feminist standpoint, "the worst problem of all" is that power-control theory is a variation of the "women's-liberation/emancipation-leads-to-crime" theories reviewed previously in this chapter (DeKeseredy & Schwartz, 1996). Of course, Hagan (1989) and Hagan et al. (1987) do not explicitly state that women's liberation causes female crime. Still, they strongly suggest that "mother's liberation" in joining the paid labor force causes daughters to commit crimes. There is an obvious problem with this: there has been a major increase in the number of women in the paid work force over the past decade, with no corresponding increase in female delinquency (Chesney-Lind, 1989).

Power-control theory, like the perspectives developed by Adler (1975), Simon (1975), and other mainstream theorists (e.g., Cohen, 1955), is what Beirne and Messerschmidt (1995, p. 549) refer to as an example of "the disregard and misrepresentation of gender and women in criminological theory." Feminist theories are specifically designed to overcome this problem, and they warrant considerable attention here.

Feminist Theories

Before reviewing several feminist theories of female crime and delinquency, it is first necessary to define feminism. *Feminism* is defined here as "a set of theories about women's oppression *and* a set of strategies for change" [emphasis in original] (Daly & Chesney-Lind, 1988, p. 502). Contrary to popular belief, the goal of feminist criminologists is "not to push men out so as to pull women in, but rather to gender the study of crime and criminal justice" (Renzetti, 1993, p. 232). The following five elements of feminist thought distinguish it from theories that misrepresent gender and feminism:

- Gender is not a natural fact but a complex social, historical, and cultural product; it is related to, but not simply derived from, biological sex difference and reproductive capacities.

- Gender and gender relations order social life and social institutions in fundamental ways.

- Gender relations and constructs of masculinity and femininity are not symmetrical but are based on an organizing principle of men's superiority to and social and political-economic dominance over women.

- Systems of knowledge reflect men's view of the natural and social world; the production of knowledge is gendered.

- Women should be at the center of intellectual inquiry, not peripheral, invisible, or appendages to men (Daly & Chesney-Lind, 1988, p. 504).

Neither feminism nor criminology is a monolithic enterprise, and this is why some scholars assert that a feminist criminology does not exist (Daly & Chesney-Lind, 1988). So, scholars use a variety of feminist theories to explain a variety of crimes and techniques of social control. There are at least eight types of feminist theory, each of which takes a distinct approach to understanding gender issues, asks different types of questions, and offers different theories of crime and its control (Beirne & Messerschmidt, 1995). Nevertheless, the four theories most often discussed in the feminist literature on criminology are (1) *liberal feminism*, (2) *Marxist feminism*, (3) *radical feminism*, and (4) *socialist feminism*. These perspectives are briefly described by Daly and Chesney-Lind (1988, pp. 537-538) in Box 3.6.

Box 3.6

Four Types of Feminist Theory

Liberal Feminist
    Causes of gender inequality: Not stated explicitly, but assumed to stem from societal inhibitions on women's full exposure to and participation in intellectual inquiry (reading and writing), physical education (competitive sports and physical fitness), and other activities in the public sphere.
    Process of gender formation: Socialization into gender roles; psychological theories such as social learning, cognitive development, or schema used.

Box 3.6, *continued*

Strategies for social change: Removal of all obstacles to women's access to education, paid employment, political activity, and other public social institutions; enabling women to participate equally with men in the public sphere; emphasis on legal change.

Key concepts: Socialization, sex (or gender) roles, equal opportunity, equal treatment of men and women, equal rights.

Marxist Feminist

Causes of gender inequality: Derived from hierarchical relations of control with the rise of private property and its inheritance by men. Class relations are primary; gender relations, secondary.

Process of gender formation: Not stated explicitly in early works, but implicitly a master-slave relationship applied to husband and wife. Some twentieth-century arguments draw from psychoanalytic theories.

Strategies for social change: In the transformation from a capitalist to a democratic socialist society, bringing women fully into economic production, socializing housework and child care, abolition of marriage and sexual relations founded on notions of private property, eradication of working-class economic subordination.

Key concepts: Capitalist oppression and working-class resistance, women as a "sex class" or a reserve army of labor for capital, husbands' exploitation of wives' labor.

Radical Feminist

Causes of gender inequality: Needs or desires of men to control women's sexuality and reproductive potential. Patriarchy—a set of social relations in which individual men and men as a group control—predating the rise of private property; "ownership" of women the precursor to ownership of territory. Some arguments assume a biological basis for men's needs or desires to control women.

Process of gender formation: Power relations between men and women structure socialization processes in which boys and men view themselves as superior to and has having a right to control girls and women. Gender power relations amplified and reinforced by heterosexual sexuality (male-defined). Psychological and psychoanalytic theories used.

Strategies for social change: Overthrowing patriarchal relations, devising methods of biological reproduction to permit women's sexual autonomy, creating women-centered social institutions (and women-only organizations). In strategies for change, dealing explicitly with the oppressive nature of sexual and familial relations for women and with their link to relations in the public sphere. Eradication of women's social subordination without obliterating gender difference. A new offshoot of radical feminism (or perhaps an amalgam of liberal and radical feminism)—cultural feminism—celebrates gender differences, especially women's special capacities or talents, but does not situate gender differences in the framework of power differences.

Key concepts: Patriarchy, women's oppression, men's control of women's bodies and minds, heterosexism.

Box 3.6, *continued*

Socialist Feminist

Causes of gender inequality: Flexible combination of radical and Marxist categories, i.e., universal male domination and historically specific political-economic relations, respectively. Focus on gender, class and racial relations of domination, in which sexuality (including reproduction) and labor (paid and unpaid) are linked. Differs from Marxist feminism in that both class and gender relations are viewed as primary.

Process of gender formation: Similar to radical feminism, but with greater emphasis on making psychological or psychoanalytical arguments historically and culturally specific and on analyzing women's agency and resistance.

Strategies for social change: Amalgam of Marxist and radical feminist strategies; simultaneous focus on transforming patriarchal and capitalist class relations (includes similar relations in self-defined socialist or communist societies).

Key concepts: Capitalist patriarchy, women's subordination and resistance to men; men's exploitation and control of women's labor and sexuality.

Source: Daly, K., & Chesney-Lind, M. (1988). "Feminism and Criminology." *Justice Quarterly* 5:497-538. Reprinted with permission.

So far, feminists who study crime have devoted most of their theoretical attention to various types of male-to-female abuse in intimate, heterosexual relationships, such as marriage and dating (Schwartz, 1991). Further, radical feminism dominates feminist perspectives on these topics (Simpson, 1989). Radical feminist theory asserts that men physically, sexually, and psychologically assault female intimates because they need or desire to control them (Daly & Chesney-Lind, 1988). British feminist Jill Radford (1987) provides a widely cited example of this perspective. She states that "it is clear that men's violence is used to control women, not just in their own individual interests, but also in the interests of men as a sex class in the reproduction of heterosexuality and male supremacy" (1987, p. 43).

Some radical feminists also try to explain the inadequate police response to victims/survivors of woman abuse described in Chapter 1. According to these theorists, instead of acting as a "value-free" agency of social control, the police organization is a "bastion of male authority and interest" that functions on behalf of men to maintain female subordination in intimate heterosexual relationships (Edwards, 1989, p. 31). One way in which the police achieve this goal is by taking a nonpunitive approach to male perpetrators of intimate violence (Radford, 1987).

Radical feminist perspectives on woman abuse played a major role in demonstrating that many women experience a broad range of abusive male behaviors in intimate relationships. However, these accounts have several shortcomings, such as assuming that all men are equally likely to abuse their female partners. Although woman abuse cuts across all socioeconomic categories, some men, such as those who adhere to the ideology of familial patriarchy and who belong to sexist male peer groups, are more likely to be abusive than others (DeKeseredy & Kelly, 1993b; DeKeseredy & Schwartz, 1998). The experiences of nonmajority groups (e.g., First Nations peoples) are also ignored, despite the fact that there are variations in the amount and type of abuse across different ethnic groups. For example, according to the Ontario Native Women's Association (1989; summary), "One in ten Canadian women has experienced a form of abuse while *eight out of ten Aboriginal women* [emphasis in original] have been abused or assaulted, or can expect to be abused or assaulted."

Radical feminist perspectives on woman abuse have several other "theoretical errors" (Messerschmidt, 1993), as do other feminist perspectives on male-to-female victimization; however, it is beyond the scope of this chapter to describe them here.[5] Because this book is mainly concerned with females in conflict with the law, the rest of this section will focus on feminist accounts of female offending and the societal reactions to their offences. Such theories are not in large supply, and those that have been developed are distinct from mainstream causal perspectives, such as Hagan et al.'s (1987) power-control theory.

Hagan et al. (1987) and other mainstream theorists tend to make "grand theoretical claims" and test their perspectives using statistical analyses of quantitative data (Vold et al., 1998). Of course, some feminist and pro-feminist scholars construct causal models and gather and analyze quantitative data. Most feminist criminologists, however, are opposed to such work. They are, according to Daly and Chesney-Lind (1988, p. 518):

> more interested in providing texture, social context, and case histories: in short, in presenting accurate portraits of how adolescent and adult women become involved in crime. This gender difference is not related to "math anxiety" but rather to a felt need to comprehend women's crime on its own terms, just as criminologists of the past did for men's crime.

Feminist theorists, then, offer an alternative way of thinking (Vold et al., 1998). Consider Messerschmidt's (1993) *structured action theory* of corporate crime, an account that builds upon his earlier socialist feminist work (see Messerschmidt, 1986).

Structured Action Theory

Recall from reading Chapter 1 that few women commit corporate crimes. According to Messerschmidt, to understand why men monopolize these "crimes of the powerful" (Pearce, 1976), we must examine the gender and racial division of labor within corporations. Men, especially white males, have the major decision-making power in corporations. Although women occupy about 38 percent of all corporate management, executive, and administrative positions in the United States, they are restricted to lower-level positions within these areas, such as personnel and affirmative action (Blau & Winkler, 1989). Since these management positions generally do not lead to more powerful positions within corporations, women have relatively few opportunities to commit criminal acts that further the goals of the corporation.

"Old-boy networks" play a key role in maintaining the gender division of labor and perpetuating corporate crime. Such networks achieve this goal by selectively recruiting junior men who share members' norms, attitudes, values, and standards of conduct. If these young executives meet their senior counterparts' expectations, they are rewarded with money, authority, corporate control, and power over women. Senior executives also teach their recruits to act according to "executive conceptions of masculinity." One of the most important practices that exemplifies these conceptions is the sacrifice of personal principles to meet corporate goals, one of which is the accumulation of profits through illegitimate means.

If young executives have "nondemanding moral codes," they are more likely to be promoted to senior positions that free them to, if necessary, commit corporate crimes. Such behavior benefits them and the corporation. According to Messerschmidt:

> Corporate crime simply assists the corporation and young upwardly mobile men reach their goals. In other words, corporate crime is a practice with which men gain corporate power through maintaining profit margins. Moreover, as corporate executives do corporate crime, they simultaneously do masculinity—construct a masculinity specific to their position in the gender, race, and occupational divisions of labor and power (1993, p. 135).

Corporate-executive masculinity is distinct from masculinities found on the street, on assembly lines, in the family, and elsewhere. For example, being a corporate "real man" entails "calculation, rationality as well as struggle for success, reward, and corporate recognition" (1993, p. 136). Male executives compete with each other and measure masculinity according to their success in the business community. Corporate crime is one technique of advancing this "gendered strategy of action."

Corporations face many obstacles in their attempts to increase profits legitimately, such as uncertain and competitive markets, fluctuating sales, government regulations, and so on (Hills, 1987). Consider the problems faced by Canadian National Hockey League (NHL) franchises described in Box 3.7. Compared to American NHL teams, Canadian clubs have to pay very high federal, provincial, and municipal taxes, and they have been negatively affected by escalating player salaries (paid in

U.S. dollars) and a weak Canadian dollar. Messerschmidt contends that these threats to profit making are also threats to white executive masculinity. Corporate crime, then, is also a solution to both of these problems. Illegal and unethical practices are means of establishing and/or maintaining a particular type of masculinity as well as profit margins.

Box 3.7

Tumultuous Times for Canadian NHL Teams

The last five years have been tumultuous times for the NHL in Canada. The country has lost two teams—Winnipeg and Québec—to the forces of U.S. relocation and the other clubs, with the exception of Toronto, have struggled financially.

Last week, even the Montreal Canadians—the most successful team in the history of the NHL—reported a $2.9 million loss over the last nine months ending Dec. 31. Owner Molson is rethinking whether or not it wants to keep the club.

Mr. Bryden (the principal owner of the Ottawa Senators) thinks Canadian NHL owners may be approaching a turning point in the public policy debate about how the game and the clubs should be treated.

"It's a matter of treating NHL hockey not with the same actual measures but in the same way we treat other industries, where their competitive capacity is assessed and their international environment is assessed."

"If there are international subsidies that are interfering with a basically sound business, the Canadian government never allows those businesses to be driven from the country by those kinds of actions."

"It always intervenes in order to preserve Canada's economy or we wouldn't have one."

Mr. Bryden thinks there may be a federal government response within weeks.

Source: This box includes excerpts from an article written by Kelly Egan for *The Ottawa Citizen* (1999, pp. A1-A2). Reprinted with permission.

Some readers may now say, "How is structured action theory different from mainstream perspectives criticized earlier in this chapter? This is a theory about men." Although the structured action theory is about men, it is a feminist perspective. It explains why so few women commit corporate crime, and it should be noted that it is hard to understand the ways in which patriarchal forces shape crime by only focusing on women. Messerschmidt's theory is also one of the first accounts of corporate crime to theorize the relationship between gender, class, and race/ethnicity.

Poverty, Unemployment, Family Violence, and Female Crime

Another group of feminist theorists focuses on three key factors that propel women into property crimes, prostitution, and drugs. These determinants, as discussed previously, are: (1) poverty, (2) unemployment, and (3) family violence. The relationship between these variables, the role of the law, and girls' crime is briefly described by Chesney-Lind (1997, pp. 28-29):

> Young women, a large number of whom are on the run from sexual abuse and parental neglect, are forced by the very statutes designed to protect them into the lives of escaped convicts. Unable to enroll in school or to take a job to support themselves because they fear detection, young female runaways are forced into the streets. Here they engage in panhandling, petty theft, and occasional prostitution to survive. Young women in conflict with their parents (often for legitimate reasons) may actually be forced by present laws into petty criminal activity, prostitution, and drug use.

This perspective is similar to the one described in Box 2.7 (see Chapter 2) by Lowman (1995). His account of becoming a street prostitute, together with Chesney-Lind's (1997) theory, informs some of the progressive policy proposals that will be described in Chapter 5. So do some feminist perspectives on criminal justice, such as Messerschmidt's (1986) socialist feminist account. As you read about his theory, consider the crime data described in Chapters 1 and 2 and Schissel's (1997a) analysis of conservative societal reactions to female young offenders.

Messerschmidt's Socialist Feminist Perspective on Social Control

Again, statistics reported in Chapters 1 and 2 show that women and girls do not constitute a major criminal threat to Canadian society. According to Messerschmidt (1986, p. 80):

> The criminal justice system deals with females as it does with marginalized males: its task is to control nontraditional behavior. Publicizing and exaggerating women's involvement in serious crime and linking it to the women's movement serves to delegitimize the general expansion of women into nontraditional roles in several ways. First, since criminal justice personnel are more likely today to label a female engaged in violence as criminal, female involvement in serious crime is exaggerated. Second, just as the state publicizes female involvement in criminality, it hides the criminality of *powerful males* (emphasis in original). The overall contribution of women to serious crime is thereby magnified. Third, black and poor females in particular are publicized as increasingly dangerous. As with male offenders, racism and class bias in the criminal justice system results in more black and poor females being imprisoned than their white counterparts who have committed similar crimes (Lewis, 1981).

Messerschmidt's (1986) theory is also relevant to the Canadian context. For example, aboriginal women are more likely than female members of the dominant culture (e.g., those of European decent) to be arrested and spend time in penal institutions for not paying fines. Further, in 1991, although aboriginal women comprised less than 2 percent of Canada's population, close to one-quarter of the inmate population of Kingston Prison for Women (PFW) was native (LaPrairie, 1993). Thus, it is not surprising that most native women view the Canadian criminal justice system as racist, an issue addressed in Box 3.8 by Adelberg and the Native Women's Association of Canada (1993, pp. 81-82).

Box 3.8

Aboriginal Women's Perceptions of the Canadian Criminal Justice System

Our understandings of law, of courts, of police, of the judicial system, and of prisons are all set by lifetimes defined by racism. Racism is not simply set by the overt experiences of racism, though most of us have known this direct hatred, have been called "dirty Indians" in school, or in foster homes, or by police or guards, or have seen the differences in the way we were treated and have known this is no accident. Racism is much more extensive than this. Culturally, economically, and as peoples we have been oppressed and pushed aside by whites. We were sent to live on reserves that denied us a livelihood, controlled us with rules that we did not set, and made us dependent on services we could not provide for ourselves.

The Indian Agent and the police are for us administrators of oppressive regimes whose authority we resent and deny. Like other peoples around the world who live under illegitimate political structures, we learn that the rules imposed by this authority exist to be broken, that they are not our ways, that they are only the outside and not the inside measure of the way a person should act. As children we were taught to fear white authority because of the punishments it could enforce. Faced with institutionalized neglect and overt racism, our feelings about white authority even before we encountered the criminal justice system mixed passive distrust and active hatred.

Source: From *In Conflict with the Law: Women and the Canadian Justice System*, eds. Ellen Adelberg and Claudia Currie, Press Gang Publishers, Vancouver, Canada, 1993. Reprinted with permission.

Evaluation of Feminist Theories

Feminist criminology is in its infancy (Curran & Renzetti, 1994); however, it has made major contributions to the study of crime and criminal justice. Still, feminist theories of crime and victimization have been criticized on several grounds. For example, some scholars contend that these perspectives are mainly "white-female centered" (Simpson, 1989) and ignore the differences between female members of the dominant culture and female members of minority groups (e.g., aboriginals, Hispanics, etc.). Of course, this criticism can also be leveled against the overwhelming majority of criminological theories (DeKeseredy & Schwartz, 1996).

This is not to say that all feminist theorists focus only on gender (Renzetti, 1994). A growing number of them are examining how gender intersects with other key variables, such as race, class, and sexual orientation (Hirsch & Keller, 1990). Examples of such feminist scholars are Danner (1996), Chesney-Lind (1997), and Messerschmidt (1993).

Feminist theorists have also not paid much attention to white-collar and corporate crime. Some feminists are addressing this concern (e.g., Daly, 1989; DeKeseredy & Hinch, 1991; Messerschmidt, 1993); however, much more work is required (Simpson, 1989). Feminists also need to develop a sophisticated theory of women's aggression and violence that situates these behaviors in the context of patriarchy (Chesney-Lind, 1999).

Some criminologists (and, not surprisingly, they are male mainstream or conventional scholars) contend it is "difficult to find direct empirical tests of feminist hypotheses" (Akers, 1997, p. 201). This, however, is not a problem for most feminist theorists because they do not want to develop accounts (like Hagan et al.'s (1987), that make "global or grand theoretical statements" and generate hypotheses that are tested using "high-tech statistical analyses" (Daly & Chesney-Lind, 1988, p. 518). Nevertheless, some feminist scholars have tested hypotheses derived from feminist theories of woman abuse. For example, the late Michael D. Smith (1990), a Canadian sociologist, gathered victimization survey data from a sample of 604 women in Toronto and tested the feminist hypothesis that wife beating results from abusive husbands' adherence to the ideology of familial patriarchy.

A similar Canadian study was done by DeKeseredy and Kelly (1993b). Using data derived from a national representative sample survey of 1,307 male university/college students, these researchers tested hypotheses derived from Smith's (1990) study and DeKeseredy and Schwartz's (1993) male peer support model. DeKeseredy and Kelly (1993b) found that males who report abusing their dating partners are more likely to espouse the ideology of familial patriarchy than those who do not report abusive behavior. These men are even more likely to abuse their partners when supported by their male peers. The theoretical framework that informed DeKeseredy and Kelly's (1993a) study is briefly described in Box 3.9 (1993b, p. 28).

Box 3.9

Familial Patriarchy, Male Peer Support, and Woman Abuse in University and College Dating Relationships

Which group of men are prone to developing an ideology that perpetuates and legitimates woman abuse in university/college dating relationships? According to DeKeseredy and Schwartz (1993), the answer lies in the empirical work on pro-abuse male peer groups. Building upon DeKeseredy's (1988) male peer support model, these researchers contend that some men experience considerable stress when their dating partners reject or fail to live up to the ideals of familial partriarchy. These women are also regarded as appropriate targets for physical, sexual, and psychological abuse by some of the male friends of these men. Peers tell their friends to mistreat dating partners who challenge their authority and/or refuse to provide them with sexual gratification.

Several studies have documented male university social networks that approve of sexual assaults on certain dating partners,[6] such as those who are defined as 'teasers,' 'economic exploiters,' 'bar pick-ups,' and 'loose women' who do not want to engage in sexual intercourse (Kanin, 1985). Some male homo-social cohorts often provide sexually aggressive members with a 'vocabulary of adjust-

> ### Box 3.9, *continued*
>
> ment" so that their violent actions do not alter their conceptions of themselves as normal, respectable men (Kanin, 1967).
>
> Similar theories have been advanced to explain the linkage between familial patriarchy and wife beating (Bowker, 1983, 1985; Smith, 1991).

Source: DeKeseredy, W. and Kelly, K. (1993). "The Incidence and Prevalence of Woman Abuse in Canadian University and College Dating Relationships." *Canadian Journal of Sociology*, 18, 137-159.

Like all research methods (e.g., surveys, participant observation, etc.), all theories have their limitations. Feminist perspectives are no exception. It should be noted, however, that attempts to address the criticisms raised here are already underway (Lorber, 1998). Further, feminist theories of crime will play a key role in mapping the future of criminology. Hopefully, many more criminologists will answer Daly and Chesney-Lind's (1988) call to apply these perspectives to all aspects of crime and criminal justice.

SUMMARY

The main objective of this chapter was to review several widely read and cited theories of women and girls' involvement in crime. The term *theory* was also defined and a substantial amount of attention was devoted to describing the practical significance of theory. Most of the crime control policies now in place in Canada are not based on sociological perspectives that focus on the major factors that propel women and girls into crime. Clearly, alternative approaches are necessary. These initiatives will be made explicit in Chapter 5.

Sociological theories are deemed by many scholars to be superior to the individualistic work done by Lombroso and Ferrero (1895) and Pollack (1950). This is not to say that all sociological perspectives on crime take women, gender, and sexuality seriously. In fact, most do not, and perspectives developed by Cohen (1955) and Hirschi (1969) are examples of gender-blind sociological theories of crime. Although they are not gender-blind, the sociological liberation/emancipation and power-control theories reviewed here are also problematic. For example, there is no evidence that women's liberation leads to crime or that working mothers cause female delinquency. Thus, a growing number of scholars call for the application of feminist theories to the problem of women and girls in conflict with the law.

There are various strands of feminist thought; however, only four are typically applied to the issues addressed in the criminological literature: (1) liberal feminism, (2) Marxist feminism, (3) radical feminism, and (4) socialist feminism. Feminist theories have widened criminological debates and it is likely that we will see new perspectives emerging in the near future (White & Haines, 1996). Nevertheless, several pitfalls need to be addressed in future feminist theoretical work, such as neglecting to take into account the experiences of female members of nonmajority groups (e.g., aboriginal women).

NOTES

[1] Reruns of this show are televised in the United States on *Nick at Nite's TV Land*, a cable television network.

[2] Parliament abolished the death penalty in 1976.

[3] "Malestream," which refers to the masculinist assumptions of mainstream sociological thought, is a word used in feminist literature. See Gelsthorpe and Morris (1988) for further reading.

[4] See Belknap (1996), Chesney-Lind and Shelden (1998), DeKeseredy and Schwartz (1996), and Pollack (1999) for in-depth critiques of individualistic perspectives on female crime.

[5] See DeKeseredy and MacLeod (1997), DeKeseredy and Schwartz (1996), Liddle (1989), and Messerschmidt (1993) for more in-depth critiques of radical feminist perspectives on woman abuse.

[6] See DeKeseredy and Schwartz (1998) and Schwartz and DeKeseredy (1997) for reviews of these studies.

DISCUSSION QUESTIONS

1. What is the practical value of theory?

2. Why do most theories of crime ignore women's experiences?

3. What are the limitations of early theories of female crime?

4. What is the value of the sociological imagination?

5. What are the similarities and differences between liberation/emancipation theories and Hagan et al.'s (1987) power-control theory?

6. What is the difference between Marxist feminism and radical feminism?

7. What are the major limitations of feminist theories of crime?

PROBLEM-SOLVING SCENARIOS

1. Generate a group discussion on the practical value of developing theory on female involvement in crime.

2. In a group, develop crime control and prevention policies informed by the four strands of feminist theory described in this chapter.

3. When you watch television or read the newspapers over the next week, keep a record of stories that link women's liberation to female crime. Do these stories include elements of the theoretical work done by Adler (1975) and Simon (1975)?

4. In a group, develop a feminist theory of female violence.

5. Modify Cohen's theory of delinquent boys to take into account female delinquency.

6. Generate a group discussion on the ways in which patriarchy contributes to female crime and the criminal justice system's response to female offenders.

7. In a group, discuss the policy implications of Hagan et al.'s power-control theory. Are they positive or negative?

SUGGESTED READINGS

Adler, F. (1975). *Sisters in Crime*. New York: McGraw-Hill.

In this book, Adler describes her liberation/emancipation theory.

Curran, D.J., & Renzetti, C. (1994). *Theories of Crime*. Needham Heights, MA: Allyn & Bacon.

This textbook provides a comprehensive overview of theories of crime. Chapter 1, which focuses on the importance of theory, is especially useful for those seeking more information on the practical significance of theory.

Daly, K., & Chesney-Lind, M. (1988). "Feminism and Criminology." *Justice Quarterly*, 5, 497-438.

This journal article is essential reading for students and faculty alike interested in learning about the main elements of feminist thought and their relevance to criminology and criminal justice studies.

Hagan, J. (1989). *Structural Criminology*. New Brunswick, NJ: Rutgers University Press.

This award-winning book is a "must read" for those interested in acquiring a more sophisticated understanding of power-control theory.

Lorber, J. (1998). *Gender Inequality: Feminist Theories and Politics*. Los Angeles: Roxbury.

Although not a criminology text, this book provides students with a highly intelligible overview of various strands of feminist theory.

MacLean, B.D., & Milovanovic, D. (eds.) (1997). *Thinking Critically About Crime*. Vancouver: Collective Press.

Chapters 5, 6, and 7 in this collection of readings offer outstanding overviews of feminist contributions to the study of crime, justice, and social control. Chapters are useful for undergraduate students, graduate students, and faculty seeking to learn more about feminist criminology.

An inmate and her three-year-old son
spend time together at a women's prison
in Québec. Most incarcerated Canadian
women have more than one child, and a
large number of them serve
as their children's primary caregiver.

Chapter 4

The Canadian Criminal Justice System's Response to Women and Girls in Conflict with the Law

INTRODUCTION

What is to be done about the crimes committed by Canadian girls and women? If you ask the general public this question, most people would probably give you one or more answers informed by the neoclassical criminology described in Chapter 3. As in the United States, many Canadian politicians, journalists, lobby groups, and voters call for more prisons, longer sentences, harsher treatment of young offenders, and capital punishment (Currie, 1998; Silverman & Kennedy, 1993). Despite the fact that these "tough on crime" policies have had a negative effect on a large number of women and girls and that these strategies have proved to be ineffective, (Miller, 1998), ironically, many females (including some feminists) either publicly or secretly strongly support punitive means of crime control. As Renzetti (1998, p. 186) reminds us, this is because "[t]he get-tough crime control rhetoric often appeals directly

> We are finally and fully confronted by the harsh reality that criminal justice *is about women, all women* (emphasis in original). Although it occasionally operates as an important resource for women, the criminal justice system most frequently represents a form of oppression in women's lives. It attacks most harshly those women with the least power to resist it.
>
> (Danner, 1998, p. 11)

to women, playing on our fears and promising us safety." Consider the description of the proposed Canadian victims-of-crime legislation in Box 4.1. It seems that this legislation also plays heavily on women's fear of crime, especially wife beating and sexual assault (see the second and eleventh paragraphs).[1]

Box 4.1

Crooks to Pay for Their Crimes, Fines Will Give $12m to Victims

Crooks are literally going to pay for their crimes under a new system of hefty automatic fines to be announced by Justice Minister Anne McLellan.

The mandatory fine surcharges, to be included in new victims-of-crime legislation, will raise an estimated $12 million. The revenues are targeted for provinces to funnel to victim assistance programs ranging from battered women's shelters, to sexual assault centres and services helping crime victims get through painful court experiences.

This is not about punishment. It's about making sure the system has the ability to care for victims and to fund the programs they need," a federal justice official said yesterday.

The legislative package of Criminal Code changes giving victims a louder voice in the justice system is likely to be tabled Thursday (April 15, 1999) in the Commons if cabinet gives it the green light today as expected. The substance of the reforms was outlined by Ms. McLellan last December.

But details of the key ingredient to penalize criminals in the pocketbook were only worked out recently with provincial lawmakers.

Criminals have been subject to extra penalties since 1988, but they are often forgotten or neglected by judges or Crown prosecutors on sentencing.

The new deal means a "major increase" in revenues for all provinces to enhance or add services for victims. The Justice Department estimates it will add up to an extra $5 million a year for Ontario programs.

An automatic 15-per-cent levy is to be tacked on to any fine under the amendments. Anyone convicted of an indictable offence would be targeted at least an extra $100 for victim programs. Someone guilty of a minor summary offence that escapes a fine would still be nailed with a minimum $50 surcharge.

The amounts could be increased, but not lowered at the discretion of a judge. The surcharge could be waived if the offender is a deadbeat and collection efforts would cost too much.

Under the legislation, a mugger sent to jail would also be liable for a $100 surcharge. A convicted drunk driver fined $600 for the offence would owe an additional $90 to be used for victim services.

Danielle Aubry, co-chair of the Alberta Association of Sexual Assault Centres, welcomed the initiative, saying, "We're constantly struggling for money."

In Alberta, the most vigilant province, only $324,000 was collected in 1997 from federal offences. Ontario figures are so low they aren't traceable.

The changes will promote national consistency of services and provide stable funding which victims groups can count on, said Steve Sullivan, executive director of the Canadian Resource Centre for Victims of Crime.

The long-awaited legislation will also let victims read impact statements in court, shelter young crime victims from cross-examination by assailants, and force judges to consider the safety of victims before releasing an accused prior to trial.

Source: Ovenden, N. (1999). "Crooks to Pay for Their Crimes." *Ottawa Citizen*, April 13, p. A6. Reprinted with permission.

Another reason why many Canadians—men and women alike—support harsh punishment is because, like their neighbors south of the border, they "are continually bombarded with the myths, misconceptions, and half-truths that dominate public discussion, while the real story is often buried in a specialized technical literature that is increasingly difficult for most people to follow" (Currie 1998, pp. 6-7). Box 4.2 provides a recent example of how the Canadian federal government has contributed to this problem in its attempt to garner public support for the new *Youth Criminal Justice Act*.

Box 4.2

Reporters were Suckers for Federal Flim-Flam

Over the past two weeks, Canadians have been managed, misinformed and manipulated by a campaign of political spin. The general quietly directing the campaign is the federal government. But we, the media, have been the unwitting foot soldiers. We were used. And we failed the public.

The issue is youth crime and Justice Minister Anne McLellan's new *Youth Criminal Justice Act*. For several years now, the political centre on young offenders has been shifting to the right. Increasingly, the public believes youth crime is worsening, that young criminals aren't punished properly, the *Young Offenders Act* is a joke. The federal liberals are aware of this shift and they know they must shift with it— or at least make it appear so. Ms. McLellan chose the second option, and the spin campaign began.

It started with "leaks" to the media in the week before the new youth crime bill was to be placed before Parliament. On March 6, the *National Post*, the *Globe and Mail*, and most Southam papers, including the *Citizen*, ran long stories on the contents of the new bill.

The *Post* emphasized that the new bill would jail parents who willfully fail to supervise children released on bail if the children reoffend. It also stated that the age at which young offenders could receive adult sentences would be lowered from 16 to 14. A "senior Justice Department official" was quoted saying the idea of the new bill was to deal with violent offenders "more firmly" while finding alternatives to jail for others. This was the key line in the spin campaign.

The Southam papers reported the new bill would "deal more harshly" with violent offenders, particularly by lowering the age at which young offenders may receive adult sentences from 16 to 14.

The *Globe* story of the same day, attributed to anonymous "sources," repeated that the bill would "crack down" on violent offenders while finding alternatives for others.

The *Globe* stated that the bill would give adult sentences to youth "as young as 14" who commit murder or one of several other violent crimes.

What readers wouldn't know from the reports— what the reporters apparently didn't know— is that most of what they cited as new changes already existed in the *Young Offenders Act*.

Box 4.2, *continued*

Under the *YOA*, offenders as young as 14 can be given adult sentences for any indictable crime (one that is punishable by more than two years in jail). The Crown simply has to convince the judge that, because of the nature of his crime, the offender's maturity, his previous convictions or other factors, an adult sentence is appropriate.

The *YOA* also has a presumption that offenders aged 16 or 17 who commit murder or other very serious violent crimes will get an adult sentence. In that case, it's up to the defence lawyer to convince the judge that an adult sentence is not appropriate.

The only change in giving adult sentences to youths in the new bill is in that second category: The presumption of an adult sentence will be extended to 14- and 15-year-olds that commit the most violent crimes. (It also adds a new category to the list of crimes that raise the presumption: a pattern of serious violent crimes).

But even this shift in presumption isn't terribly important. When the Crown and defence clash over whether a case should be taken to adult court, where a conviction means an adult sentence, they both muster all the evidence they can and the judge decides based on the evidence. So as a practical matter, whether the formal presumption is in favour of a youth or adult sentence doesn't make much difference. In the words of Ottawa Lawyer Carey MacLellan, a specialist in youth crime, "It's not consequential. The judge will do what they do."

As for the jailing of parents who fail to live up to their supervision agreements, that too is permitted under the *YOA*, though it is rarely done. The new law will allow for a second form of the same charge to be laid, one that would carry a maximum two-year sentence instead of the current maximum of six months. But this won't make it any more likely that the charge will actually be used.

These facts were almost entirely absent in the initial reports, and even the stories in the following days continued to repeat the original mistakes. But where the facts were scant, buzz-phrases like "crackdown" and "get tough" abounded. Editorialists and columnists, without any exception I could find, picked up the errors of the news stories compounding the false impression that tough new changes were coming.

So who was to blame for the mistakes of the week leading up to the new bill's release? Did the "sources" of the leaks mislead reporters, either explicitly or implicitly, in describing what was coming? Or did the reporters simply misunderstand what "sources" told them? I can't answer that. But what happened next shows how government could bolster the false impression of tough changes not by lying, but by spinning.

On Thursday, March 11, the new *Youth Criminal Justice Act* (*YCJA*) was introduced in Parliament. Despite errors in the previous week's news coverage, the government press releases did nothing to clarify the truth. In fact, the wording of the press releases added to the confusion by seeming to confirm the key mistake the press had been making.

In the main press release, a series of bullet points highlighted the key features of the new *Youth Criminal Justice Act*. The very first bullet said the *YCJA* would "allow an adult sentence for any youth 14 years old or more . . ." for any

Box 4.2, *continued*

indictable crime. Any reporter or reader would, quite fairly, assume that meant this was unique to the *YCJA*— that it was a change from the old *YOA*. It doesn't exactly say that, of course. The government didn't lie. But the placement and the ambiguous wording encouraged reporters to continue to make the crucial mistake they had been making for the past week.

The only clue to the truth about sentencing under the *YOA* was to be found in the more detailed backgrounder release, which says the *YCJA* will "maintain" the possibility of adult sentences for those 14 and older. One word, buried in the press releases: That was all the government offered to clear up a mistake they knew was being made repeatedly. For reporters scrambling to summarize a complex story on deadline, that was no help at all. Which was exactly the point.

With a misleading press release, and with mistakes repeated over and over in the press, it wasn't surprising that news stories written after the bill's release still failed to straighten out the facts. And editorials continued to rely on the mistakes of the news reports passionately condemning or supporting fictitious "get tough" sentencing changes. Even now, a week after their release, columns continue to appear repeating the same errors.

In reviewing nearly 100 stories and opinion pieces published by Ontario-based newspapers, I found fewer than five that came close to properly explaining the sentencing of parents to jail for failing to supervise their offending children. As for the issue of giving adult sentences to young offenders, I did not find a single story that accurately explained the law.

I spoke with Alan Young, professor of criminal law at Osgoode Hall Law School, about the spin and errors of the past two weeks. Neither of us believes that youth crime is worsening or the "get-tough" policies are wise and, frankly, we're happy Anne McLellan didn't go that route in reality. It the cynical manipulation of image and fact that bothers me. Mr. Young was more circumspect. It's part of a "pretty common pattern," he said. Governments "use the media as their handmaiden for influencing public opinion."

That's a depressing assessment, but at least in this instance, it's undeniable that we were used, whether like handmaidens or in some less genteel capacity. We were used, the public was manipulated, and the generals of the spin campaign had the victory.

Source: This box includes excerpts from an article by Dan Gardner for *The Ottawa Citizen*. (1999, pp. A1-A2). Reprinted with permission.

It is beyond the scope of this chapter to provide a more in-depth analysis of the factors that contribute to widespread Canadian support for get-tough crime control initiatives. Rather, the main objective is to focus on two criminal justice system responses to girls and women in conflict with the criminal law: (1) court processing, and (2) sentencing. Because data on charges laid by the police are described in Chapters 1 and 2, these statistics will not be repeated here.

WOMEN AND GIRLS PROCESSED THROUGH CANADIAN COURTS

Women Processed Through Courts

The data presented in this section are derived from the *Adult Criminal Court Survey* (ACCS). This national database is briefly described in Box 4.3. Table 4.1, which presents ACCS statistics, shows that at the national level, the number of Canadian women processed through the court system for violent, drug, property, and other crimes decreased slightly from 1994-95 to 1996-97. At the regional level, however, all regions reported a slight decrease in processing except the Atlantic and Pacific regions. The former increased significantly, while the latter only marginally increased (see Table 4.2). It should also be noted that 85 percent of the adult court caseload in 1996-97 involved men (Stevenson et al., 1998).

Box 4.3

A Brief Description of the Adult Criminal Court Survey

- A national database of statistical information on charges, cases and persons involving accused who are aged 18 years or older, companies and youths that have been raised to adult criminal court.

- The Canadian Centre for Justice Statistics collects the data on completed federal statute charges in collaboration with provincial and territorial government departments responsible for provincial criminal courts.

- The primary unit of analysis is the case, which is defined as one or more charges laid against an individual and disposed of in court on the same day.

- Coverage is of provincial criminal courts in seven provinces and two territories (representing approximately 80% of the national provincial criminal court caseload). They are Newfoundland (2.0%), Prince Edward Island (0.4%), Nova Scotia (4.1%), Québec (20.6%), Ontario (50.9%), Saskatchewan (6.5%), Alberta (14.3%), Yukon (0.5%) and the Northwest Territories (0.7%).

- Data for federal statute offenses heard in Québec's municipal courts are not currently available. It is estimated that approximately 20 percent of federal statute charges in Québec are heard in municipal court.

- In Québec, sex is determined on the basis of the accused's name, producing a relatively higher rate of sex unknown.

Source: Dell, C., & Boe, R. (1998). *Adult Female Offenders in Canada: Recent Trends*. Ottawa: Correctional Service of Canada, p. 45. Reprinted with permission.

Table 4.1
Women Processed Through the Court System,* Canada

(The Canada total does not include British Columbia, Manitoba and New Brunswick for 1994/1995 and 1995/1996 and the Northwest Territories for 1996/97)

	1994/1995		1995/1996		1996/1997	
Offense	Actual Number	Rate Per** 10,000	Actual Number	Rate Per 10,000	Actual Number	Rate Per 10,000
Crime of Violence	9,926	10.9	9,960	10.8	9,619	10.3
Property Crimes	24,916	27.3	23,968	25.9	22,825	24.4
Drugs***	3,864	4.2	3,640	3.9	3,492	3.7
Other****	19.070	20.9	19,143	20.7	18,485	19.8
TOTAL	57,776	63.3	56,771	61.3	54,421	58.2

*	Source: Adult Criminal Court Survey
**	Rate per 10,000 total adult female (aged 18+ years) population
***	Drugs = Drug Related Offenses
****	Other = Other Federal Statutes & Other Criminal Code Violations (Traffic offenses are excluded)

Source: Dell, C., & Boe, R. (1998). *Adult Female Offenders in Canada: Recent Trends*. Ottawa: Correctional Service of Canada, p. 9. Reprinted with permission.

Table 4.2
Women Processed Through the Court System,* Regions

(The regional totals do not include British Columbia in the Pacific region, Manitoba in the Prairie region and New Brunswick in the Atlantic Region for 1994-95 and 1995/96 and the Northwest Territories in the Prairie region for 1996/97)

	1994/1995		1995/1996		1996/1997	
	Actual Number	Rate Per** 10,000	Actual Number	Rate Per 10,000	Actual Number	Rate Per 10,000
ATLANTIC						
Crimes of Violence	482	7.6	654	10.3	690	10.8
Property Crimes	1,472	23.3	1,729	27.2	1,790	28.0
Drugs***	141	2.2	173	2.7	136	2.1
Other****	849	13.4	1,081	17.0	1,077	16.8
Atlantic—Total	2,944	46.5	3,637	57.2	3,693	57.7

continued

Table 4.2, *continued*

	1994/1995		1995/1996		1996/1997	
	Actual Number	Rate Per** 10,000	Actual Number	Rate Per 10,000	Actual Number	Rate Per 10,000
QUÉBEC						
Crimes of Violence	885	3.0	954	3.3	899	3.1
Property Crimes	2,483	8.7	1,945	6.7	1,841	6.3
Drugs	620	2.2	732	2.5	772	2.6
Other	2,126	7.4	2,320	8.0	2,185	7.5
Québec— Total	6,114	21.3	5,951	20.6	5,697	19.5
ONTARIO						
Crimes of Violence	6,319	14.9	6,061	14.0	5,659	12.9
Property Crimes	13,881	32.6	13,540	31.4	12,897	29.4
Drugs	2,291	5.4	2,083	4.8	1,948	4.4
Other	12,206	28.7	11,629	27.0	11,089	25.3
Ontario—Total	34,697	81.6	33,313	77.2	31,593	72.1
PRAIRIE						
Crimes of Violence	2,205	16.0	2,232	16.0	2,319	16.6
Property Crimes	7,032	50.9	6,694	47.9	6,233	44.5
Drugs	801	5.8	631	4.5	623	4.5
Other	3,830	27.7	4,026	28.8	4,077	29.1
Prairie—Total	13,868	99.9	13,583	97.1	13,252	94.7
PACIFIC						
Crimes of Violence	35	3.4	59	5.6	52	4.7
Property Crimes	48	4.7	60	5.7	64	5.8
Drugs	11	1.2	21	2.0	13	1.2
Other	59	5.7	87	8.2	57	5.2
Pacific—Total	153	14.9	227	21.4	186	16.9
TOTAL	57,776	63.3	56,711	61.3	54,421	58.2

*   Source: Adult Criminal Court Survey
**   Rate per 10,000 total adult female (aged 18+ years) population
***   Drugs = Narcotics Control Act & Food and Drugs Act
**** Other = Other Federal Statutes & Other Crime (Traffic offenses are excluded)
It should be noted that figures may not add to totals due to rounding

Source: Dell, C., & Boe, R. (1998). *Adult Female Offenders in Canada: Recent Trends*. Ottawa: Correctional Service of Canada, p. 12. Reprinted with permission.

Girls Processed Through the Youth Court System

The data presented in the first part of this section are derived from the *Youth Court Survey*, which is briefly described by Dell and Boe (1997, p. 54) in their report to the Correctional Service of Canada:

> A **case** is one or more charges against a young person which are presented in court on the same date (emphasis in original). Basic charge data are used to "create" cases, a case being all the charges against a young person that have the same date of first appearance. Identifiers used to link charges to cases are the coded name, sex, date of birth, date of first court appearance and court location code. This report uses case counts as the unit of analysis.

As pointed out in Table 4.3, overall, there has been a small decrease in the number of girls' cases processed through the youth court system between 1991-92 and 1994-95. (However, there was an increase in 1993-94 that was followed by a decrease in 1994-95.) There was a decline in property crimes and there was a minor increase in violent crimes (following a slight decrease in 1994-95). Further, as described in Table 4.4, there was no major increase in crimes by girls at the regional level. In fact, the rate was stable in most regions. Still, the rate marginally increased in the Atlantic region from 1992-93 to 1994-95, while the overall number of cases processed through the Pacific region youth court system slightly decreased during the same time period.

Table 4.3
Female Youth Processed Through the Canadian Court System*

Offense	1991/1992		1992/1993		1993/1994		1994/1995	
	Actual Number	Rate Per** 10,000	Actual Number	Rate Per 10,000	Actual Number	Rate Per 10,000	Actual Number	Rate Per 10,000
Crimes of Violence	3,436	32.2	3,830	34	4,551	39.9	4,327	37.6
Property Crimes	10,832	101	10,356	92	10,124	88.8	8,710	75.7
Drugs***	327	3	342	3	394	3.5	513	4.5
Other****	3,976	37	4,092	36	4,333	38	4,111	35.7
Young Offenders Act	2,023	18.9	2,156	19.1	2,490	21.8	2,497	21.7
TOTAL	20,594	192.8	20,776	184.4	21,892	191.9	20,158	175.2

*	Source: Youth Court Statistics
**	Rate per 10,000 total female youth (aged 12-17 years) population
***	Drugs = Narcotics Control Act & Food and Drugs Act
****	Other = Other Federal Statutes & Other Crimes

Source: Dell, C., & Boe, R. (1997). *Female Young Offenders in Canada: Recent Trends*. Ottawa: Correctional Service of Canada, p. 9. Reprinted with permission.

Table 4.4
Female Youth Processed The Youth Court System,* Regions

	1992/1993		1993/1994		1994/1995	
	Actual Number	Rate Per** 10,000	Actual Number	Rate Per 10,000	Actual Number	Rate Per 10,000
ATLANTIC						
Crimes of Violence	254	24.4	306	29.7	348	34.1
Property Crimes	617	59.1	624	60.5	634	62.2
Drugs***	8	0.8	6	0.6	17	1.7
Other****	179	17.2	160	15.5	188	18.4
Young Offenders Act	121	11.6	129	12.5	150	14.7
Atlantic—Total	1,179	113	1,225	118.7	1,337	131.1
QUÉBEC						
Crimes of Violence	213	7.5	188	6.5	215	7.4
Property Crimes	256	9	215	7.4	242	8.3
Drugs	27	0.9	53	1.8	103	3.5
Other	84	2.9	100	3.5	76	2.6
Young Offenders Act	42	1.5	44	1.5	49	1.7
Québec— Total	622	21.8	630	21.8	685	23.6
ONTARIO						
Crimes of Violence	1,914	47.6	2,245	55.2	2,078	50.7
Property Crimes	4,939	122.9	4,953	121.8	3,987	97.3
Drugs	157	3.9	184	4.5	226	5.5
Other	19,33	48.1	2,102	51.7	1,855	45.3
Young Offenders Act	729	18.1	889	21.9	869	21.2
Ontario—Total	9,672	240.7	10,373	255.1	9,015	219.9
PRAIRIE						
Crimes of Violence	1,168	57.3	1,469	71.3	1,393	66.8
Property Crimes	3,342	164	3,309	160.6	2,880	138.1
Drugs	78	3.8	86	4.2	101	4.8
Other	1,568	77	1,651	80.1	1,652	79.2
Young Offenders Act	921	45.2	1,061	51.5	1,069	51.2
Prairie—Total	7,077	347.3	7,576	367.6	7,095	340.1

Table 4.4, *continued*

	1992/1993		1993/1994		1994/1995	
	Actual Number	Rate Per** 10,000	Actual Number	Rate Per 10,000	Actual Number	Rate Per 10,000
PACIFIC						
Crimes of Violence	398	30.5	480	35.5	450	32.4
Property Crimes	1,242	95	1,047	77.5	977	70.3
Drugs	76	5.8	75	5.6	73	5.3
Other	216	16.6	178	13.2	229	16.5
Young Offenders Act	293	22.4	308	22.8	297	21.4
Pacific—Total	2,225	170.2	2,088	154.6	2,026	145.8
TOTAL	20,776	184.4	21,892	191.9	20,158	175.2

*   Source: Youth Court Statistics
**   Rate per 10,000 total female youth (aged 12-17) population
***   Drugs = Narcotics Control Act & Food and Drugs Act
****   Other = Other Federal Statutes & Other Crime

Source: Dell, C., & Boe, R. (1997). *Female Young Offenders in Canada: Recent Trends.* Ottawa: Correctional Service of Canada, p. 12. Reprinted with permission.

Table 4.4 also shows that the Prairie region had the highest rate of girls processed through the courts, followed by Ontario, Pacific, Atlantic, and Québec regions. The Prairie region's aboriginal population is higher than that of other regions listed in Table 4.4 (Siggner, 1992), which may account, in large part, for why this region had the highest rate of girls processed through courts. For example, similar to disenfranchised African-Americans, native and Métis youth are "unfairly targeted for legal scrutiny" (Schissel, 1993, p. 61).

Boys appear in courts more often than do girls. For example, in 1996-97, males accounted for 80 percent (88,113) of the caseload. Further, in 1996-97, most of the female youth court cases (5%) involved 15-year-old girls (Stevenson et al., 1998), and girls who appear before courts had fewer charges against them than did boys (Pate, 1999).

SENTENCING

The Sentencing of Women

There are far more Canadian men than women sentenced to federal and provincial/territorial correctional facilities. For example, in 1995-96, men accounted for 97 percent of the federal correctional population and 91 percent of the provincial/territorial population. During that year, 10,540 women were sent to provincial/territorial institutions, and 130 were admitted to federal ones (Goff, 1999), while 103,982 men were sent to provincial/territorial facilities and 4,272 were admitted to federal ones. However, during the past 20 years, the percentage increase in women sent to correctional facilities was much higher than that of men (Boritch, 1997). For example:

- Between 1978-79 and 1995-96, the number of women admitted to provincial/territorial institutions increased by 57 percent, compared to a 17 percent increase for males.

- Between 1983-84 and 1995-96, there was a 30 percent increase in the number of women sent to federal institutions, compared to a two percent increase for males (Goff, 1999).

These figures should be read with caution, though, because the female statistics, as pointed out by Goff (1999, pp. 156–157) in Box 4.4, are founded on very small base figures. Box 4.4 also provides a recent profile of Canadian women in the federal correctional system.

Box 4.4

A Recent Profile of Incarcerated Canadian Women

[O]n March 31, 1997, 2.5 percent of all incarcerated inmates in the federal correctional system were women. This meant that 357 women were serving a sentence of two years or more at some institution in Canada on that day. Most information collected on federally sentenced women has been demographic and descriptive in its orientation. According to the latest information produced by the Solicitor General of Canada (1997), federally sentenced women in 1997 shared the following common characteristics: they were between 20 and 34 years of age, single, Caucasian, with most only receiving a high school education at best, serving their first federal sentence for a period of less than six years in length, and most having more than one child, with many of the women being the primary caregiver.

Most federally sentenced women (205, or 57.4 percent) identified themselves as Caucasian, 66 (or 18.5 percent) were aboriginal, 35 (or 10.1 percent) were black, nine (or 2.5 percent) were Asiatic, while the remaining 41 stated they belonged to another race (eight individuals, or 2.2 percent); 33 (or 9.2 percent) did not identify their race. The highest percentage of federally sentenced aboriginal women offenders (48.1 percent) were located in the Prairie Region of the Correctional Service of Canada, while the largest number of black women sentenced to a federal term of incarceration were located in Ontario (16.8 percent) and the Atlantic Region (13.9 percent).

Box 4.4, *continued*

Most women (74.8 percent) were serving their first period of federal incarceration. Seventy-one (or 19.9 percent) of all federally sentenced women in 1997 were serving a life sentence for murder. The most common sentence for women was between three and six years (35.3 percent) followed by between two and three years (22.7 percent), life (19.9 percent), six to 10 years (17.4 percent), 10 years or more (4.2 percent) and an indeterminate sentence (.5 percent).

In Canada, women represent a small percentage of offenders sentenced to a period of incarceration in either a provincial/territorial or federal correctional facility. According to the Canadian Centre for Justice Statistics (1997, p. 9), women accounted for 3 percent of all admissions to federal facilities and 9 percent of all admissions to provincial/territorial facilities during 1995-96. In 1991, very few women (a total of 141) were sentenced to a federal facility. Currently, the total population of federally sentenced women is approximately 350, in comparison to about 12,000 men. This means that women represent about 2.8 percent of the federal offender population, a ratio that has remained relatively stable since 1975. The rate of incarceration of women per 100,000 population remained stable between 1975 and 1985 (between 0.9 and 1.2), while for men it increased from 37.4 to 47.0 per 100,000 population (Johnson, 1986).

At the federal level, the number of women incarcerated has increased by about 50 percent since 1975, while the number of men has also increased by approximately 50 percent. However, these percentages are misleading because they are founded on such small base figures. The increase amounts to an approximate increase of 175 women, compared with an increase of 3,500 men.

At the provincial level of custody, a slight increase of the percentage of women admitted to custody occurred in the decade between 1978-79 and 1989-90. The number of women increased by a little more than 100 percent while the percentage for men was approximately 20 percent. Once again, however, the actual numbers for women were much lower than for men. During 1989-90, the number of women admitted to a provincial custody facility was 9,209, in comparison to 105,905 men.

These much smaller numbers of women serving a sentence indicate women's lower incidence of offending overall, as well as the less serious nature of their offences. Women tend to receive shorter sentences than men, a statistic related to the less serious nature of their crime and the fact that they have been convicted for fewer previous criminal offences.

Source: Goff, C. (1999). *Corrections in Canada.* Cincinnati: Anderson.

Excluded from Box 4.4 are data showing that many women in Canadian prisons were also physically and/or sexually assaulted as children by family members or other people. For example, the Canadian Task Force on Federally Sentenced Women found that 68 percent of the 191 federal female inmates interviewed reported that they had been physically abused, while 53 percent reported having been sexually abused at some point in their lives. Abuse statistics generated from aboriginal female inmates were much higher, with 90 percent of them reporting physical abuse and 61 percent reporting sexual abuse (Shaw, 1994). Research on women incarcerated in provincial institutions uncovered similar data (see Comack, 1993; Faith, 1993a). Women in penal institutions report higher rates of abuse than those in the female general population.

Several studies show that women are more likely than men to receive nonprison sentences, such as probation.[2] In fact, for all offences, except for "morals" and "other federal statutes," Canadian women were more likely to receive probation as the most serious disposition (Birkenmayer & Besserer, 1997; Dell & Boe, 1998; Goff, 1999). Adult Criminal Court Survey data show that fines are the second most common sanction for Canadian women, followed by incarceration and then by sentences in the category of "other," which includes absolute or conditional discharge, suspended sentence, payment of legal costs, and suspension of driver's license. The least common sanction is restitution/compensation to the offenders' victims (Dell & Boe, 1998).

Contrary to what you might think, except for being charged with a violent crime, the severity of an offence is not a major determinant of women being incarcerated; nor is a prior record (Boritch, 1997). Rather, sentence severity is more heavily determined by a woman's "respectability." For example, judges are more likely to hand down lenient sentences if a female offender is married, has children, and is financially dependent on her spouse or the government (Boritch, 1977; Daly, 1987; Kruttschnitt, 1982, 1984; Kruttschnitt & Green, 1984). On the other hand, those who violate patriarchal gender-role expectations are given more severe dispositions. So, it seems that in addition to enforcing the law, the Canadian criminal justice system, like its United States counterpart, is deeply concerned about enforcing patriarchal or traditional gender-role expectations (Chesney-Lind, 1986).

The Sentencing of Girls

Sentences for Canadian youths are described in Box 4.5. Of all dispositions, probation is the most common for both boys and girls. However, in 1996-97, girls were more likely than boys to receive this sentence. Probation was the most common sanction in 57 percent of the girls' cases, compared with 49 percent of the boys' cases. Further, during this same year:

- boys were more likely to receive custodial sentences than were girls (36% vs. 25%);
- boys (5%) were slightly more likely than girls (4%) to receive a fine;

- boys (19%) were more likely to be sentenced to open custody than were girls (15%);

- boys (17%) were more likely to be sentenced to secure custody than were girls (10%);

- girls (8%) were more likely to receive community service dispositions than were boys (6%); and

- girls (3%) were slightly more likely than boys (2%) to receive an absolute discharge (Stevenson et al., 1998).

Box 4.5

Sentences for Canadian Youths

In Canada, there are two categories of sentences in youth court: custody- and community-based. The dispositions that fall under these categories are described below.

Custody Sentences
Custody sentences require a youth to spend time in a designated correctional institution, and there are two types:

Secure (Closed) Custody: a youth is committed to a facility specifically designated for the secure detention of youths.

Open Custody: a youth is committed to a community residential center, child care institution, forest or wilderness camp, or any other similar facility.

Community Dispositions
Community dispositions can be served in a youth's community, and there are a variety of such sentences:

Probation: a youth must abide by a set of conditions for a maximum period of two years. At a minimum, he or she must keep the peace, be of good behavior and appear in court when required to do so. Probation is often combined with other types of sentences.

Fine: a youth is ordered to pay up to $1,000 within a set time period. However, credits for work performed in lieu of payment can be earned.

Community Service: a youth is ordered to perform community service work for a specified number of hours without pay for the benefit of the community.

Absolute Discharge: a youth is found guilty of the offence and is discharged absolutely, which means that he or she does not have to serve a sentence for his or her offence. Still, a record is kept of the decision.

Other: various dispositions including conditional discharge, compensation, compensation in kind, pay purchaser (money for the innocent purchaser of stolen goods), restitution, prohibition/seizure/forfeiture, essays, apologies and counseling programs may be ordered.

Source: Stevenson, K., Tufts, J., Hendrick, D., & Kowalski, M. (1998). *A Profile of Youth Justice in Canada*, Catalogue No. 85-544, p. 38. Reprinted with permission.

Disposition data described so far in this section tell us nothing about whether girls are getting more serious sentences today than prior to the *Young Offenders Act* (*YOA*), which came into force in 1984 and which eliminated *status offences*. Status offences depended on the juvenile status of the offender and included behaviors that, if engaged in by adults, would not be officially designated as crimes (Boritch, 1997). They include behaviors such as running away from home, immorality, truancy, and violations of liquor laws (Reitsma-Street, 1993). As in the United States (see Chesney-Lind, 1997), Canadian girls were far more likely than boys to be given custodial dispositions for status offences, which have been used to control girls' sexuality and to punish them for "unfeminine" behavior (Boritch, 1997). Further, girl status offenders were sentenced to longer periods of incarceration than were boys who committed status offences.

Status offences were basically "'buffer charges' for suspected sexuality when applied to girls" (Chesney-Lind, 1997, p. 65). Consider the following statement made by a United States judge who sentenced girls to custody for status offences: "I figure if a girl is about to get pregnant, we'll keep her until she's sixteen and ADC[3] will pick her up" (Rogers, 1972, p. 227). With the abolition of status offences in Canada, it would be logical to assume that fewer girls are in custody today than prior to the YOA. However, this is not the case. According to Reitsma-Street (1993), prior to 1984, less than 500 Canadian girls were sent to secure custody or admitted to a welfare institution, while after 1984, custody increased steadily from 6.7 percent in 1984-85 to 12.7 percent in 1988-89. Things have not gotten better. In fact, they are getting worse, as described in Table 4.5, which presents more recent Youth Court Survey data.

Table 4.5 shows that the numbers of girls sent to secure custody has increased from 1991-92 to 1994-95. Further, more girls were admitted to open custody facilities, while the number of girls who received less serious dispositions, such as fines, restitution, absolute discharges, and community service orders decreased during this same time period. It should also be noted that in some parts of Canada, such as British Columbia, there has been an increase in the number of girls remanded into custody pending disposition of a charge. For example, in this province, between 1992-93 and 1995-96, the rate increased from 1.5 to 2.8 (Dell & Boe, 1997).

Table 4.5
Canadian Female Youth Dispositions, 1991-92 to 1994-95*

Disposition**	1991-92	1992-93	1993-94	1994-95
Secure Custody	706	8	1,086	1,095
Detention for Treatment	1	–***	–	–
Open Custody	1,468	1,565	1,896	1,795
Probation	5,547	5,809	5,886	6,952
Fine	868	828	838	686
Compensation	24	17	17	20
Pay Purchaser	4	6	7	5
Compensation (Kind)	4	–	–	–
Community Service Order	1,854	2,109	2,108	1,123
Restitution	16	12	17	7
Prob./Seizure/ Forfeit	4	10	12	2
Absolute Discharge	921	835	767	668
Other	571	653	760	255
TOTAL	**11,987**	**12,675**	**13,394**	**12,609**

*Source: Youth Court Survey

**Disposition is the most serious disposition for a person or case. The seriousness of the disposition is determined by the effect it has on the young person. The dispositions above are ordered from most to least serious. If the disposition with the highest priority is a fine, compensation on pay purchases, and there is a combination of these, the disposition with the largest dollar value is selected as the most significant. In the event that multiple charges result in multiple custody orders, the highest priority is assigned to the largest custody order. The same situation applies in the case of multiple probation orders.

***– is nil or zero.

Source: Dell C., & Boe, R. (1997). *Female Young Offenders in Canada: Recent Trends*. Ottawa: Correctional Service of Canada, p. 37.

Why didn't the *YOA* decrease the number of Canadian incarcerated girls? Boritch (1997) contends that this can be partially explained by the fact that criminal justice officials have reclassified status offenders into categories that are available in the *YOA*, such as *order-maintenance offences* and *administrative offences*. The former include *breach of probation* and *breach of undertaking*, while the latter include offences such as *escaping from custody*, *failure to appear in court*, and *contempt of court*. Consider the following data uncovered by Reitsma-Street (1993):

- By 1991, one in four charges laid against Canadian girls in youth courts are against the administration of justice; and

- Over one-fifth of girls in Canadian open or secure custody facilities were charged with violations against administrative laws.

The reclassification of status offenders tell us that in Canada, as in the United States, there is "tremendous and high-level resistance to the notion that youth who have not committed any criminal act should not be held in institutions" (Chesney-Lind, 1997, p. 82). Further, the increase in the number of Canadian girls incarcerated is partially the result of the criminal justice system being more likely today to label a girl engaged in crime as a young offender. Recall from reading Chapter 2 that some behaviors that used to be viewed as "incorrigibility" are now being labeled assault.

Kim Pate (1999, p. 2), Executive Director of the Canadian Association of Elizabeth Fry Societies, describes other factors that have contributed to the increase in the number of Canadian girls sent to secure custody facilities:

> Young women are disproportionately disadvantaged as a result of a lack of gender-focused community and institutional programming and services, and extremely limited access to open custody settings. The majority of young women who receive open custody dispositions must serve their sentences in secure custody and/or co-ed correctional facilities. Girls and young women also tend to have more limited access to the services and programs, both in the community and in institutions. In many young offender centres across the country, incidences of sexual assault and/or pregnancies during custody had led to further segregation of young women in correctional facilities. Young women are in real need of women-centred approaches in the youth justice system, their needs are often ignored or at best subsumed by those of young men.

Much of this chapter has thus far been devoted to describing punishments meted out to Canadian girls and women who are officially designated as criminals. But, do these punishments work? Do they help reduce crimes committed by girls and women? It is beyond the scope of this chapter to evaluate the effectiveness of all of the dispositions reviewed here. Because prisons, jails, and youth custodial facilities are of central concern to many Canadians, the bulk of the rest of this chapter will focus on the problems with these correctional institutions.

THE PITFALLS OF INCARCERATION IN CORRECTIONAL FACILITIES

Correctional institutions, such as prisons, are contexts of involuntary confinement. Some people view them as necessary means of social control, while others, like myself, agree with Faith (1993a, p. 151), who views them as small totalitarian societies, with rules affecting almost every intimate aspect of an inmate's life. As briefly described in Chapter 3, prisoners experience several major "pains of imprisonment" (Johnson & Toch, 1982). A more detailed list is provided in Box 4.6. Further, some female inmates experience a considerable amount of abuse, such as being made to participate in experiments involving hallucinogenic drugs (see Box 4.7), as well as physical, verbal, and sexual abuse at the hands of correctional staff (Chesney-Lind, 1997; Pate, 1999). For example, in April 1994, following a four-day period in which some inmates at Kingston's Prison for Women (P4W) attacked guards, lighted fires, and hurled human waste, Corrections Canada ordered a male riot squad to intervene. This squad subjected some women to what Justice Louise Arbour referred to as a "cruel, inhumane and degrading" strip search, and some women were kept in segregation cells for days (Bronskill, 1996).

Box 4.6

The "Jumbled Accumulation of Agonies" Behind Bars

Below is a list of "conventional features" of life behind bars compiled by Faith (1993a, pp. 151-153):

- the stigma of incarceration;
- the claustrophobia of confinement;
- craving fresh air or the feeling of rain on the face;
- the deadly boredom;
- strict limitations on physical movement and the aggravation of needing an "inmate pass" to move from one part of the institution to another;
- anxiety about one's children (and frequently the devastation of losing them);
- loneliness for close family members, sweethearts and community support systems;
- nervousness from being under constant scrutiny and supervision;
- physical and emotional problems that accompany withdrawal from alcohol and street drugs;
- lack of anyone to serve advocacy for one's needs;
- lack of privacy and the tensions that erupt between people in "total institutions" who haven't chosen to be confined together;
- endless line-ups;
- inability to get straight answers to questions;
- paranoia about breaking what seem like arbitrary, tyrannical or, at best coercive institutional rules;
- fears of being punitively segregated in isolation for behavioral infractions, or likewise segregated in a prison-within-the prison for "medical observation" or "protective" or "administrative" custody;
- insensitivities and abuses of power both by staff and other prisoners;

Box 4.6, *continued*

- mail and phone censorship and the risk of losing these "privileges";
- lack of choice in such simple matters as when to eat, sleep or watch television;
- little or no choice of diet;
- weight-gain;
- chain-smoking as a coping mechanism;
- having to be locked in one's cell periodically throughout the day and facing the slot in the door for routine "body counts," to ensure no one has escaped;
- the inability to escape from the cacophony of radios, television, people hollering at each other, the rattling of keys and clanging of electronic doors;
- never getting a good night's sleep because of the sounds of the institution, including the snoring, coughing, weeping and wailing of other prisoners, and because for security reasons it's never fully dark;
- depressions and mood swings produced by prescribed behavior-modifying drugs;
- cognitive dissonance from not knowing how or whether to show feelings (if you laugh too much you must be stoned on contraband drugs; if you're too quiet you must be depressed and in need of medicine);
- dependency and infantilization processes that accrue when one is denied the right to make any decision concerning one's own life; and
- the uncertainty of when you will be released and the realization of very limited choices in the "free" world when the time comes.

Source: From *Unruly Women* by Karlene Faith, Press Gang Publishers, Vancouver, Canada, 1993. Reprinted with permission.

Box 4.7

LSD Tested on Female Prisoners: Scientists Experimented on Inmates at Kingston's Prison for Women in the 1960s

Twenty-three inmates at Kingston's Prison for Women were given LSD as part of a psychology experiment in the early 1960s, the *Citizen* has learned.

The study involving the powerful hallucinogenic drug was conducted with the full knowledge of the prison's superintendent and federal corrections officials. The subjects included a 17-year-old girl who was unable to give informed consent to the experiment and who still suffers from periodic acid flashbacks.

"This use of LSD with inmates in the Prison for Women was a risky undertaking," says a report into the LSD use completed in January by Correctional Services. "We conclude that the administration of LSD at the Prison for Women, particularly when it was administered at the prison rather than the Institute of Psychotherapy, could lead to substantial, debilitating long-term negative effects."

The report recommends that all the women involved receive a fully apology and a "settlement package" from the federal government.

> ## Box 4.7, *continued*
>
> But locating the women who were part of the study may prove difficult.
>
> The investigators who wrote the report discovered that many inmate files were either missing or had been destroyed.
>
> "The access to administrative and inmate files has been unsatisfactory," the report states.
>
> "The inability to obtain relevant administrative files and most inmate files made it impossible to provide a full account of the use of LSD or ECT (electroshock therapy) at the Prison for Women."
>
> Investigators interviewed two of the women and uncovered documents that referred to an additional 21 who were part of the pilot study by a psychologist and psychiatrist. Both women complained of long-term effects that continue to plague them decades after their first exposure to LSD.
>
> The report says the women suffer from a recognized psychiatric syndrome called Post-Hallucinogen Perceptual Disorder.
>
> "It's a very sad indictment of our commitment to human rights and social justice, and a number of principles I think Canadians hold dear," said Kim Pate, the Executive Director of the Canadian Association of Elizabeth Fry Societies." We're happy to parade around the globe maintaining this is one of the best countries to live in. The reality is: not when you go into the bowels of some of our institutions. You certainly don't see the short fingers of the rule of law creeping in there to protect prisoners."

Source: This box includes excerpts from an article by Mike Blanchfield for *The Ottawa Citizen*. (1998, pp. A1-A2). Reprinted by permission.

There are many other "atrocity tales" that could be told here about the plight of Canadian women in correctional institutions (Goffman, 1961), while describing the history of Canadian correctional facilities for women and girls. Because that information is described in great depth elsewhere (see Boritch, 1997; Faith, 1993a; Goff, 1999), it is beyond the objectives of this chapter to reproduce this information here. Of more importance here are the reasons why correctional facilities are inadequate means of dealing with female offenders of all ages.

An Expensive and Ineffective Means of Preventing Crime

Correctional facilities, such as prisons, are expensive. As Ruth Morris (1995, p. 5) points out:

> Any way you look at it, anywhere in the world, incarceration is the most costly alternative we have in responding to crime. The costs vary from country to country, and prisons are a lot cheaper in Latin America, but they still are several times as costly as any community placement. If you compute in the higher failure rate of prisons, they become one of the most amazing dollars-down-the-drain investments of countries today.

Consider the following costs of Canadian adult corrections:

- In 1996-97, $946 million was spent on operating the federal corrections system, while provincial/territorial costs amounted to $970 million.

- The average annual cost of incarcerating an offender in a federal correctional facility during 1995-96 was $50,375.

- During 1995-96, the average annual cost of incarceration in women's institutions was $74,965 (Solicitor General of Canada, 1997).

Could money be better spent on superior means of curbing crime? This question is especially important when one considers that most women and girls are not serving time for serious violent offences. Rather, the majority have committed minor crimes, and close to one-third of the adult female admissions to provincial institutions were for fine defaults (Boritch, 1997).

These and other data on the costs of corrections (see, for example, Goff, 1999) show that governments and many members of the general population are willing to spend millions of dollars "closing the barn doors after the horses have left." Might we be better off devoting more attention and resources to preventing crimes from being committed in the first place? How many social services could be created across Canada that help prevent women and girls from engaging in crime with the "$78.1 million it would cost us to build and maintain a cage for 400 our fellow Canadians for just one year" (Morris, 1995, p. 6)? The answer is "a lot." The next chapter provides examples of ways in which funds could be used to create effective prevention strategies.

Failure to Address the Broader Cultural, Social, and Economic Forces that Influence Women and Girls to Commit Crime

All of the women and girls who commit crimes are not economically or socially disenfranchised, but most are. Further, many have a host of other major problems, especially a history of abuse at the hands of family members, acquaintances, or others (Chesney-Lind, 1997). Thus, it is not surprising that custodial facilities do not deter many people from committing crime—a finding of almost every responsible North American study in the past 25 years (Currie, 1998; DeKeseredy & Schwartz, 1996). For example, in 1985, 50 percent of the 8,000 women sentenced to Canadian provincial/territorial institutions had served at least one prior jail term (Boritch, 1997; Chunn & Gavigan, 1991). Further, 25.2 percent of the women who, on March 31, 1997, were serving term of federal incarceration served at least one previous term of such imprisonment (Solicitor General of Canada, 1997).

It should also be noted that aboriginal women in federal custody are more likely to be readmitted than are non-aboriginal offenders, as uncovered by a study conducted by Belcourt et al. (1993). These researchers found that of the aboriginal women who served their first sentence in a federal institution and who were released between 1978 and 1988, 44 percent returned to federal custody, compared to only 19 percent of their non-aboriginal counterparts. This figure becomes more alarming when one considers that aboriginal offenders made up only 14 percent of the 968 women in Belcourt et al.'s (1993) sample. Aboriginal women were also more likely than non-aboriginal women to be readmitted more than once between 1978 and 1988, with 28.8 percent being multiple offenders.

Penal institutions are ineffective because they ignore two important factors. First, they ignore the family and community networks of which an offender is part. To the extent that any individual is influenced in the first place to take drugs or commit crimes by relatives, friends, and neighbors, he or she will be returning after incarceration to the same people. Will they be a different influence this time? Incarceration involves spending a lot of money and attention try to "correct" or "rehabilitate" a person, but does little to deal with family or neighborhood problems, such as joblessness, poverty, and family violence (DeKeseredy & Schwartz, 1996).

Second, incarceration disregards the broader structural aspects of society that help create an atmosphere in which crime can be committed. In the case of prostitution, this includes high youth unemployment, extreme levels of social inequality and poverty, and the lack of meaningful jobs for many people. However, it is not simply the lack of money or a job that influences people to commit crime. If this were the case, as Currie (1998) reminds us, then university students would be committing many violent crimes. Rather, it is that:

> the experience of life year in, year out at the bottom of a harsh, depriving, and excluding social system wears away at the psychological and communal conditions that sustain healthy human development. It stunts children's intellectual and emotional growth, undercuts parents' ability to raise children caringly and effectively, increases the risks of child abuse and neglect, and diminishes the capacity of adults to supervise the young. It creates neighborhoods that are both dangerous and bereft of legitimate opportunities and role models, makes forming and maintaining families more difficult, and makes illicit activities far more alluring for teenagers and adults. Life, in short, is harder, bleaker, less supportive, and more volatile at the bottom. And those conditions, in ways both direct and indirect, both obvious and subtle, breed . . . crime (Currie, 1998, p. 135).

What is the point of sending those who break the law to correctional facilities with the hope that they will never commit crimes again if these people have to return to deprived neighborhoods or violent families? As stated several times in this book, these contexts perpetuate and legitimate crime and will continue to do so until we seriously consider the policy proposals suggested in Chapter 5.

Important Considerations

Many more limitations of using correctional facilities to deal with women and girls in conflict with the law could be discussed here, such as the lack of effective educational and vocational programs in penal institutions (Faith, 1993a; Goff, 1999). However, the most important point to consider is that it is impossible, for reasons described here and elsewhere,[4] to incarcerate our way out of a female or male crime problem. Further, in attempting to do so, we are wasting our money, squandering resources, and destroying lives (Currie, 1998). If the federal and provincial governments, as well as the general population, want to take some effective steps toward lowering the rate of female crime, then they should target gender inequality and other broader social forces that influence girls and women to break the law (Boritch, 1997). This, however, is not likely to happen in the near future. Like their counterparts in the United States, Canadian politicians do not want to appear to be "soft on crime" for fear of not being re-elected and/or they "cannot see beyond the next sound bite" (Chesney-Lind, 1997, p. 173). Moreover, as in the United States, crime control in Canada is "big business" for some people and has created a growing and politically influential constituency of people whose jobs and status depend on the expansion of get-tough strategies (Currie, 1998).

There is some evidence that alternative solutions to crime, such as community-based programs, are being seriously considered by a growing number of North Americans. For example, a 1997 survey done by the California Wellness Foundation found that:

- the "vast majority" of Californians would rather spend money on youth violence prevention programs than on further incarceration;

- four out of five respondents reported that the "biggest priority" should be investing in strategies that prevent youths from joining gangs, becoming violent, or ending up behind bars; and

- three out of five respondents stated that they supported diverting money from the prison construction budget to community-based violence prevention projects (cited in Currie, 1998).

What do these findings tell us? At the very least, we can conclude that many people are receptive to change. Perhaps, like the Californians in the survey above, more Canadians will respond positively to the suggestions offered in the next chapter.

SUMMARY

The main objective of this chapter was to review Canadian research on the court processing of women and girls and the sentences given to females convicted of breaking the law. What can we conclude from the data presented in this chapter? First, most of the Canadian adult court caseload involves men (85%), and at the national level, the number of women processed through courts has slightly decreased over the last few years. Second, boys appear in youth courts much more than do girls, and girls who appear before courts have fewer charges against them than do boys.

Third, overall, there has been a slight decrease the number of girls' cases processed through youth courts between 1991-92 and 1994-95. Moreover, there was no major increase at the regional level. We can also conclude that the number of Canadian girls and women admitted to correctional facilities is increasing. Still, women are more likely to receive nonprison sentences than are men, and girls are less likely to be sent to custodial facilities than are boys.

This chapter yields several other important conclusions. For example, the *Young Offenders Act*, which eliminated status offences, did not decrease the number of girls given custodial dispositions. In fact, more girls have been given secure and open custody dispositions, while the number of girls who receive less serious sentences (e.g., fines) is decreasing.

Another, albeit highly controversial, conclusion is that incarceration is expensive, is an ineffective crime prevention technique, and ignores the broader cultural, social, and economic forces that influence girls and women to commit crime. Nevertheless, many Canadians strongly support "get tough" strategies; thus, we are not likely to see a significant decrease in the number of girls and women sentenced to penal institutions in the near future. This is not to say that a growing number of people are not receptive to change, and a California study summarized in this chapter suggests that a critical mass of North Americans may be willing to consider the alternative solutions proposed in Chapter 5.

NOTES

[1] As Renzetti (1998) correctly points out, however, women are not a homogenous group. In fact, many women, especially those of color who are lesbian survivors of intimate violence do not support harsh criminal justice policies because they view them as racist and homophobic. Moreover, they do not want to subject their partners to the abuse that the police and other criminal justice officials have historically inflicted on visible minorities and gays and lesbians.

[2] See Boritch (1997) for a review of these studies.

[3] Aid to Dependent Children.

[4] For example, see Currie (1998) for an in-depth, compelling critique of incarceration.

DISCUSSION QUESTIONS

1. Why do most Canadians support "get tough on crime" policies?

2. Why does the Prairie region have the highest rate of girls processed through youth courts?

3. What is a major problem with Québec data generated by the Adult Criminal Court Survey?

4. Under what conditions are judges likely to hand down lenient sentences to adult female offenders?

5. Why didn't the abolition of status offences result in fewer girls being sent to custodial facilities?

6. Why is incarceration an ineffective means of preventing crime?

PROBLEM-SOLVING SCENARIOS

1. Get together with a group of students and debate the strengths and limitations of incarceration.

2. Over the next month, clip articles from newspapers, which demonstrate that the federal and provincial governments occasionally construct myths about female crime and criminal law.

3. In a group, discuss and debate the value of having convicted youths who have committed relatively minor offences perform community service work.

4. In a group, discuss and debate the value of spending more government money on crime prevention strategies.

5. Generate a group discussion on the reasons why many women support get-tough crime control strategies.

6. Generate a group discussion on the strengths and limitations of mandatory fine surcharges described in Box 4.1.

SUGGESTED READINGS

Currie, E. (1998). *Crime and Punishment in America: Why the Solutions to America's Most Stubborn Social Crisis Have Not Worked— and What Will.* New York: Metropolitan Books.

> This book includes an in-depth critique of imprisonment and offers several effective alternatives to incarceration, including prevention.

Goff, C. (1999). *Corrections in Canada.* Cincinnati: Anderson.

> This is an excellent resource for students seeking an in-depth overview of the Canadian federal corrections system. Chapter 4 is especially useful for those interested in learning more about Canadian women and corrections.

Miller, S.L. (ed.). (1998). *Crime Control and Women: Feminist Implications of Criminal Justice Policy.* Thousand Oaks, CA: Sage.

> This collection of readings includes feminist critiques of "get tough" crime control approaches, such as boot camps and the war on drugs.

Solicitor General of Canada. (1997). *Basic Facts About Corrections in Canada.* Ottawa: Solicitor General of Canada.

> This short book provides basic statistical information on Canadian adult corrections from April 1, 1996, to March 31, 1997. Criminal justice students are likely to find this book to be a useful reference. It is available free of charge from the federal government.

Stevenson, K, Tufts, J., Hendrick, D., and Kowalski, M. (1998). *A Profile of Youth Justice in Canada.* Ottawa: Statistics Canada.

> This book provides a recent statistical overview of youth crime in Canada and the ways in which this problem it is dealt with by the justice system.

Victims of domestic violence live in crowded conditions at a women's refuge. Again and again we see family violence figuring in the histories of female offenders. Reducing family violence should be a priority in the control and prevention of crime by women and girls.

Chapter 5

Rethinking the Control and Prevention of Female Crime in Canada

INTRODUCTION

At the time of writing this chapter, Ontario was nearing the end of a provincial election campaign. Not surprisingly, in a bid to get re-elected on June 3, 1999, Premier Mike Harris publicly "pushed the crime button" by demanding tougher laws for young offenders (Eaton & Hutchison, 1999). As expected, many Ontarians were pleased with his "political grandstanding" (Chesney-Lind, 1998), which is an example of "the triumph of ideology over evidence in the short history of neoconservative thought" (Currie, 1985, p. 167). Because he won the election, it is fair to assume that Premier Harris's "get tough" discourse helped him get many votes. Box 5.1 provides a list of some other crime and social control measures proposed by Harris during his election campaign.

Will Harris and other North American politicians help reduce crimes like those addressed in this book by getting tough? Many people, such as feminist criminologist Susan Miller (1998, p. xxiii), do not think so; for them, "reducing crime is about getting smart, not about getting tough." This is a valid point. As Walker (1998, p. 5) points out, "One of the major obstacles in the search for sensible crime policies is the fact that there are many bad ideas," and a simplistic solution like simply increasing the costs of committing crime is a prime example

In a civilized society what matters is not just whether we reduce crime, but how (emphasis in original). *And how seriously and honestly we confront that question in the coming years will be a test of our character as a nation.*

(Currie, 1998, p. 193)

of a bad idea. For example, a large body of research has failed to generate conclusive evidence showing that incarcerating many people leads to major reductions in crime (DeKeseredy & Schwartz, 1996; Walker, 1998).

Box 5.1

Promises, Promises
Here's What the Harris Conservatives Said
They'd Do to Address Crime and Social Control

- Change the Mental Health Act to make it easier to force a mentally ill person to seek treatment; institute community treatment orders to allow doctors to force someone back into hospital if they stop taking medication.

- Impose a province-wide code of conduct, which will set minimum standards of behavior in schools and spell out the consequences of breaking the rules.

- Mandatory criminal background checks for all school staff.

- Give majority of parents at any school in Ontario the power to impose a dress code or require a uniform for students.

- Establish strict discipline schooling programs for students who have been expelled from regular classes.

- Those on welfare could be required to clean up parks or maintain highways.

- Test welfare recipients to see if they are illiterate or are abusing drugs or alcohol. If they fail, they would have to take remedial training, or join a rehabilitation program, or risk losing benefits.

- Require people on parole to take drug tests. They would be sent back to jail if they fail.

- Streamline the eviction of people who allow their rental units to be used for drug dealing.

- Revoke liquor licenses or business permits of establishments where drugs are used or sold.

- Give municipalities the power to shut down crack houses.

- Outlaw squeegee kids and panhandlers by making "threatening and harassing" behavior, such as blocking people on sidewalks, a provincial offence.

- Create a registry of sex offenders. Allow police to notify communities about sex offenders in their neighborhoods.

- Make parents financially responsible for property damage caused by their children.

- Double the number of domestic violence courts.

- Lobby the federal government for a tougher *Young Offenders Act*.

- Bill criminals for the cost of their custody.

- Create "elder shelters" for victims of assault.

Source: This box includes excerpts from an article by Maria Bohuslawsky for *The Ottawa Citizen* (1999, p. B2). Reprinted with permission.

There is, however, conclusive evidence that incarceration costs a great deal of money (see Chapter 4) that could be better spent on more effective means of curbing crimes committed by girls and women (as well as those committed by boys and men). Conservative Politicians, such as Mike Harris, probably know this, but they adopt neoclassical solutions to win elections (DeKeseredy & Schwartz, 1996).

As many criminology and deviance students point out when neo-classical policies are attacked, "It is always easy to criticize." They ask, "What would you do? Do you have any better ideas?" Following Harvard University sociologist William Julius Wilson (1996), one of the world's leading experts on poverty and joblessness, in this chapter I call for a "broader vision."[1] This entails suggesting policies that target the key social, cultural, and economic forces that propel women and girls into crime, such as family violence, poverty, and unemployment. Such an approach might seem too radical for some readers because it moves the discussion of crime prevention and control out of the realm of criminal justice and into that of social and economic policy (Walker, 1998). However, crime is an outrageous problem that requires outrageous solutions (Gibbons, 1995), especially those that address unemployment, families and children, and neighborhoods (Currie, 1985).

The policies that make up the broader vision advanced here are not likely to be well received by many Canadians who support "right-wing ideological agendas," such as the one promoted by Mike Harris. In addition to what is described in Box 5.1, his agenda includes: the elimination of public responsibility for social services, lowering wages and decreasing employees' rights, closing schools and hospitals, and increasing university and college tuition (Lightman, 1997). Supporters of such neo-conservative policies often respond to alternative solutions by stating that they cannot work because they require too much money, which should be used to lower the deficit (Wilson, 1996). If money has not been too tight to build five new Canadian regional correctional facilities for women,[2] then money can be found for these solutions too—if that is what people want. Government spending is always directly related to political priorities. What we need now is a "radical readjustment" in thinking about our priorities (Faith, 1993a; Wilson, 1996).

NEW DIRECTIONS IN CRIME CONTROL AND PREVENTION

In addition to being heavily guided by William Julius Wilson's (1996) concept of a broader vision, most of the policies suggested here are informed by *critical criminology*. This perspective views class, ethnic, and gender inequality to be the major sources of crime.[3] Obviously, these types of inequities are not going to be eliminated in the near future

(Messerschmidt, 1986). Consequently, some critical criminologists (including this author) contend that we need to implement *short-term, progressive policies* that "chip away" at the forces that motivate people to commit crime. Further, many critical criminologists do not call for the elimination of police, courts, or even correctional facilities. For example, few critical criminologists are willing to allow serial or mass murderers to walk freely on the streets.

Critical criminologists, however, do not believe that the criminal justice system should have the sole responsibility for dealing with crime. This is a problem that Currie (1985, p. 18) refers to as compartmentalizing "social problems along bureaucratic lines." Rarely, if ever, will you find the federal Minister of Finance, a person who manages economic problems that contribute to criminal activity, considering how his or her economic decisions could affect crime rates. Nor will you will find him or her discussing economic issues, such as factory closures, the North American Free Trade Agreement (NAFTA), or cuts in welfare or unemployment benefits with the federal Minister of Justice, the Solicitor General of Canada, or police chiefs or officers. Consequently, many policies are adopted without taking into account the ultimate effect on crime. Thus, police, prison officials, and other criminal justice personnel are called in to "clean up the mess" made by the rest of society (Currie, 1985).

Real life, as we know, does not play itself out along the above bureaucratic lines set up by government agencies. For example, what you eat or drink can affect how you behave (for example, if you consume vast quantities of beer). The fact that Health Canada is located in a separate building from the Justice Department does not affect that truth. In real life, nutrition, employment, child care, and many other events affect your life. It is mainly in textbooks that they are separated (DeKeseredy & Schwartz, 1996).

Thousands of alternative proposals informed by critical criminological thought could be provided here. However, only those that are directly relevant to four key determinants of female involvement in crime will be discussed. These factors are: (1) family violence, (2) woman abuse in dating, (3) poverty, and (4) unemployment. Critical criminologists will differ on how best to deal with these factors. Nevertheless, the first step is to recognize that these determinants have much more to do with reducing female involvement in crime than does increasing the rate of incarceration (Irwin & Austin, 1997). It is to progressive steps aimed at reducing family violence that we turn first.

Reducing Family Violence[4]

As Currie (1998, p. 82) reminds us, "The first priority is to invest serious resources in the prevention of child abuse and neglect." Data presented in this book show that many Canadian female offenders, like their American counterparts, have a history of child physical and sexual abuse, as well as child neglect. Further, the background of many women in Canadian federal correctional facilities "underscores the important links between women's childhood victimization and their later criminal careers" (Chesney-Lind, 1997, p. 27). Consider data gleaned from Widom's (1989) United States study, which show that abused or neglected girls were twice as likely as than other girls in the study to have an adult criminal record. Thus, it appears that if we can prevent child abuse and neglect, we can reduce adult crime (Currie, 1998). Preventing male-to-female violence in marital/cohabiting relationships can also make a difference because many adult female offenders have been beaten and sexually assaulted by their male intimate partners.

How can we curb family violence and child neglect? Space limitations preclude a detailed discussion on the ways in which the above and other types of family violence (e.g., sibling violence)[5] can be prevented. In fact, one could write (and several people have written) entire books on control and prevention issues surrounding family violence (e.g., Finkelhor et al., 1988; Thorne-Finch, 1992). The following suggestions, informed by Gelles and Cornell (1985, p. 144) and others (e.g., Barnett et al., 1997), are important steps to take:

- Eliminate the norms that encourage and legitimate violence in our society and families. For example, spanking, as a means of raising children, should be against the law as it is in Sweden. Media violence, which glorifies and legitimates violence, should also be eliminated.

- Create and implement effective ways of reducing violence-provoking stress created by society, such as poverty, gender inequality, and unemployment. Some strategies to achieve this goal are briefly discussed further on in this chapter.

- Integrate families into a network of kin and community. The reduction of isolation can help alleviate stress and other problems that lead to family violence, including child sexual abuse (Barnett et al., 1997; Russell, 1984). *Home visitation* is one effective way of reducing isolation and providing parents with assistance. The Prenatal–Early Infancy Program (PEIP), created in the late 1970s in Elmira, New York, is an excellent example of home visitation; it is described by Currie in Box 5.2 (1998, pp. 84-85).

- Eliminate the patriarchal nature of society. The adherence to the ideology of familial and societal patriarchy is one of the most powerful determinants of male-to-female partner abuse and other types of family violence, such as child abuse.

- End the cycle of violence in the family. Physical punishment of children is perhaps the most effective way of teaching violence. Eliminating it would be an important step in crime prevention.

Box 5.2

The Elmira Prenatal–Early Infancy Progam (PEIP)

The Elmira Program served vulnerable women—mostly white, poor, young, and unmarried—in a semirural community with some of the highest levels of child abuse and neglect in the state. The project had several related goals: to ensure more healthy pregnancies and births, improve the quality of parental care, and enhance the women's own development—in school, at work, and in family life. Registered nurses visited each woman during her pregnancy and for two years after the birth of her child. The visits took place weekly for the first six weeks after birth, decreasing to every six weeks by the last four months of the program. Five nurses, each working with twenty to twenty-five families, spent an average of about an hour and fifteen minutes with the mothers, providing parenting education, linking the families with other social services as needed, and generally building a long-term supportive relationship with women who had usually been allowed to fall through the cracks of the social-service system.

Unlike many programs aimed a low-income parents, this one was carefully evaluated from the start. Mothers who received home visits before giving birth were compared with a control group who did not. The control group did, however, have access to an infant development specialist who screened the children for specific problems and, if necessary, referred them to other specialized services. Some of the control group mothers were also given free transportation to regular prenatal and well-child care at local doctors' offices. The study group, therefore, was not being compared with families who got no help at all but with families who were offered considerably more help during and after pregnancy than most low-income families routinely get.

Yet the differences in outcomes between the groups, during the time they spent in the program were dramatic. Mothers in the treatment group were much less likely to have another pregnancy and much more likely to enter the labor force. Their children were growing up in less hazardous and more stimulating homes, were less often punished, and were much less likely to need emergency-room treatment than the control group's children. Most encouragingly, there was an impressive reduction in official reports to child-protective agencies of abuse or neglect of children in the experimental group. Among the mothers deemed at highest risk—those who were poor, unmarried, and teenaged—19 percent of the control group, versus just 4 percent of the mothers in the program had confirmed cases of abuse or neglect.

Source: Currie, E. (1998). *Crime and Punishment in America: Why the Solutions to America's Most Stubborn Social Crisis Have Not Worked—And What Will*, pp. 84-85. © 1998 by Elliott Currie. Reprinted with permission of Henry Holt and Company, LLC.

Preventing Woman Abuse in Dating

Data described in Chapters 1 and 2 show that intimate violence is not restricted to families or marriage/cohabitation. Many adolescents and girls in their early twenties are also physically, sexually, and psychologically assaulted by their boyfriends and dating partners, which contributes to a large number of them getting in trouble with the law (Chesney-Lind & Shelden, 1998). Thus, programs specifically tailored to deal with male-to-female victimization in courtship are required, such as New Directions for Young Women, which is based in Seattle, Washington (NiCarthy, 1983). This program focuses on the relationship between *addictive love* and woman abuse in teenage dating relationships. Addictive love is when one or two youths in a relationship "believe that they can't survive without each other, and the desire to be together every minute develops into the need or demand that the partner be continually available (NiCarthy, 1983, p. 120).

Girls in addictive relationships are at great risk of being abused, and to prevent this problem, New Directions strives to get girls in the program to:

- Become aware of the pervasiveness of violence and abuse in intimate relationships.

- Recognize signs of addictive love in intimate relationships.

- Recognize emotional, sexual, and physical abuse. Understand the relationship of addictive love and abuse.

- Understand the roles of power and sex roles in abuse.

- Know their rights, including the right not to be abused.

- Learn about alternatives to abuse (negotiation, assertiveness, and separation).

- Learn about resources for battered women (cited in Chesney-Lind & Sheldon, 1998, p. 231).

To supplement programs such as New Directions, booklets such as *Today's Talk About Sexual Assault* should be distributed to teenage girls at schools, community centers, and elsewhere. Developed in British Columbia by the Victoria Women's Sexual Assault Centre (VWSAC) (1994), the *Today's Talk* booklet attempts to get girls to recognize *healthy relationships* versus *unhealthy relationships*, and it includes a wealth of practical information on other issues, such sexual assault and AIDS. According to the VWSAC (1994, p. 22), healthy relationships are when you:

- Listen to each other.

- Feel good about yourself.

- Have fun together.
- Trust each other.
- Care about each other.
- Can talk about your feelings.
- Try to work things out.
- Feel equal to each other.
- Want to have sex.
- You feel safe having sex.
- You agree on birth control and on safer-sex protection.

Unhealthy relationships, according to the VWSAC (1994, p. 22), are when:

- One person has more power than the other.
- There is jealousy and possessiveness.
- You don't listen to each other.
- You feel bad about yourself.
- One or both partners try to control the other.
- You feel criticized or picked on.
- You don't trust each other.
- There is pressure to stay in the relationship.
- You are forced to have sex.
- There is a lot of anger, fighting, or violence.
- You can't talk about your feelings.

As described in Box 5.3 (1994, p. 23), the VWSAC booklet also includes advice on how to avoid abusive boys. However, some ask if it is males who are the primary perpetrators of dating violence, shouldn't there be programs, booklets, videos, and the like designed to prevent them from raping, beating, and psychologically abusing their girlfriends and dating partners? Further, because it is men who are the abusers, shouldn't it be men—as opposed to women—who change their attitudes, beliefs, and behaviors? These are important points that are strongly adhered to by *pro-feminist* men. Their philosophy is best described below by Thorne-Finch (1992, pp. 234-235):

> Raising awareness about male violence and working toward its eradication are major goals for pro-feminist men. Contrary to the conservative or the New Age men's perspective, pro-femi-

nist men argue that male dominance of women is not a function of suppressed male essence, genes, natural selection, or inadequate socialization. From a pro-feminist perspective, male violence against women is caused by a society in which male violence against women is generally encouraged and legitimized and its effects minimized. Pro-feminist men, adopting a social constructionist[6] approach, criticize social forces and institutions like pornography, the military, the media, and the family, for creating violent men. Their perspective is pro-feminist, gay affirmative, and male supportive. They also emphasize that the existing masculinities and femininities are socially created and thus have the potential for change.

Box 5.3

Guys to Avoid

There are many good, understanding, and respectful men who care about women and treat them well. Unfortunately, there are also men who don't care about women and think it's no big deal to hurt them. As a young woman, guys you probably want to avoid are those who:

- Ignore you, interrupt you, tease you or make fun of things that are important to you. These guys have no respect for you.

- Are possessive or jealous or try to control who you see or who you talk to.

- Stand or sit too close to you or make you feel uncomfortable by the way they look at you.

- Drink a lot or abuse drugs.

- Have a bad attitude towards women or express anger or violence towards women. For example, guys who say things like: "Women should be quiet," "Women are bitches," "Women should stay at home."

- Have a reputation for 'making it.' To keep up their reputation, they might force you into sex.

- Are nice to you when you two are alone, but start acting like jerks when friends are around. Or the opposite: guys who are nice when you are together with friends, but treat you badly when no one's around.

Source: *Today's Talk About Sexual Assault: A Booklet for Teens* (1994, p. 23). Reprinted with permission of the Victoria Women's Sexual Assault Centre.

There are a variety of individual and collective pro-feminist strategies that should be considered.[7] The following strategies suggested by the VWSAC (1994, pp. 30-31) are specifically tailored for boys. They focus on male-female interactions and are also appropriate for older males:

- Accept the fact that no means no. If a girl tells you that she doesn't want to have sex, STOP.

- Don't try to read your girlfriend or dating partner's mind. Rather, ask her what she wants. She may just want to be close and cuddle; this is not the same as wanting to have sexual intercourse.

- Check out what you both want from the relationship. Ask her questions about what her needs and desires are and encourage her to ask you. Communicating with each other may prevent a lot of problems and will help you decide if you both want the same thing from the relationship.

- If you are getting mixed message from a woman, speak up! Tell her you are confused and ask her to tell you clearly what it is she wants.

- Don't assume that your girlfriend will be like women in magazines and on television—she won't! Those women are characters who are playing certain roles for money. Your girlfriend is a real person with real feelings.

Below are some useful pro-feminist means of interacting with other boys, also suggested by the VWSAC (1994, pp. 30-31). If slightly modified, they are also relevant to older males:

- Listen to other guys and how they talk about women. Ask yourself how you feel about what they say. Are these guys respectful or not? Decide for yourself if you want to be part of the conversation. Being male doesn't mean you have to talk tough.

- Decide what kind of friends you want. It's important to be accepted and everyone wants to have friends, but choose your friends carefully. Do they think the same way as you do? Are they friends who pressure you to talk and behave in a certain way.

- Set an example by using words that describe women in a respectful manner. Use a girl's name, not words that refer to her in a sexual way. For example, say "Mary" instead of "that babe," etc.

- Remember that it is all right to *not* talk about your sex life (emphasis in original). You can tell your friends that what you do is your business.

- Speak out against abuse when you see it. Help to educate other guys about sexual, physical, and psychological abuse. If your friends are behaving in an abusive way, let them know.

Older males also need to become part of the struggle to reduce woman abuse in dating and other intimate relationships (e.g., marriage/cohabitation). They could use slightly modified versions of the above pro-feminist strategies, as well as the following individual and collective steps informed by Funk (1993, pp. 105-128):

- Ensuring that survivor or victim service organizations have funds to stay open.

- Actively and caringly support survivors of woman abuse.

- Participating equally in household chores.

- Respecting women's space.

- Not viewing pornography.

- Not interrupting women.

- Talking with other men about woman abuse.

- Confronting expressions of sexism.

- Exposing the connections between sexism, racism, hetero-sexism, and other expressions of oppression in the ways they all support a culture of woman abuse.

- Actively listening to women and reading literature on their issues, problems, concerns, etc.

- Building, sustaining, and maintaining men against woman abuse groups.

- Developing a commitment to nonviolence.

- Doing anti-woman abuse education.

Getting men to help prevent woman abuse is not an easy task because many of them do not want to give up their patriarchal power and privilege (DeKeseredy & Schwartz, 1998). A critical mass of men are attracted to anti-feminist backlash[8] arguments about political correctness (Hornosty, 1996). Some men are opposed to sexism and woman abuse but do not do anything to prevent or stop it because they do not know what to do, they do not know other men who are trying to curb male-to-female victimization, or for a host of other reasons described by DeKeseredy and Schwartz (1998) and Funk (1993). Nevertheless, research shows that pro-feminist men's efforts can help make a difference (Klein et al., 1997).

Reducing Poverty and Unemployment[9]

As stated previously in this chapter, poverty and unemployment are powerful determinants of various types of violence against women in intimate or family relationships (DeKeseredy et al., in press a; Hotaling

& Sugarman, 1986; Klein et al., 1997; Tolman & Bennett, 1990). Consider the plight of many socially and economically disenfranchised women who live in Canadian public housing estates and their immediate surroundings. These are key arenas where gendered power relations are played out (Connell, 1987; DeKeseredy et al., in press b; Messerschmidt, 1993). Others assert that the influx of "hard drugs" (e.g., crack) into these contexts has exacerbated the degradation and abuse of women (Bourgois & Dunlap, 1993; Maher, 1995; Miller, 1997). Further, joblessness, unbalanced gender ratios, poverty, and men's attempts to resist women's struggles for gender equity have all enhanced cultural support for the abuse of women in these urban pockets of concentrated disadvantage (Bourgois, 1995; Miller, 1997; Oliver, 1994; Rainwater, 1990; Wilson, 1996).

Canadian support for the above assertions is provided by DeKeseredy et al.'s (in press a) Quality of Neighborhood Life Survey (QNLS). This survey was administered in the summer of 1998 in six public housing estates in the west end of an urban center in Eastern Ontario. The majority of the women in the QNLS sample live in what Kasarda (1992) calls *severely distressed households*, which simultaneously exhibit five characteristics: low income, less than high school education, poor work history, single parenthood, and dependency on government assistance. For example, the total number of women in the sample is 216, and Table 5.1 shows that:

- nearly one-half of the women reported that their major source of income was welfare payments;

- 27 percent stated that they were on disability payments;

- only 31 percent had completed high school, while 58 percent dropped out of high school or attended a vocational school; and

- about one-half of these women reported being single, divorced, widowed, or separated, with at least one child at home under the age of 17.

DeKeseredy et al. (in press a) found that 19.3 percent of the women in their sample stated they were, in the past year, victimized by one or more of the types of intimate partner violence described in Table 5.2. Further, 3 percent were physically assaulted by a stranger, and 1.5 percent were sexually assaulted by a stranger during the same time period. Moreover, 26 percent of the women reported experiencing one or more of the types of public harassment reported in Table 5.3 in the year before the survey.

Table 5.1
Selected Sociodemographic Characteristics Of QNLS Female Respondents

Average Age		42	
Median Personal Income		$8,000 (n=39)	
Median Household Income		12,600 (n=39)	
Major Source of Income		**Percent**	**N**
	From job	18	30
	From employment insurance	2	3
	From welfare	47	80
	Disability payments	27	45
	From family or friends	7	11
Marital Status		**Percent**	**N**
	Single	21.6	45
	Dating someone	9.6	20
	Living with someone	6.7	14
	Married	22.1	46
	Divorced	17.8	37
	Separated	12.5	26
	Widowed	9.6	20
Ethnic Identification		**Percent**	**N**
	Central American	.5	1
	French Canadian	16.4	34
	English Canadian	49.8	103
	Aboriginal	2.4	5
	British	1.4	3
	Eastern European	.5	1
	Southern Europe	1.0	2
	Far Eastern	2.4	5
	African	11.1	23
	Caribbean	6.8	14
	Middle Eastern	6.3	13
	Latin American	1.4	3

Source: DeKeseredy, W.S., Alvi, S., Schwartz, M.D., & Perry, B. (in press a). "Violence Against and the Harrassment of Women in Canadian Public Housing: An Exploratory Study." *Canadian Review of Sociology and Anthropology*. Reprinted with permission.

If poverty and unemployment are strongly associated with female victimization, the same can be said about female crime. If we can eliminate or minimize poverty, we will ultimately overcome or minimize many of the problems described throughout this text. How can we achieve this goal? Below are some examples of policies that can help. You are invited to discuss and debate the effectiveness of the following strategies advanced by some progressive sociologists, policy analysts, and community activists.[10]

- Job creation and training programs, including publicly supported community-oriented job creation.

- Higher minimum wage level.

- Day care.

- Housing assistance.

- Introducing entrepreneurial skills into the high school curriculum.

- Creating linkages between schools, private business, and government agencies.

Those people caught up in "deficit mania" (McQuaig, 1987) would probably ask "What would all this cost" (Devine and Wright, 1993)? This is a fair question. These and other strategies aimed at alleviating poverty and unemployment would probably cost billions of dollars. However, the cost of these and related social problems, such as crime, is much higher (Currie, 1985, 1993). For example, Devine and Wright estimate that the direct and indirect cost of poverty in the United States is half a trillion dollars a year! In light of this, spending billions of dollars to solve poverty, unemployment, intimate violence, female crime, and other social problems is a solid investment. As pointed out in the literature on poverty (e.g., Alvi et al., 2000; W. Wilson, 1996), "the urban underclass is a time bomb ticking. It would be prudent . . . to defuse the bomb while there is still something to save" (Devine and Wright, 1993:217).

Table 5.2
Intimate Physical Violence Against Women Incidence Rates

Physical Violence	Yes		No	
	N	%	N	%
Grab you	26	14.5	153	85.5
Push or shove you	25	14.0	154	86.0
Throw something at you that could hurt	6	3.4	172	96.6
Slap you	11	6.2	166	93.8
Twist your arm or pull your hair	10	5.6	169	94.4
Kick you	7	3.9	171	96.1
Punch or hit you with something that could hurt	5	2.8	173	97.2
Slam you against a wall	8	4.5	169	95.5
Choke you	4	2.2	174	97.8
Burn or scald you on purpose	0	0.0	178	100.0
Beat you up	6	3.4	171	96.6
Use a knife or gun on you	1	0.6	176	99.4

Source: DeKeseredy, W.S., Alvi, S., Schwartz, M.D., & Perry, B. (in press a). "Violence Against and the Harrassment of Women in Canadian Public Housing: An Exploratory Study." *Canadian Review of Sociology and Anthropology*. Reprinted with permission.

Table 5.3
Verbal Harassment of Women in Public Places Incidence Rates

	Yes		No	
	N	%	N	%
Ever insult you because they thought you were gay or lesbian	4	2.0	196	98.0
Ever insult you because they did not like your skin color or religion	19	9.5	182	90.5
Ever make sexual remarks about you or to you that made you feel uncomfortable	42	21.0	158	79.0

Source: DeKeseredy, W.S., Alvi, S., Schwartz, M.D., & Perry, B. (in press a). "Violence Against and the Harassment of Women in Canadian Public Housing: An Exploratory Study." *Canadian Review of Sociology and Anthropology*. Reprinted with permission.

Community-Building as Crime Control[11]

Crime, regardless of whether it is committed by boys, girls, women, or men, cannot be solely attributed to an individual's family history. Nor can it be solely attributed to one's position in the socioeconomic ladder. Although these are two major determinants of crime, the crimes examined in this text are also functions of neighborhood or community social and organizational characteristics (Sampson et al., 1998). For example, urban neighborhoods that are characterized by *collective efficacy* have lower crime rates than those that are not (Sampson et al., 1997). Collective efficacy refers to "mutual trust among neighbors combined with a willingness to intervene on behalf of the common good, specifically to supervise children and maintain public order" (Sampson et al., 1998, p. 1). A growing body of research on the relationship between collective efficacy and crime shows that the community—not the police or other formal agents of social control—curbs crime. More specifically, it is people who live in places where neighbors can depend on each other for social support and informal means of social control (DeLeon-Granados, in press).

What does a community characterized by collective efficacy look like? The following is a "textbook" example described by DeLeon-Granados (in press; p. 186):

> [C]ity leaders dedicated to building community; police officers trained to exploit community power; citizens ready, willing, and able to walk their streets, to help one another during crises; a shared culture that values community and altruistic behavior; spatial environments designed to make people feel part of a community; and neighborhoods and cities planned in such a fashion that they induce people to get to know one another, to rub shoulders, and form community in all the glorious ways imaginable.

Although Sampson et al.'s (1997, 1998) research shows that collective efficacy can make a difference, some communities are so shattered by joblessness, poverty, and other social problems that it is highly unlikely that people living in these areas will work closely together to curb crime (W. Wilson, 1996). For example, Sampson et al. (1998) found that collective efficacy was low in Chicago communities where concentrated poverty was high. Thus, while it is necessary to develop community-based, informal crime prevention strategies, such approaches should not be viewed as a substitute for economic strategies and public spending (Currie, 1985; Sampson et al., 1998). To nourish a community, and to develop one that is rich in collective efficacy, jobs and effective social programs are therefore required (Currie, 1985; W. Wilson, 1986). As Currie (1985, p. 263) reminds us, "In the long run, a commitment to full and decent employment remains the keystone of any successful anticrime policy."

Eliminating Gender Inequality

Female crime, female victimization, female poverty, and sexist criminal justice practices, such as the reclassification of girl status offenders (see Chapter 4), are all symptoms of a much larger problem: gender inequality (Boritch, 1997). In addition to implementing the strategies described thus far in this chapter, it is also necessary to eliminate sexism in all aspects of women's lives. Thus, there should be gender equality in the workplace, family, schools, athletics, and so on. Many Canadians (including a large number of women), however, sharply disagree with this assertion and contend that Canadian women have achieved equality and that the call for equity is simply "radical feminist rhetoric" that is divorced from reality.

Similar responses have been made to calls for gender equity in the United States, as described below by Faludi (1991, p. ix):

> To be a woman in America at the close of the 20th century—
> what good fortune. That's what we keep hearing, anyway. The
> barricades have fallen, politicians assure us. Women have
> "made it," Madison Avenue cheers. Women's fight for equality
> has "largely been won," *Time Magazine* announces. Enroll at
> any university, join any law firm, apply for credit at any bank.
> Women have so many opportunities now, corporate leaders say,
> that we don't really need equal opportunity policies. Women are
> so equal now, lawmakers say, that we no longer need an Equal
> Rights Amendment. Women have "so much," former President
> Ronald Reagan says, that the White House no longer needs to
> appoint them to higher office. Even American Express ads are
> saluting a woman's freedom to charge it. At last, women have
> received their full citizenship papers.

And yet . . .

If, as some people contend, the "battle has been won," then why are an alarming number of Canadian girls and women sexually and physically abused by men and boys? Why are married and cohabiting women still mainly responsible for household chores (Armstrong & Armstrong, 1994)? Further, if women "have made it," why do so many of them experience the problems described by *National Post* journalist Anne Giardini (1999, pp. B1, B3) in Box 5.4. If you still think there is no gender inequality in Canada, consider the following statistics from the Canadian Labor Congress (1997):

- Only 20 percent of Canadian women have full-time, full-year jobs, which pay more than $30,000 per year, compared to 40 percent of men.

- Canada has the second highest incidence of low-paid employment for women, (34.3%) among all industrialized (OECD) countries. Only Japan (37.2%) was worse.

- While women account for less than 20 percent of those in the top 10 paying job categories, they represent more than 70 percent in the lowest paying jobs.

- The unemployment rate for young women (under the age of 24) is 15.6 percent; for "visible minority" women: 13.4 percent; for aboriginal women: 17.7 percent; and for women with disabilities: 16.6 percent. The Disabled Women's Network of Canada shows that 65 percent of women with disabilities who were unemployed wanted to work.

- In less than 20 years, the number of women part-time workers has increased by 200 percent. Throughout that period, women made up 70 percent of the part-time workforce. More than one-third of part-time workers wanted to work full-time, but could only find part-time work.

- One in 10 jobs are now temporary. Over a period of 15 years, the number of women working more than one job increased by 372 percent.

In sum, the data presented in this book and in other sources (e.g., Alvi et al., 2000; Armstrong & Armstrong, 1994; Renzetti & Curran, 1995) show that Canada and the United States are still characterized by gender inequality. Moreover, crimes committed by women and girls are "glaring examples of gender inequality in Canadian society" (Boritch, 1997, p. 14). Nevertheless, there are reasons to be optimistic; although Canada is a patriarchal country, every major social institution, such as the family, the workplace, the military, and so on, has been affected by laws and other means of eliminating sexism. Further, public opinion polls reveal that most North Americans support gender equality in most parts of social life (Renzetti & Curran, 1995).

Box 5.4

Feminism is Not a Dirty Word
Women's Rights May Not Be in Vogue,
But the Fight for Them Isn't Over Yet

No one admits to being a feminist any more. The problem may be partly due to the word itself.

"Feminist" careens along your tongue and comes to a plosive stuttering stop in the same way as "racist" and "sexist." Just as the word racist brings to your mind's eye the picture of a lardy old boy, white and freckled, with the proverbial red neck and a ponderous beer belly, the word feminist summons up a strident, hirsute woman with a wagonload of axes to grind. Some women I know dodge the word and its associations by avoiding the issue of feminism entirely.

Then there the people—including many women—who take the view that the battle has been won, sister, so let's stop rocking the boat. You don't have to look far for evidence that such complacency is ill-considered and the world is still a man's world. Examples range from the ridiculous to the depressing.

A short four years ago, my father, the Dean of Engineering at a Canadian university, announced that in order to remedy the gender imbalance in his faculty (77 men and two women) he would strive to ensure that women would fill the next few positions that came open. The uproar! You would think that he had proposed that half of the faculty be subjected to sex-change operations to be conducted by undergraduate biology students using rusty protractors for scalpels. One local paper ran the story on its front page under a headline guaranteed to cause more lamentation and gnashing of teeth: "No Men Allowed."

Academia is fertile ground for this kind of backlash. This paper ran a report a few weeks ago about the sad plight of one Martin Loney, a social policy consultant who had managed to crank out "10 scholarly books," but who, despite this prodigious output, lost out on an academic position at Carleton University to a "woman with no books to her name." By my count, based on a visit to the Carleton University Web site, both the departments of political science and sociology have faculties overwhelmingly dominated by men. Clearly men are being hired and even promoted—the chairs of both departments are male. Could it be, could it just possibly be, that the woman who was hired in Loney's stead was better qualified than he was?

Then there was the groundswell of support (most memorably from the ninnies who make up the Alberta klatch of "Real Women") for Steve Ewanchuk, the pressing and would-be Lothario whom the Supreme Court of Canada recently found guilty of sexual assault for having forced his attentions on a young female job applicant. Ewanchuk coyly declined to testify at his trial, presumably on the basis that his testimony would tend to incriminate rather than exonerate him. After the Supreme Court decision, Ewanchuk launched a petition for a new hearing. His argument? If I had known, he complained, that I was going to be found guilty, I would have told you my side of the story.

Box 5.4, *continued*

Well, at least his argument—that when he said no, he didn't want to testify, what he really meant was yes—is consistent. This is, after all, a man for whom the question: "Which part of 'no' did you not understand?" is a brainteaser of Mensa proportions.

The list goes on. Women make up only about 8% of the membership boards of Canadian companies and hold only one in five seats in Parliament. Even in the books that I read to my children females are under-represented—one friend has told me that when he reads to his young daughters he makes a point of changing some of the male pronouns to female.

Convinced that we need to keep the objectives of feminism around for a while longer, and looking for some new terminology, I checked in my computer's thesaurus for substitutes for the word feminist. Here is the list it came up with: Like a woman. Womanly. Feminine. Female. Ladylike. Effeminate. Womanish. Nurturing. Gentle.

I guess I will have to keep looking for a word to describe a woman like me, who wants to raise her daughter in a world that is as much hers as her brothers.

Source: Giardini, A. (1999). "Feminism is Not a Dirty Word." *National Post*, June 8, B1, B3.

SUMMARY

The alternative strategies suggested here are by no means exhaustive. Many more progressive initiatives could have been included here. You are encouraged to examine the policies called for by the authors listed in the suggested readings section of this chapter. Rather than provide a long list of effective solutions to the problems examined in this text, as with Messerschmidt (1986), the main objective of this book was to show that there are effective alternatives to the "get tough" approach.

Some readers may contend that these policies are utopian. Like the progressive strategies suggested by Currie (1993) to curb the inner-city drug crisis in the United States, they are from being utopian. In fact, some of them are actually in place in other countries, such as Sweden. It is time for a "broader vision" (Wilson, 1996). We have, after all, tried almost everything else and have had little, if any, success. As Currie (1993, p. 332) reminds us, "We have tried moral exhortation. We have tried neglect. We have tried punishment. We have even, more grudgingly, tried treatment. We have tried everything but improving lives."

NOTES

[1] "A Broader Vision" is the title of Chapter 8 in W. Wilson's (1996) widely read and cited book *When Work Disappears: The World of the New Urban Poor.*

[2] These prisons are to replace Kingston's Prison for Women and are located in: Truro, Nova Scotia; Kitchener, Ontario; Joliette, Québec; Edmonton, Alberta; and Maple Creek-Nekaneet, Saskatchewan.

[3] There are various types of critical criminology, such as feminism, postmodernism, anarchism, abolitionism, left realism, and peacemaking. For more information on these perspectives, see DeKeseredy and Schwartz (1996) and MacLean and Milovanovic (1991, 1997b).

[4] This section includes some material from DeKeseredy (1996).

[5] See DeKeseredy and Ellis (1997) for more social scientific information on sibling violence in Canada.

[6] Social constructionist theorists are sociologists who: emphasize subjective judgments in the definition of a condition or behavior as a social problem; define social problems as a process of making claims about putative (supposed) social conditions; and attempt to explain claims-making and not the social conditions referred to by claims-makers (Alvi et al., 2000).

[7] See DeKeseredy and Schwartz (1998), Funk (1993), Schwartz and DeKeseredy (1997), and Thorne-Finch (1992) for more in-depth information on pro-feminist men's efforts to curb woman abuse.

[8] See Faludi (1991) for an excellent analysis of the anti-feminist backlash. Also, see DeKeseredy (2000) for an in-depth analysis of the anti-feminist backlash against Canadian woman abuse surveys.

[9] This section includes modified sections of articles published previously by DeKeseredy et al. (in press a; in press b).

[10] For more information on these strategies, see Alvi et al. (2000), Currie (1985, 1993), DeKeseredy and Schwartz (1996), and W. Wilson (1996).

[11] This subheading is derived from the subtitle of DeLeon-Granados' (in press) book *Travels Through Crime and Place: On the Trail of Community-Building as Crime Control.*

DISCUSSION QUESTIONS

1. How would reducing the rate of family violence contribute to a reduction in female crime?

2. How does job creation help foster neighborhood collective efficacy?

3. Why do many people believe that Canada is not characterized by gender inequality?

4. What are the limitations of compartmentalizing social problems along bureaucratic lines?

5. What advances have been made recently in Canada to eliminate gender inequality?

6. What are the characteristics of severely distressed households?

PROBLEM-SOLVING SCENARIOS

1. In a group, develop a set of strategies designed to enhance collective efficacy in your neighborhood. Identify the strengths and limitations of your proposals.

2. Get together with a few students and discuss ways in which you can help curb family violence in your neighborhood.

3. In a group, discuss ways of eliminating gender inequality in the workplace and in universities.

4. Design a job creation plan for unemployed youths and discuss and/or debate your plan with other students.

5. In a group, develop strategies aimed at minimizing or overcoming resistance to the policy proposals suggested in this chapter.

6. In a group, discuss the strengths and limitations of the crime and social control policies promised by Ontario Premier Mike Harris.

SUGGESTED READINGS

Barnett, O.W., Miller-Perrin, C.L., & Perrin, R.D. (1997). *Family Violence Across the Lifespan*. Thousand Oaks, CA: Sage.

> This book is especially useful for those seeking an in-depth interdisciplinary understanding of various types of family violence and effective means of preventing and controlling them.

Currie, E. (1993). *Reckoning: Drugs, the Cities, and the American Future*. New York: Hill and Wang.

> Although this book focuses mainly on the inner-city drug crisis in the United States, some of the alternative policies advanced by Currie are relevant to most of the crime problems examined in this text, especially those discussed in Chapter 6.

Renzetti, C.M., & Curran, D.J. (1995). *Women, Men, and Society*, 3rd ed. Boston: Allyn & Bacon.

> This book provides students with an overview of recent empirical and theoretical work on gender and gender-related issues. Gender inequality and progressive means of eliminating this problem in major social institutions are also examined in great detail.

Walker, S. (1998). *Sense and Nonsense about Crime and Drugs: A Policy Guide*, 4th ed. Belmont, CA: West/Wadsworth.

> This book provides a highly intelligible critique of liberal and conservative crime control policies.

Wilson, W.J. (1996). *When Work Disappears: The World of the New Urban Poor*. New York: Knopf.

> This book is essential reading for anyone seeking a rich sociological understanding of inner-city poverty. Some of the policy proposals discussed in this chapter are informed by those suggested in Chapter 6.

References

Addiction Research Foundation (1995). *Ontario Student Drug Use Survey*. Toronto: Addiction Research Foundation.

Adelberg, E., & Currie, C. (eds.). (1993). *In Conflict with the Law: Women and the Canadian Justice System*. Vancouver: Press Gang.

Adelberg, E., & Native Women's Association of Canada (1993). "Aboriginal Women and Prison Reform." In E. Adelberg & C. Currie (eds.) *In Conflict with the Law: Women and the Canadian Justice System* (pp. 95-116). Vancouver: Press Gang.

Adler, F. (1975). *Sisters in Crime: The Rise of the New Female Criminal*. New York: McGraw-Hill.

Akers, R.L. (1997). *Criminological Theories: Introduction and Evaluation, 2nd ed.* Los Angeles: Roxbury.

Alberta Report (1995a). Table of Contents. July 31, 1.

Alberta Report (1995b). "You've Come a Long Way, Baby: Prodded by Feminism, Today's Teenaged Girls Embrace Antisocial Male Behaviour. July 31, 24.

Alvi, S. (2000). *Youth and the Canadian Criminal Justice System*. Cincinnati: Anderson.

Alvi, S., & DeKeseredy, W.S. (1997). "Youth Unemployment and Entrepreneurial Culture: Improving the Odds?" *Teach*, March/April, 38-40.

Alvi, S., DeKeseredy, W.S., & Ellis, D. (2000). *Contemporary Social Problems in North America*. Toronto: Prentice Hall.

Armstrong, P., & Armstrong, H. (1994). *The Double Ghetto: Canadian Women and Their Segregated Work, 3rd ed.* Toronto: McClelland & Stewart.

Atlas, R., & Pepler, D. (1997). *Observations of Bullying in the Classroom*. Manuscript submitted for publication. LaMarsh Centre on Violence and Conflict Resolution. York University.

Badgley, R. (1984). *Report of the Committee on Sexual Offences Against Children and Youths*. Ottawa: Supply and Services Canada.

Bala, N. (1997). *Young Offenders Law*. Concord, ON: Irwin Law.

Barnett, O.W., Miller-Perrin, C.L., & Perrin, R.D. (1997). *Family Violence Across the Lifespan*. Thousand Oaks, CA: Sage.

Barrett, M., & McIntosh, M. (1982). *The Anti-social Family*. London: Verso.

Beare, M.J. (1996). *Criminal Conspiracies: Organized Crime in Canada*. Toronto: Nelson.

Becker, H.S. (1973). *Outsiders: Studies in the Sociology of Deviance*. New York: Free Press.

Beirne, P., & Messerschmidt, J.W. (1995). *Criminology, 2nd ed*. New York: Harcourt Brace.

Belcourt, R., Nouwens, T., & Lefebvre, L. (1993). "Examining the Unexamined: Recidivism Among Female Offenders." *Correctional Service of Canada Forum*, 5, 10-14.

Belknap, J. (1996). *The Invisible Woman: Gender, Crime, and Justice*. Belmont, CA: Wadsworth.

Birkenmayer, A., & Besserer, S. (1997). *Sentencing in Adult Provincial Courts: A Study of Nine Jurisdictions, 1993 and 1994*. Ottawa: Statistics Canada

Blanchfield, M. (1998). "LSD Tested on Female Prisoners." *Ottawa Citizen*, February 28, A1-A2.

Blau, R., & Winkler, A. (1989). "Women in the Labor Force: An Overview." In J. Freeman (ed.) *Women: A Feminist Perspective* (pp. 265-286). Palo Alto, CA: Mayfield.

Bohuslawsky, M. (1999). "Promises, Promises: Common Sense Revolution, Part II." *Ottawa Citizen*, June 4, B2.

Boritch, H. (1997). *Fallen Women: Female Crime and Criminal Justice in Canada*. Toronto: Nelson.

Bourgois, P. (1995). *In Search of Respect: Selling Crack in El Barrio*. Cambridge, UK: Cambridge University Press.

Bourgois, P. & Dunlap, E. (1993). "Exorcising Sex-for-Crack: An Ethnographic Perspective from Harlem." In M.S. Ratner (ed.) *Crack Pipe as Pimp: An Ethnographic Investigation of Sex-for-Crack Exchanges* (pp. 97-132). New York: Lexington.

Bowker, L. (1983). *Beating Wife-Beating*. Lexington, MA: Lexington Books.

Bowker, L. (1985)."The Effects of National Development on the Position of Married Women in the Third World: The Case of Wife-Beating." *International Journal of Comparative and Applied Criminal Justice*, 9, 1-13.

Bowlby, G., Levesque, J.M., & Sunter, D. (1997). "Youths and the Labour Market." *Labour Force Update*, Catalogue No. 71-005-XPB, 1(1). Ottawa: Statistics Canada.

Bracey, D.H. (1979). *Baby Pros*. New York: John Jay Press.

Braithwaite, J. (1989). *Crime, Shame and Reintegration*. New York: Cambridge University Press.

Brinkerhoff, M., & Lupri, E. (1988). "Interspousal Violence." *The Canadian Journal of Sociology*, 13, 407-434.

Bronskill, J. (1996). "Female Inmates Win Better Protection." *Ottawa Citizen Archives* at *http://www.ottawacitizen.com/ARCHIVE_1996/june5/nat/nat5/nat5.htm* (May 30, 1999).

Brook, J.S., & Brook, D.W. (1996). "Risk and Protective Factors for Drug Use: Etiological Considerations." In C.L. McCoy, L.R. Metsch, & J.A. Inciardi (eds.) *Intervening with Drug-Involved Youth* (pp. 23-44). Thousand Oaks, CA: Sage.

Browne, A. (1987). *When Battered Women Kill*. New York: Free Press.

Bursik, R.J., & Grasmick, H.G. (1995). "Defining Gangs and Gang Behavior." In M.W. Klein, C.L. Maxson, & J. Miller (eds.) *The Modern Gang Reader* (pp. 8-13). Los Angeles: Roxbury.

Campbell, A. (1990). "Female Participation in Gangs." In C.R. Huff (ed.) *Gangs in America* (pp. 163-182). Newbury Park, CA: Sage.

Canadian Centre for Justice Statistics. (1997). *Adult Correctional Services in Canada, 1995-96*. Ottawa: Statistics Canada.

Canadian Labor Congress. (1997). *Women's Work: A Report*. Ottawa: Canadian Labour Congress.

Carrigan, D.O. (1998). *Juvenile Delinquency in Canada: A History*. Concord, ON: Irwin.

Carrington, P. (1995). "Has Violent Crime Increased? Comment on Corrado and Markwart." *Canadian Journal of Criminology*, 37, 61-74.

Carroll, W. (1987). "Which Women are More Proletarianized? Gender, Class and Occupation in Canada." *Canadian Review of Sociology and Anthropology*, 24, 45-70.

Cernkovich, S., & Giordano, P. (1979). "A Comparative Analysis of Male and Female Delinquency." *Sociological Quarterly*, 20, 131-145.

Cherney, E. (1999). "Fewer than Half of Canada's Teens Find Part-time Work." *National Post*, January 19, A6.

Chesney-Lind, M. (1986). "Women and Crime: The Female Offender." *Signs: Journal of Women in Culture and Society*, 12, 78-96.

Chesney-Lind, M. (1989). "Girls' Crime and Women's Place: Toward a Feminist Model of Female Delinquency." *Crime & Delinquency*, 35, 5-29.

Chesney-Lind, M. (1997). *The Female Offender: Girls, Women and Crime*. Thousand Oaks, CA: Sage.

Chesney-Lind, M. (1998). Foreword. In S.L. Miller (ed.) *Crime Control and Women: Feminist Implications of Criminal Justice Policy* (pp. ix-xii). Thousand Oaks, CA: Sage.

Chesney-Lind, M. (1999). "Review of Patricia Pearson's *When She Was Bad: Violent Women and the Myth of Innocence*." *Women & Criminal Justice*.

Chesney-Lind, M., & Bloom, B. (1997). "Feminist Criminology: Thinking about Women and Crime." In B.D. MacLean & D. Milovanovic (eds.) *Thinking Critically about Crime* (pp. 45-55). Vancouver: Collective Press.

Chesney-Lind, M., & Shelden, R.G. (1992). *Girls: Delinquency and Juvenile Justice*. Belmont, CA: Brooks/Cole.

Chesney-Lind, M., & Shelden, R.G. (1998). *Girls: Delinquency and Juvenile Justice, 2nd ed.* Belmont, CA: West/Wadsworth.

Chisholm, P. (1997). "Bad Girls: A Brutal B.C. Murder Sounds an Alarm about Teenage Violence." *MacLean's* at *http://www.macleans.ca/newsroom120897/cov1120897.htm* (May 26, 1998).

Chunn, D., & Gavigan, S.A.M. (1991). "Women and Crime in Canada." In M.A. Jackson & C.T. Griffiths (eds.) *Canadian Criminology: Perspectives on Crime and Criminality* (pp. 275-314). Toronto: Harcourt Brace Jovanovich.

Chunn, D., & Menzies, R. (1996). "Canadian Criminology and the Woman Question." In N. Hahn Rafter & F. Heidensohn (eds.) *International Feminist Perspectives in Criminology* (pp. 139-166). Philadelphia: Open University Press.

Clinard, M., & Quinney, R. (1973). *Criminal Behavior Systems, Revised ed.* New York: Holt, Rinehart and Winston.

Cobb, C. (1998). "Divorce Panel 'Taunts' Women: Women Who Report Abuse are Intimidated, MP Charges." *Ottawa Citizen*, June 15, A3.

Cohen, A. (1955). *Delinquent Boys: The Culture of the Gang.* New York: Free Press.

Comack, E. (1993). *Women Offenders' Experiences of Physical and Sexual Abuse: A Preliminary Report.* Criminology Research Centre, University of Manitoba.

Conklin, J.E. (1998). *Criminology, 6th ed.* Needham Heights, MA: Allyn & Bacon.

Connell, R.W. (1987). *Gender and Power.* Stanford, CA: Stanford University Press.

Craig, W., & Pepler, D. (1997). *Naturalistic Observations of Bullying and Victimization on the Playground.* Unpublished Report. LaMarsh Research Centre on Violence and Conflict Resolution, York University.

Craig W., Peters, R., & Konarski, R. (1998). *Bullying and Victimization Among Canadian School Children.* Paper presented at Investing in Children: A National Research Conference, Ottawa.

Crawford, M., & Gartner, R. (1992). *Woman Killing: Intimate Femicide in Ontario, 1974-1990.* Report prepared for the Women We Honour Action Committee and the Ontario Women's Directorate, Toronto.

Crompton, V. (1991). "A Parent's Story." In B. Levy (ed.) *Dating Violence: Young Women in Danger* (pp. 21-27). Seattle: Seal Press.

Crook, N. (1984). *A Report on Prostitution in the Atlantic Provinces.* Working Papers on Prostitution and Pornography, Report No. 12. Ottawa: Department of Justice.

Curran, D. (1984). "The Myth of the New Female Delinquent." *Crime & Delinquency,* 30, 386-399.

Curran, D.J., & Renzetti, C.M. (1994). *Theories of Crime.* Boston: Allyn & Bacon.

Currie, E. (1985). *Confronting Crime.* New York: Pantheon.

Currie, E. (1993). *Reckoning: Drugs, the Cities, and the American Future.* New York: Hill & Wang.

Currie, E. (1998). *Crime and Punishment in America: Why the Solutions to America's Most Stubborn Social Crisis Have Not Worked—and What Will.* New York: Metropolitan Books.

Daly, K. (1987). "Discrimination in the Criminal Courts: Family, Gender, and the Problem of Equal Treatment." *Social Forces,* 66, 152-175.

Daly, K. (1989). "Gender and Varieties of White Collar Crime." *Criminology,* 27, 769-764.

Daly, K., & Chesney-Lind, M. (1988). "Feminism and Criminology." *Justice Quarterly*, 5, 497-538.

Danner, M.J. (1996). "Gender Inequality and Criminalization: A Socialist Feminist Perspective on the Legal Control of Women." In M.D. Schwartz & D. Milovanovic (eds.) *Race, Gender, and Class in Criminology: The Intersection* (pp. 29-48). New York: Garland.

Danner, M.J. (1998). "Three Strikes and it's Women Who Are Out: The Hidden Consequences for Women of Criminal Justice Policy Reforms." In S.L. Miller (ed.) *Crime Control and Women: Feminist Implications of Criminal Justice Policy* (pp. 1-14). Thousand Oaks, CA: Sage.

Decker, S. & Kempf-Leonard, K. (1995). "Constructing Gangs: The Social Definition of Youth Activities. In M.W. Klein, C.L. Maxson, & J. Miller (eds.) *The Modern Gang Reader* (pp. 14-23). Los Angeles: Roxbury.

DeKeseredy, W.S. (1988). "Woman Abuse in Dating Relationships: The Relevance of Social Support Theory." *Journal of Family Violence*, 3, 1-13.

DeKeseredy, W.S. (1996). "Patterns of Family Violence." In M. Baker (ed.) *Families: Changing Trends in Canada, 2nd ed* (pp. 249-272). Toronto: McGraw-Hill Ryerson.

DeKeseredy, W.S. (1999). "Tactics of the Anti-Feminist Backlash Against Canadian National Woman Abuse Surveys." *Violence Against Women*, 5, 1258-1276.

DeKeseredy, W.S., Alvi, S., Schwartz, M.D., & Perry, B. (in press a). "Violence Against and the Harassment of Women in Canadian Public Housing: An Exploratory Study." *Canadian Review of Sociology and Anthropology*.

DeKeseredy, W.S., Alvi, S., Schwartz, M.D., & Tomaszewski, A. (in press b). "Joblessness, Poverty, Gender, and Inner-city Crime: The Current State of Canadian Sociological Knowledge." In A. Godenzi (ed.) *Conflict, Gender and Peace*. Fribourg, Switzerland: Fribourg University Press.

DeKeseredy, W.S., & Ellis, D. (1997). "Sibling Violence: A Review of Canadian Sociological Research and Suggestions for Further Empirical Research." *Humanity & Society*, 21, 397-411.

DeKeseredy, W.S., & Hinch, R. (1991). *Woman Abuse: Sociological Perspectives*. Toronto: Thompson.

DeKeseredy, W.S., & Kelly, K. (1993a). "The Incidence and Prevalence of Woman Abuse in Canadian University and College Dating Relationships." *Canadian Journal of Sociology*, 18, 137-159.

DeKeseredy, W.S., & Kelly, K. (1993b). "Woman Abuse in University and College Dating Relationships: The Contribution of the Ideology of Familial Patriarchy." *Journal of Human Justice*, 4, 25-52.

DeKeseredy, W.S., & MacLean, B.D. (1991). "Exploring the Gender, Race and Class Dimensions of Victimization: A Left Realist Critique of the Canadian Urban Victimization Survey." *International Journal of Offender Therapy and Comparative Criminology*, 35, 143-161.

DeKeseredy, W.S., & MacLeod, L. (1997). *Woman Abuse: A Sociological Story*. Toronto: Harcourt Brace.

DeKeseredy, W.S., Saunders, D.G., Schwartz, M.D., & Alvi, S. (1997). "The Meanings and Motives for Women's Use of Violence in Canadian College Dating Relationships: Results from a National Survey." *Sociological Spectrum*, 17, 199-222.

DeKeseredy, W.S., & Schwartz, M.D. (1993). "Male Peer Support and Woman Abuse: An Expansion of DeKeseredy's Model." *Sociological Spectrum*, 13, 393-414.

DeKeseredy, W.S., & Schwartz, M.D. (1994). "Locating a History of Some Canadian Woman Abuse in Elementary and High School Dating Relationships." *Humanity & Society*, 18, 49-63.

DeKeseredy, W.S., & Schwartz, M.D. (1996). *Contemporary Criminology*. Belmont, CA: Wadsworth.

DeKeseredy, W.S., & Schwartz, M.D. (1998). *Woman Abuse on Campus: Results from the Canadian National Survey*. Thousand Oaks, CA: Sage.

DeLeon-Granados, W. (in press). *Travels Through Crime and Place: On the Trail of Community-Building as Crime Control*. Boston: Northeastern University Press.

Dell, C., & Boe, R. (1997). *Female Young Offenders in Canada: Recent Trends*. Ottawa: Correctional Service of Canada.

Dell, C., & Boe, R. (1998). *Adult Female Offenders in Canada: Recent Trends*. Ottawa: Correctional Service of Canada.

Desroches, F.J. (1995). *Force and Fear: Robbery in Canada*. Toronto: Nelson.

Devine, J.A., & Wright, J.D. (1993). *The Greatest of Evils: Urban Poverty and the American Underclass*. Hawthorne, NY: Aldine de Gruyter.

Dexter, L. (1958). "A Note on the Selective Inattention in Social Science." *Social Problems*, 6, 176-182.

Dobash, R.E., & Dobash, R. (1979). *Violence Against Wives: A Case Against the Patriarchy*. New York: Free Press.

Donziger, S. (ed.). (1996). *The Real War on Crime*. New York: Harper Perennial.

Duffy, A., & Momirov, J. (1997). *Family Violence: A Canadian Introduction*. Toronto: Lorimer.

Eaton, B., & Hutchison, C. (1999). "Tories Weak on Crime Initiatives." *Ottawa Citizen*, June 1, B5.

Edwards, S. (1989). *Policing "Domestic" Violence: Women, the Law and the State*. London: Sage.

Egan, K. (1999). "Give Hockey a Tax Break, Politicians Told." *Ottawa Citizen*, March 2, A1-A2.

Ellis, D. (1987). *The Wrong Stuff: An Introduction to the Sociological Study of Deviance*. Toronto: Collier Macmillan.

Ellis, D., & DeKeseredy, W.S. (1996). *The Wrong Stuff: An Introduction to the Sociological Study of Deviance, 2nd ed*. Toronto: Allyn & Bacon.

Ellis, D., & DeKeseredy, W.S. (1997). "Rethinking Estrangement, Interventions, and Intimate Femicide." *Violence Against Women*, 3, 590-609.

Esbensen, F., & Winfree, L.T. (1998). "Race and Gender Differences Between Gang and Nongang Youths: Results from a Multisite Survey." *Justice Quarterly*, 15, 505-525.

Ewing, C.P. (1990). *Kids Who Kill*. Lexington, MA: Lexington Books.

Fairstein, L. (1993). *Sexual Violence: Our War Against Rape*. New York: Morrow.

Faith, K. (1993a). *Unruly Women: The Politics of Confinement and Resistance*. Vancouver: Press Gang.

Faith, K. (1993b). "Media, Myths and Masculinization: Images of Women in Prison." In E. Adleberg & C. Currie (eds.) *In Conflict with the Law: Women and the Canadian Justice System* (pp. 174-211). Vancouver: Press Gang.

Faludi, S. (1991). *Backlash: The Undeclared War Against American Women*. New York: Crown.

Farge, B., & Rahder, B. (1991). *Police Response to Incidents of Wife Assault*. Report prepared for the Assaulted Women's Helpline and the Metro Toronto Committee Against Wife Assault. Toronto.

Fedorowycz, O. (1995). *Homicide in Canada*. Ottawa: Statistics Canada.

Fekete, J. (1994). *Moral Panic: Biopolitics Rising*. Montreal: Robert Davies.

Feldman, H.W., Espada, F., Penn, S., & Byrd, S. (1993). "To the Curb: Sex Bartering and Drug Use Among Homeless Crack Users in Los Angeles." In M.S. Ratner (ed.) *Crack Pipe as Pimp: An Ethnographic Investigation of Sex-for-Crack Exchanges* (pp. 133-59). New York: Lexington.

Finkelhor, D., Hotaling, G.T., & Yllo, K. (1988). *Stopping Family Violence: Research Priorities for the Coming Decade*. Beverly Hills: Sage.

Finkelhor, D., & Yllo, K. (1985). *License to Rape: Sexual Abuse of Wives*. New York: Free Press.

Finnegan, W. (1998). *Cold New World: Growing Up in a Harder Country*. New York: Random House.

Foran, T. (1995). "A Descriptive Comparison of the Demographic and Family Characteristics of the Canadian and Offender Populations. *Forum on Corrections Research*, 7, 3-5.

Forcese, D. (1997). *The Canadian Class Structure, 4th ed*. Toronto: McGraw-Hill Ryerson.

Fraser Committee. (1985). *Pornography and Prostitution in Canada*. Ottawa: Department of Supply and Services.

Friedrichs, D.O. (1996). *Trusted Criminals: White Collar Crime in Contemporary Society*. Belmont, CA: Wadsworth.

Funk, R. (1993). *Stopping Rape: A Challenge for Men*. Philadelphia: New Society.

Gagné, M., & Lavoie, F. (1993). "Young People's Views on the Causes of Violence in Adolescents' Romantic Relationships." *Canada's Mental Health*, 41, 11-15.

Gardner, D. (1999). "Reporters were Suckers for Federal Flim-flam." *Ottawa Citizen*, March 19, A1-A2.

Gartner, R. (1995). "Homicide in Canada." In J.I. Ross (ed.) *Violence in Canada: Sociopolitical Perspectives* (pp. 186-222). Toronto: Oxford University Press.

Gartner, R., & Doob, A. (1994). *Trends in Criminal Victimization, 1988-93*. Ottawa: Statistics Canada.

Gavigan, S.A.M. (1983). "Women's Crime and Feminist Critiques." *Canadian Criminology Forum*, 6, 75-90.

Gavigan, S.A.M. (1993). "Women's Crime: New Perspectives and Old Theories." In E. Adelberg & C. Currie (eds.) *In Conflict with the Law: Women and the Canadian Justice System* (pp. 215-234). Vancouver: Press Gang.

Gelles, R.J., & Cornell, C.P. (1985). *Intimate Violence in Families*. Beverly Hills: Sage.

Gelsthorpe, L., & Morris, A. (1988). "Feminism and Criminology in Britain." *British Journal of Criminology*, 28, 93-110.

Gemme, R., Payment, N., & Malenfant, L. (1984). *A Report on Prostitution in Quebec*. Working Papers on Prostitution and Pornography, Report No. 11. Ottawa: Department of Justice.

Giardini, A. (1999). "Feminism is Not a Dirty Word." *National Post*, June 8, B1, B3.

Gibbons, D. (1995). "Unfit for Human Consumption: The Problem of Flawed Writing in Criminal Justice and What to Do about It. *Crime & Delinquency*, 41, 246-266.

Gimenez, M. (1990). "The Feminization of Poverty: Myths or Reality." *Social Justice*, 17, 43-69.

Goff, C. (1997). *Criminal Justice in Canada*. Toronto: Nelson.

Goff, C. (1999). *Corrections in Canada*. Cincinnati: Anderson.

Goffman, E. (1961). *Asylums: Essays on the Social Situation of Mental Patients and Other Inmates*. New York: Anchor.

Gomme, I.M. (1993). *The Shadow Line: Deviance and Crime in Canada*. Toronto: Harcourt Brace Jovanovich.

Gomme, I.M., Morton, M., & West, W.G. (1984). "Rates, Types, and Patterns of Male and Female Delinquency in an Ontario County. *Canadian Journal of Criminology*, 26, 313-24.

Gordon, R. (1993). *Incarcerated Gang Members in British Columbia: A Preliminary Study*. Victoria, BC: Ministry of Attorney-General.

Hackler, J. (1994). *Crime and Canadian Public Policy*. Toronto: Prentice Hall.

Hagan, J. (1989). *Structural Criminology*. New Brunswick, NJ: Rutgers University Press.

Hagan, J., Gillis, A., & Simpson, J. (1987). "Class in the Household: A Power-Control Theory of Gender and Delinquency." *American Journal of Sociology*, 92, 788-816.

Hagan, J., & McCarthy, B. (1997). *Mean Streets: Youth Crime and Homelessness*. New York: Cambridge University Press.

Haran, J.F., & Martin, J.M. (1984). "The Armed Urban Bank Robber." *Federal Probation*, 48, 47-53.

Hatch, A.J., & Faith, K. (1991). "The Female Offender in Canada: A Statistical Profile." In R.A. Silverman, J.J. Teevan, & V.F. Sacco (eds.) *Crime in Canadian Society, 4th ed.* (pp. 70-78). Toronto: Butterworths.

Hatfield, M. (1997). *Concentrations of Poverty and Distressed Neighborhoods in Canada.* Ottawa: Human Resources Development Canada.

Health Canada. (1995). *Canada's Alcohol and Other Drug Survey.* Ottawa: Ministry of Supply and Services.

Heide, K.M. (1992). *Why Kids Kill Parents: Child Abuse and Adolescent Homicide.* Columbus, OH: Ohio University Press.

Hill, G., & Atkinson, M. (1988). "Gender, Familial Control, and Delinquency." *Criminology,* 26, 127-150.

Hills, S. (ed.). (1987). *Corporate Violence: Injury and Death for Profit.* Totowa, NJ: Rowman & Littlefield.

Hirsch, M., & Keller, E.F. (eds.). (1990). *Conflicts in Feminism.* New York: Routledge.

Hirschi, T. (1969). *Causes of Delinquency.* Berkeley: University of California Press.

Holmes, J., & Silverman, E. (1992). *We're Here, Listen to Us!* Ottawa: Advisory Council on the Status of Women.

Holmlund, C. (1994). "A Decade of Deadly Dolls: Hollywood and the Woman Killer." In H. Birch (ed.) *Moving Targets: Women, Murder and Representation* (pp. 127-151). Berkeley: University of California Press.

Hornosty, J.M. (1996). "A Look at Faculty Fears and Needed University Policies Against Violence and Harassment." In C. Stark-Adamec (ed.) *Violence: A Collective Responsibility* (pp. 31-56). Ottawa: Social Science Federation of Canada.

Horowitz, R. (1990). "Sociological Perspectives on Gangs: Conflicting Definitions and Concepts." In C.R. Huff (ed.) *Gangs in America* (pp. 37-54). Newbury Park, CA: Sage.

Huff, C.R. (1993). "Gangs in the United States." In A.P. Goldstein & C.R. Huff (eds.) *The Gang Intervention Handbook* (pp. 3-20). Champaign, IL: Research Press.

Hotaling, G.T., & Sugarman, D.B. (1986). "An Analysis of Risk Markers and Husband to Wife Violence: The Current State of Knowledge." *Violence and Victims,* 1, 102-124.

Huizinga, D. (1997). "Gangs and the Volume of Crime." Paper presented at the annual meeting of the Western Society of Criminology, Honolulu.

Inciardi, J., Lockwood, D., & Pottieger, A.E. (1993). *Women and Crack-Cocaine.* New York: Macmillan.

Irwin, J., & Austin, J. (1997). *It's About Time: America's Imprisonment Binge.* Belmont, CA: Wadsworth.

Jackson, P.G. (1989). "Theories and Findings about Youth Gangs." *Criminal Justice Abstracts,* June, 313-329.

James, J., & Thornton, W. (1980). "Women's Liberation and the Female Delinquent." *Journal of Research in Crime and Delinquency,* 20, 230-244.

Jensen, G., & Thompson, K. (1990). "What's Class Got to Do with It? A Further Examination of Power-Control Theory." *American Journal of Sociology,* 95, 1009-1023.

Jiwani, Y. (1998). "Reena Virk: The Erasure of Race." *The Freda Centre for Research on Violence against Women and Children* at *http://www.harbour.sfu.ca/freda/articles/virk.htm* (May 26, 1998).

Joe, K., & Chesney-Lind, M. (1993). *Just Every Mother's Angel: An Analysis of Gender and Ethnic Variations in Youth Gang Membership*. Paper presented at the annual meeting of the American Society of Criminology, Miami.

Joe, K., & Chesney-Lind, M. (1995). "Just Every Mother's Angel: An Analysis of Gender and Ethnic Variations in Youth Gang Membership." *Gender & Society*, 9, 408-430.

Johnson, D. (1998). "Seven Flaws of Capital Punishment." *Ottawa Citizen*, February 10, A15.

Johnson, H. (1996). *Dangerous Domains: Violence Against Women in Canada*. Toronto: Nelson.

Johnson, H., & Sacco, V.F. (1995). "Researching Violence Against Women: Statistics Canada's National Survey." *Canadian Journal of Criminology*, 37, 281-304.

Johnson, R., & Toch, H. (eds.). (1982). *The Pains of Imprisonment*. Beverly Hills, CA: Sage.

Jones, A. (1994). *Next Time She'll Be Dead: Battering and How to Stop It*. Boston: Beacon.

Kanin, E.J. (1967). "An Examination of Sexual Aggression as a Response to Sexual Frustration." *Journal of Marriage and the Family*, 29, 428-433.

Kanin, E.J. (1985). "Date Rapists: Differential Sexual Socialization and Relative Deprivation." *Archives of Sexual Behavior*, 14, 219-231.

Kantor, G.K., & Straus, M.A. (1990a). "The 'Drunken Bum' Theory of Wife Beating." In M.A. Straus & R.J. Gelles (eds.) *Physical Violence in American Families: Risk Factors and Adaptations to Violence in 8,145 Families* (pp. 203-224). New Brunswick, NJ: Transaction.

Kantor, G.K., & Straus, M.A. (1990b). "Response of Victims and Police to Assault on Wives." In M.A. Straus & R.J. Gelles (eds.) *Physical Violence in American Families: Risk Factors and Adaptations to Violence in 8,145 Families* (pp. 473-487). New Brunswick, NJ: Transaction.

Kappeler, V.E., Blumberg, M. & Potter, G.W. (1996). *The Mythology of Crime and Criminal Justice, 2nd ed*. Prospect Heights, IL: Waveland.

Karmen, A. (1990). *Crime Victims: An Introduction to Victimology, 2nd ed*. Pacific Grove, CA: Brooks/Cole.

Kasarda, J.D. (1992). "The Severely Distressed in Economically Transforming Cities." In A.V. Harrell & G.E. Peterson (eds.) *Drugs, Crime, and Social Isolation: Barriers to Urban Opportunity* (pp. 45-98). Washington, D.C.: Urban Institute Press.

Kennedy, L.W., & Dutton, D.G. (1989). "The Iincidence of Wife Assault in Alberta." *Canadian Journal of Behavioral Science*, 21, 40-54.

Klein, E., Campbell, J., Soler, E., & Ghez, M. (1997). *Ending Domestic Violence: Changing Public Perceptions/Halting the Epidemic*. Thousand Oaks, CA: Sage.

Klein, M. (1995). *The American Street Gang: Its Nature, Prevalence, and Control*. New York: Oxford University Press.

Kruttschnitt, C. (1982). "Women, Crime and Dependency." *Criminology*, 19, 495-513.

Kruttschnitt, C. (1984). "Sex and Criminal Court Dispositions: The Unresolved Controversy." *Research in Crime and Delinquency*, 21, 213-232.

Kruttschnitt, C., & Green, D.E. (1984)." The Sex-Sanctioning Issue: Is it History?" *American Sociological Review*, 49, 54-551.

LaPrairie, C. (1993). "Aboriginal Women and Crime in Canada: Identifying the Issues." In E. Adelberg & C. Currie (eds.) *In Conflict with the Law: Women and the Canadian Justice System* (pp. 235-246). Vancouver: Press Gang.

Lefkowitz, B. (1997). *Our Guys*. New York: Vintage.

Lewis, D.K. (1981). "Black Women Offenders and Criminal Justice." In M.Q. Warren (ed.) *Comparing Female and Male Offenders*. Beverly Hills: Sage.

Liddle, A. (1989). "Feminist Contributions to an Understanding of Violence Against Women: Three Steps Forward, Two Steps Back." *Canadian Review of Sociology and Anthropology*, 26, 759-775.

Lightman, E.S. (1997). "It's Not a Walk in the Park: Workfare in Ontario." In E. Shragge (ed.) *Workfare: Ideology for a New Under-class* (pp. 85-108). Toronto: Garamond.

Lombroso, C., & Ferrero, W. (1895). *The Female Offender*. New York: Philosophical Library.

Loper, A.B., & Cornell, D.G. (1996). *Homicide by Girls*. Paper presented at the annual meeting of the National Girls Caucus, Orlando, FL.

Lorber, J. (1998). *Gender Inequality: Feminist Theories and Politics*. Los Angeles: Roxbury.

Lowman, J. (1984). *Vancouver Field study of Prostitution*. Working Papers on Pornography and Prostitution, Report No. 8. Ottawa: Department of Justice.

Lowman, J. (1986). "You Can Do It, but Don't Do It Here." In J. Lowman, M.A. Jackson, T.S. Palys, & S. Gavigan (eds.) *Regulating Sex* (pp. 193-214). Burnaby: School of Criminology, Simon Fraser University.

Lowman, J. (1989). *Street Prostitution: Assessing the Impact of the Law: Vancouver*. Ottawa: Department of Justice Canada.

Lowman, J. (1992). "Street Prostitution." In V.F. Sacco (ed.) *Deviance: Conformity and Control in Canadian Society* (pp. 49-94). Toronto: Prentice Hall.

Lowman, J. (1995). "Prostitution in Canada." In M.A. Jackson & C.T. Griffiths (eds.) *Canadian Criminology: Perspectives on Crime and Criminality*, 2nd ed. (pp. 333-359). Toronto: Harcourt Brace.

Lowman, J., & Fraser, L. (1995). *Violence Against Persons Who Prostitute: The Experience in British Columbia*. Ottawa: Department of Justice.

Lupri, E. (1990). "Male Violence in the Home." In C. McKie and K. Thompson (eds.) *Canadian Social Trends* (pp. 170-172). Toronto: Thompson Educational Publishing.

Lupsha, P. (1986). "Organized Crime in the United States." In R.J. Kelly (ed.) *Organized Crime: A Global Perspective*. New Jersey: Roman and Littlefield.

MacLean, B.D. (1994). "Gender Inequality in Dispositions under the Young Offenders Act." *Humanity & Society*, 18, 64-81.

MacLean, B.D., & Milovanovic, D. (eds.). (1991). *New Directions in Critical Criminology*. Vancouver: Collective Press.

MacLean, B.D., & Milovanovic, D. (1997a). "Thinking Critically about Criminology." In B.D. MacLean & D. Milovanovic (eds.) *Thinking Critically about Crime* (pp. 11-16). Vancouver: Collective Press.

MacLean, B.D., & Milovanovic, D. (eds.). (1997b). *Thinking Critically about Crime*. Vancouver: Collective Press.

Mahan, S. (1996). *Crack Cocaine, Crime, and Women: Legal, Social and Treatment Issues*. Thousand Oaks, CA: Sage.

Maher, L. (1995). "In the Name of Love: Women and Initiation into Illicit Drugs." In R.E. Dobash, R.P. Dobash, & L. Noaks (eds.) *Gender and Crime* (pp. 132-166). Cardiff: University of Wales Press.

Maher, L. (1997). *Sexed Work: Gender, Race, and Resistance in a Brooklyn Drug Market*. London: Clarendon Press.

Mathews, F. (1993). *Youth Gangs on Youth Gangs*. Toronto: Central Toronto Youth Services.

McCormack, T. (1987). "Feminism, Women's Studies and the New Academic Freedom." In J. Gaskell & A. McLaren (eds.) *Women and Education: A Canadian Perspective*. Calgary: Detselig.

McKenzie, D., & Single, E. (1997). "Licit and Illicit Drugs." In D. McKenzie, B. Williams, & E. Single (eds.) *Canadian Profile: Alcohol, Tobacco & Other Drugs* (pp. 89-132). Toronto: Canadian Centre on Substance Abuse.

McQuaig, L. (1987). *Behind Closed Doors*. Toronto: Penguin Books.

Meloff, W., & Silverman, R.A. (1992). "Canadian Kids Who Kill." *Canadian Journal of Criminology*, January, 15-34.

Mercer, S. (1988). "Not a Pretty Picture: An Exploratory Study of Violence Against Women in High School Dating Relationships." *Resources for Feminist Research*, 17, 15-23.

Merton, R.K. (1938). "Social Structure and Anomie." *American Sociological Review*, 3, 672-682.

Messerschmidt, J.W. (1986). *Capitalism, Patriarchy, and Crime: Toward a Socialist Feminist Criminology*. Totowa, NJ: Roman and Littlefield.

Messerschmidt, J.W. (1993). *Masculinities and Crime: Critique and Reconceptualization of Theory*. Lanham, MD: Roman & Littlefield.

Miller, E. (1983). "A Cross-Cultural Look at Women and Crime: An Essay Review." *Contemporary Crises*, 7, 59-70.

Miller, J. (1997). *Assessing the Nature of Violence Against Young Women in an Urban African-American Community*. Unpublished manuscript. Department of Criminology and Criminal Justice, University of Missouri at St. Louis.

Miller, J. (1998). "Up It Up: Gender and the Accomplishment of Street Robbery." *Criminology*, 36, 37-66.

Miller, J., & Schwartz, M.D. (1994). "Rape Myths and Violence Against Street Prostitutes." *Deviant Behavior*, 16, 1-23.

Miller, S.L. (ed.). (1998). *Crime Control and Women: Feminist Implications of Criminal Justice Policy*. Thousand Oaks, CA: Sage.

Miller, S.L. (1998). "Introduction." In S.L. Miller (ed.) *Crime Control and Women: Feminist Implications of Criminal Justice Policy* (pp. xv-xxiv). Thousand Oaks, CA: Sage.

Mills, C.W. (1959). *The Sociological Imagination*. New York: Oxford University Press.

Morash, M., & Chesney-Lind, M. (1991). "A Re-formulation and Partial Test of the Power-Control Theory of Delinquency." *Justice Quarterly*, 8, 347-377.

Morris, A. (1987). *Women, Crime, and Criminal Justice*. Oxford, UK: Basil Blackwell.

Morris, R. (1995). *Penal Abolition: The Practical Choice*. Toronto: Canadian Scholars' Press.

Naffine, N. (1987). *Female Crime: The Construction of Women in Criminology*. Sydney, Australia: Allen & Unwin.

NiCarthy, G. (1983). "Addicted Love and Abuse: A Course for Teenage Women." In S. Davidson (ed.) *The Second Mile: Contemporary Approaches in Counseling Young Women*. Tucson: New Directions for Young Women.

Oliver, W. (1994). *The Violent Social World of Black Men*. New York: Lexington Books.

Olweus, D. (1987). "School-yard Bullying: Grounds for Intervention." *School Safety*, 6, 4-11.

Ontario Native Women's Association. (1989). *Breaking Free: A Proposal for Change to Aboriginal Family Violence*. Thunder Bay, ON: Ontario Native Women's Association.

Ouellet, L.J., Wiebel, W.W., Jimenez, A.D., & Johnson, W.A. (1993). "Crack Cocaine and the Transformation of Prostitution in Three Chicago Neighborhoods." In M.S. Ratner (ed.) *Crack Pipe as Pimp: An Ethnographic Investigation of Sex-for-Crack Exchanges* (pp. 69-98). New York: Lexington.

Ovenden, N. (1999). "Crooks to Pay for Their Crimes." *Ottawa Citizen*, April 13, A6.

Pate, K. (1999). "Why Do We Think Young Women Are Committing More Violent Offences?" *http://www.elizabethfry.ca/violent/page1.htm* (April 26, 1999).

Pateman, C. (1988). *The Sexual Contract*. Cambridge: Polity Press.

Pearce, F. (1976). *Crimes of the Powerful: Marxism, Crime and Deviance*. London: Pluto Press.

Pearson, P. (1997). *When She Was Bad: Violent Women and the Myth of Innocence*. Toronto: Random House.

Pettiway, L.E. (1997). *Workin' It: Women Living Through Drugs and Crime*. Philadelphia: Temple University Press.

Pfohl, S. (1994). *Images of Deviance and Social Control, 2nd ed.* New York: McGraw-Hill.

Pollack, O. (1950). *The Criminality of Women*. New York: Barnes.

Pollack, O., & Freidman, A.S. (eds.). (1969). *Family Dynamics and Female Delinquency*. Palo Alto, CA: Science and Behavior Books.

Pollock, J.M. (1999). *Criminal Women*. Cincinnati: Anderson.

Prejean, H. (1993). *Dead Man Walking*. New York: Vintage.

Purvis, A. (1997). "Fury of Her Peers: A Teenager's Brutal Assault and Drowning Raise Questions in a Quiet Canadian Town. *Time* at *http://bubblemouth.pathfinder.com/time/ma.../1997/int/971208/crime.fury_of_her_p.htm* (May 26, 1998).

R. v. Lavallee. (1990). 1 S.C.R., 852-900.

Radford, J. (1987). "Policing Male Violence—Policing Women." In J. Hanmer & M. Maynard (eds.) *Women, Violence and Social Control* (pp. 30-45). Atlantic Highlands, NJ: Humanities Press International.

Rainwater, L. (1990). *Behind Ghetto Walls*. Chicago: Aldine de Gruyter.

Ratner, M.S. (ed.) (1993). *Crack Pipe as Pimp: An Ethnographic Investigation of Sex-for-crack Exchanges*. New York: Lexington.

Reitsma-Street, M. (1993). "Canadian Youth Court Charges and Dispositions for Females Before and After the Implementation of the Young Offenders Act." *Canadian Journal of Criminology*, 35, 437-458.

Renzetti, C.M. (1993). "On the Margins of the Malestream (Or, They *Still* Don't Get It, Do They): Feminist Analyses in Criminal Justice Education." *Journal of Criminal Justice Education*, 4, 219-234.

Renzetti, C.M. (1994). "On Dancing with a Bear: Reflections on Some of the Current Debates Among Domestic Violence Theorists."*Violence and Victims*, 9, 195-200.

Renzetti, C.M. (1998). "Connecting the Dots: Women, Public Policy, and Social Control." In S.L. Miller (ed.) *Crime Control and Women: Feminist Implications of Criminal Justice Policy* (pp. 181-189).

Renzetti, C.M., & Curran, D.J. (1995). *Women, Men, and Society*. Boston: Allyn & Bacon.

Rodgers, K. (1994). *Wife Assault: The Findings of a National Survey*. Ottawa: Statistics Canada.

Rogers, K. (1972). "For Her Own Protection...: Conditions of Incarceration for Female Juvenile Offenders in the State of Connecticut." *Law and Society Review*, Winter, 223-246.

Roland, E. (1989). "Bullying: The Scandinavian Research Tradition." In D. Tattum & D. Lane (eds.) *Bullying in Schools*. Stoke-on-Trent: Trentham.

Russell, D.E.H. (1984). *Sexual Exploitation: Rape, Child Sexual Abuse, and Workplace Harassment*. Beverly Hills: Sage.

Russell, D.E.H. (1986). *The Secret Trauma: Incest in the Lives of Girls and Women*. New York: Basic Books.

Salamon, A. (1984). *Kept Women: Mistresses in the '80s*. London: Orbis.

Sampson, R.J., Raudenbush, S.W., & Earls, F. (1997). "Neighborhoods and Violent Crime: A Multilevel Study of Collective Efficacy." *Science*, 277, 918-924.

Sampson, R.J., Raudenbush, S.W., & Earls, F. (1988). *Neighborhood Collective Efficacy—Does It Help Reduce Violence?* Washington, D.C.: U.S. Department of Justice.

Schissel, B. (1993). *Social Dimensions of Canadian Youth Justice.* Toronto: Oxford University Press.

Schissel, B. (1997a). *Blaming Children: Youth Crime, Moral Panics and the Politics of Hate.* Halifax: Fernwood.

Schissel, B. (1997b). *The Roots of Disadvantage: The Differential Effects of Poverty on Rural and Urban Youth.* Report prepared for the Centre for Rural Studies and Enrichment, St. Peter's College. Muenster, Saskatchewan: St. Peter's College.

Schulman, M.A. (1979). *A Survey of Spousal Violence Against Women in Kentucky.* Study No. 792701 conducted for the Kentucky Commission on Women. Washington, DC: U.S. Government Printing Office.

Schur, E.W. (1984). *Labeling Women Deviant: Gender, Stigma, and Social Control.* New York: Random House.

Schwartz, M.D. (1989). "Asking the Right Questions: Battered Women Are Not All Passive." *Sociological Viewpoints*, 5, 46-61.

Schwartz, M.D. (1991). "The Future of Critical Criminology." In B.D. MacLean & D. Milovanovic (eds.) *New Directions in Critical Criminology* (pp. 119-124). Vancouver: Collective Press.

Schwartz, M.D., & DeKeseredy, W.S. (1994). "'People Without Data' Attacking Rape: The Gilbertization of Mary Koss." *Violence Update*, December, 5(8), 11.

Schwartz, M.D., & DeKeseredy, W.S. (1997). *Sexual Assault on the College Campus: The Role of Male Peer Support.* Thousand Oaks, CA: Sage.

Sev'er, A. (1997). "Recent or Imminent Separation and Intimate Violence Against Women: A Conceptual Overview." *Violence Against Women*, 3, 566-589.

Shaver, F.M. (1993). "Prostitution: A Female Crime?" In E. Adelberg & C. Currie (eds.) *In Conflict with the Law: Women and the Canadian Criminal Justice System* (pp. 153-173). Vancouver: Press Gang.

Shaw, M. (1994). "Women in Prison: A Literature Review." *Forum on Corrections Research*, 6, 13-18.

Shelden, R.G., Tracy, S.K., & Brown, W.B. (1997). *Youth Gangs in American Society.* Belmont, CA: Wadsworth.

Shoham, S., & Hoffman, J. (1991). *A Primer in the Sociology of Crime.* New York: Harrow and Heston.

Short, J.F. (1990). "New Wine in Old Bottles? Change and Continuity in American Gangs. In C.R. Huff (ed.) *Gangs in America* (pp. 223-239). Newbury Park, CA: Sage.

Short, J.F. (1997). *Poverty, Ethnicity, and Violent Crime.* Boulder, CO: Westview.

Shover, N. (1996). *Great Pretenders: Pursuits and Careers of Persistent Thieves.* Boulder, CO: Westview.

Siggner, A. (1992). "The Socio-demographic Conditions of Registered Indians." In R.A. Silverman & M.O. Nielson (eds.) *Aboriginal Peoples and Canadian Criminal Justice* (pp. 19-30). Toronto: Butterworths.

Silverman, R., & Kennedy, L. (1993). *Deadly Deeds: Murder in Canada*. Toronto: Nelson.

Silverman, R.A., Teevan, J.J., & Sacco, V.F. (1996). *Crime in Canadian Society, 5th ed.* Toronto: Harcourt Brace.

Simon, R. (1975). *Women and Crime*. Lexington, MA: Lexington Books.

Simpson, S. (1989). "Feminist Theory, Crime and Justice." *Criminology*, 27, 605-632.

Sinclair, R.L., & Boe, R. (1998). *Male Young Offenders in Canada: Recent Trends*. Ottawa: Correctional Service of Canada.

Sleeth, P., & Barnsley, J. (1989). *Recollecting Our Lives: Women's Experiences of Childhood Sexual Abuse*. Vancouver: Press Gang.

Smart, C. (1976). *Women, Crime and Criminology: A Feminist Critique*. London: Routledge & Kegan Paul.

Smith, D. (1996). Keynote address. Presentation to the Western Association of Sociology and Anthropology, Kelowna, British Columbia.

Smith, M.D. (1986). *Woman Abuse: The Case for Surveys by Telephone*. LaMarsh Research Centre on Violence and Conflict Resolution Report No. 12. North York, ON: York University.

Smith, M.D. (1987). "The Incidence and Prevalence of Woman Abuse in Toronto." *Violence and Victims*, 2, 173-87.

Smith, M.D. (1989). *Woman Abuse in Toronto: Incidence, Prevalence and Sociodemographic Correlates*. LaMarsh Research Centre on Violence and Conflict Resolution Report No. 18. North York, ON: York University.

Smith, M.D. (1990). "Patriarchal Ideology and Wife Beating: A Test of a Feminist Hypothesis." *Violence and Victims*, 5, 257-73.

Smith, M.D. (1991). "Male Peer Support of Wife Abuse: An Exploratory Study." *Journal of Interpersonal Violence*, 6, 512-519.

Solicitor General of Canada. (1986). "Reported and Unreported Crimes." In R. Silverman & J. Teevan (eds.) *Crime in Canadian Society* (pp. 98-114). Toronto: Butterworths.

Solicitor General of Canada. (1997). *Basic Facts about Corrections in Canada, 1997 edition*. Ottawa: Solicitor General of Canada.

Snider, L. (1993). *Bad Business: Corporate Crime in Canada*. Toronto: Nelson.

Stanko, E.A. (1985). *Intimate Intrusions: Women's Experiences of Male Violence*. London: Routledge & Kegan Paul.

Stanko, E.A. (1990). *Everyday Violence: How Women and Men experience Sexual and Physical Danger*. London: Pandora.

Statistics Canada. (1993). *Violence Against Women Survey*. Ottawa: Statistics Canada.

Statistics Canada. (1994). *Canadian Crime Statistics, 1992*. Ottawa: Statistics Canada.

Statistics Canada. (1995). *Table 2, Canadian Crime Statistics*, Catalogue No. 85-205, 1993. Ottawa: Statistics Canada.

Statistics Canada. (1996). "Changes in Women's Occupations." *Canadian Social Trends*, Catalogue No. 11-008. Ottawa: Statistics Canada.

Statistics Canada. (1997). *National Longitudinal Survey of Children and Youth*. Ottawa: Statistics Canada.

Statistics Canada. (1998). *Youths and Adults Charged in Criminal Incidents, Criminal Code and Federal Statutes, by Sex* at *http://www.statcan.ca/english/Pgdb/State/Justice/legal14.htm* (March 13, 1998).

Steffensmeier, D.J. (1983). "Organization Properties and Sex Segregation in the Underworld: Building a Sociological Theory of Sex Differences in Crime." *Social Forces*, 61, 1010-32.

Steffensmeier, D.J. (1993). *National Trends in Female Arrests, 1960-1990: Assessment and Recommendations for Research*. Unpublished manuscript. Department of Sociology, Pennsylvania State University, College Park.

Steffensmeier, D.J., & Terry, R.M. (1986). "Institutionalized Sexism in the Underworld: A View from the Inside." *Sociological Inquiry*, 56, 304-23.

Stevenson, K., Tufts, J., Hendrick, D., & Kowalski, M. (1998). *A Profile of Youth Justice in Canada*. Ottawa: Statistics Canada.

Straus, M.A., & Gelles, R.J. (1986). "Societal Change and Change in Family Violence from 1975 to 1985 as Revealed by Two National Surveys." *Journal of Marriage and the Family*, 48, 465-479.

Straus, M.A., Gelles, R.J., & Steinmetz, S.K. (1981). *Behind Closed Doors: Violence in the American Family*. New York: Anchor Books.

Sykes, G. (1958). *The Society of Captives*. Princeton, NJ: Princeton University Press.

Sutherland, E. (1949). *White-Collar Crime*. New York: Holt, Rinehart and Winston.

Tanner, A. (1993). "Making a John Confess to His Wife Intrigues Some City Prostitution Foes." *Edmonton Journal*, August 24, A1, A7.

Tanner, J. (1996). *Teenage Troubles: Youth and Deviance in Canada*. Toronto: Nelson.

Thorne-Finch, R. (1992). *Ending the Silence: The Origins and Treatment of Male Violence Against Women*. Toronto: University of Toronto Press.

Toby, J. (1957). "Social Disorganization and Stake in Conformity: Complementary Factors in the Predatory Behavior of Young Hoodlums." *Journal of Research in Crime and Delinquency*, 48, 12-17.

Toch, H. (1992). *Mosaic of Despair: Human Breakdowns in Prison*. Hyattsville, MD: American Psychological Association.

Tolman, R.M., & Bennett, L.W. (1990). "A Review of Research on Men Who Batter." *Journal of Interpersonal Violence*, 5, 87-97.

Tunnell, K. (1992). *Choosing Crime: The Criminal Calculus of Property Offenders*. Chicago: Nelson-Hall.

Van Brunschot, E.G. (1995). "Youth Involvement in Prostitution." In R.A. Silverman & J.H. Creechan (eds.) *Canadian Delinquency* (pp. 298-310). Toronto: Prentice Hall.

van den Haag, E. (1982). "Could Successful Rehabilitation Reduce the Crime Rate?" *Journal of Criminal Law and Criminology*, 73, 1025-1035.

Victoria Women's Sexual Assault Centre. (1994). *Today's Talk about Sexual Assault: A Booklet for Teens.* Victoria, B.C.: Victoria Women's Sexual Assault Centre.

Toronto Star. (1995a). "Man Tried to Rape His Ex-wife on Street." *Toronto Star,* September 29, A9.

Toronto Star. (1995b). "Man Who Attacked, Raped Wife Jailed for Two Years Less a Day." *Toronto Star,* July 14, A22.

Vold, G.B., Bernard, T.J., & Snipes, J.B. (1998). *Theoretical Criminology, 4th ed.* New York: Oxford University Press.

Walker, L. (1979). *The Battered Woman.* New York: Harper and Row.

Walker, S. (1998). *Sense and Nonsense about Crime and Drugs: A Policy Guide, 4th ed.* Belmont, CA: West/Wadsworth.

Watt, D., & Fuerst, M.K. (1989). *The Annotated 1990 Tremeear's Criminal Code.* Toronto: Carswell.

White, R., & Haines, F. (1996). *Crime and Criminology: An Introduction.* New York: Oxford University Press.

Widom, C.S. (1989). "Child Abuse, Neglect and Violent Criminal Behavior." *Criminology,* 27, 252-271.

Wilson, J.Q. (1985). *Thinking about Crime.* New York: Vintage.

Wilson, J.Q., & Herrnstein, R. (1985). *Crime and Human Nature: The Definitive Study of the Causes of Crime.* New York: Simon and Shuster.

Wilson, M., & Daly, M. (1994). *Spousal Homicide.* Ottawa: Statistics Canada.

Wilson, M., Johnson, H., & Daly, M. (1995). "Lethal and Non-lethal Violence Against Wives." *Canadian Journal of Criminology,* 37, 331-62.

Wilson, W.J. (1996). *When Work Disappears: The World of the New Urban Poor.* New York: Knopf.

Zietz, D. (1981). *Women Who Embezzle or Defraud: A Study of Convicted Felons.* New York: Praeger.

Name Index

Adelberg, E., 25, 26, 32, 93
Adler, F., 80-82, 83, 85
Akers, R.L., 66, 84, 94
Alvi, S., 9, 29, 30, 33n14, 50, 60, 139,
    140, 141, 143, 146n10
Arbour, L., 117
Armstrong, H., 85, 143
Armstrong, P., 85, 143
Atkinson, M., 84
Atlas, R., 61n5
Aubry, D., 100
Austin, J., 67, 130

Badgley, R., 52
Bailey, M., 44
Bala, N., 45
Barnett, O.W., 131
Barnsley, J., 50
Barrett, M., 46
Beare, M.J., 31, 33n15
Becker, H.S., 24
Beirne, P., 31, 85, 86
Belcourt, R., 121
Belknap, J., 65, 73, 74, 80, 83, 96n3
Bennett, L.W., 138
Bernardo, P., 3
Besserer, S., 112
Birkenmayer, A., 112
Blanchfield, M., 119
Blau, R., 79, 90
Bloom, B., 65
Boe, R., 14, 18, 27, 31, 43, 45, 46, 49,
    104, 105, 106, 107, 108, 112, 114,
    115
Bohuslawsky, M., 128
Boritch, H., 3, 5, 18, 19, 23, 24, 32,
    32n3, 33n13, 51, 72, 110, 112,
    114, 115, 119, 120, 122, 124n2,
    142, 143

Bourgois, P., 20, 33n11, 138
Bowker, L., 95
Bowlby, G., 61n7
Bracey, D.H., 52
Braithwaite, J., 74
Brinkerhoff, M., 7
Bronskill, J., 117
Brook, D.W., 50
Brook, J.S., 50
Browne, A., 10
Bursik, R.J., 53

Campbell, A., 56, 59
Carrigan, D.O., 54, 55, 60
Carrington, P., 45
Carroll, W., 30
Cernkovich, S., 83
Cherney, E., 56
Chesney-Lind, M., 1, 6, 10, 20, 25, 27-
    28, 37, 45, 55, 56, 57, 58, 59, 60,
    61n1, 61n3, 61n10, 65, 70, 71, 72,
    75, 79, 80, 82, 83, 85, 86, 88, 89,
    91-92, 93, 94, 95, 96n3, 112, 114,
    116, 117, 120, 122, 127, 131, 133
Chisholm, P., 1, 2, 32n2, 37, 38, 40, 41
Chunn, D., 120
Clinard, M., 31
Close, G., 73
Cobb, C., 17
Cohen, A., 75, 76-79, 80
Cohen, J., 85, 95
Cohen, S., 38
Comack, E., 112
Conklin, J.E., 67
Connell, R.W., 56, 138
Cornell, C.P., 131
Cornell, D.G., 44, 45
Craig, W., 48, 61n5
Crawford, M., 8

167

Subject Index

About the Author

Walter S. DeKeseredy is Professor of Sociology at Carleton University in Ottawa, Canada. He has written more than 60 journal articles and book chapters on woman abuse, poverty and crime, and left realist criminology. He is the author of *Woman Abuse in Dating Relationships: The Role of Male Peer Support*; with Ronald Hinch, coauthor of *Woman Abuse: Sociological Perspectives*; with Desmond Ellis, coauthor of the second edition of *The Wrong Stuff: An Introduction to the Sociological Study of Deviance*; with Desmond Ellis and Shahid Alvi, coauthor of *Contemporary Social Problems in North America*; with Martin D. Schwartz, coauthor of *Contemporary Criminology*, *Sexual Assault on the College Campus: The Role of Male Peer Support*, and *Woman Abuse on Campus: Results from the Canadian National Survey*; and with Linda MacLeod, *Woman Abuse: A Sociological Story*.

In 1995, DeKeseredy received the Critical Criminologist of the Year Award from the American Society of Criminology's Division on Critical Criminology. In 1993, he received Carleton University's Research Achievement Award. Currently, he is coeditor of *Critical Criminology: An International Journal* and serves on the editorial boards of *Violence Against Women: An International and Interdisciplinary Journal* and *Women & Criminal Justice*. Together with Shahid Alvi, Martin D. Schwartz, and Andreas Tomaszewski, DeKeseredy is working on a book for University of Toronto Press titled *Under Siege: Joblessness, Poverty, and Crime in a Vulnerable Canadian Urban Community*, which will include the results of the first in-depth Canadian sociological study of crime and other major social problems in public housing.